Andrew MacLaran

The Politics of
Positive Discrimination

The Politics of Positive Discrimination

An evaluation of the
Urban Programme 1967-77

JOHN EDWARDS
and RICHARD BATLEY
Preface by
PROFESSOR JOHN GREVE

TAVISTOCK PUBLICATIONS

First published in 1978
by Tavistock Publications Limited
11 New Fetter Lane, London EC4P 4EE
Set by Red Lion Setters, Holborn, London
Printed in Great Britain at the
University Press, Cambridge

ISBN 0 422 76660 7

To Bridget and Jucélia

Contents

Preface

In May 1968 the Prime Minister (Mr Harold Wilson) announced the launching of the Urban Programme. Nine years later, on 6 April 1977, the Secretary of State for the Environment (Mr Peter Shore) unveiled a 'new policy for the inner cities' in a statement to the House of Commons. As part of the new policy the administration of the Urban Programme was to be transferred from the Home Office to the Department of the Environment, there would be a large increase in its budget (from £30 million a year to £125 million a year), its scope would be extended to cover economic and environmental projects in addition to the social projects with which it had primarily been concerned.

Other changes were also proposed — and are discussed in Chapter 8 of this book — but the most important is the absorption of the Urban Programme into the much larger programmes for which the Department of the Environment is responsible.

In this book John Edwards and Richard Batley present the first comprehensive and detailed analysis and assessment of the development and functioning of the Urban Programme. In itself, this makes it a study of unusual interest, but the authors also relate their discussion of the Programme to a wider context of policies, priorities, and values and, at the end of the book, indicate further policy options that might have been considered by the Government.

The study on which this book is based was commissioned by the Home Office and carried out between 1971 and 1975. A final report was submitted to the Home Office in January 1976. The authors worked in the Home Office alongside the Civil Servants responsible for shaping and administering the Urban Programme. They had access to papers, attended internal and interdepartmental meetings, and received invaluable help and guidance from Civil Service colleagues in the Home Office and other central departments.

Researchers and administrators engaged in a frank and penetrating examination of each others' activities which for both parties served, in general, to dissolve misconceptions, clarify intentions, encourage reappraisal, and to deepen understanding of the roles and constraints within which each played their parts. Sometimes, however, the discussions foundered in bewilderment when the conceptual, functional, and value differences between administrator and researcher proved unbridgeable — at least in the operational situation.

It was not the purpose of the discussions to effect a compromise or a consensus of views. The principal merit of the interchange between the research workers and Civil Servants was that it took place over a period of time within the context of the normal work routine while the participants were defining and interpreting the aims and methods of their respective operations in terms of policy.

That component of social policy that was labelled the 'Urban Programme' was defined in vague terms when first conceived and the book shows how, from the start, policy relating to it emerged incrementally and, in part, as a result of the actual processes of implementation.

As will be seen, while the broad objectives of the Urban Programme did not change significantly after 1968, the specific aims varied considerably during the period studied. It can be argued that the ad hoc nature of the Programme is one of its unsatisfactory features. Critics have described it as a typical British response to a challenging situation — a response bearing the familiar characteristics of stopping the gap and muddling through. There is validity in these claims, for the approach of central government to dealing with the diverse problems of urban areas — including economic and social 'deprivation' — has been fragmented and spasmodic. A number of measures have been introduced since the late 'sixties — often with more rhetoric than resources — but they have been administered by different government departments and have been inadequately co-ordinated. The Urban and

Educational Priority Areas (EPA) programmes, the Community Development Projects (CDP), the General Improvement Areas (GIAs), the Housing Action Areas (HAAs), the 'Six Cities' studies, and the Comprehensive Community Programmes (CCPs) all focus on a set of related problems and tasks, but the manner in which these schemes have been established and the nature of their administration typify the uneven and incremental evolution of social policies in Britain. It does not appear that 'new' policies for inner cities herald a genuine break with the tradition of departmental policies. In some respects, transfer of the Urban Programme to the Department of the Environment might further undermine the limited efforts that have been made to develop a more concerted formulation and execution of policy in the social field. Whatever its defects, the Urban Programme has been an enterprise involving the co-operation of several government departments.

The roles of the separate departments of central government with their sharp demarcations of responsibility and high degree of departmental autonomy remain strong. It is not the purpose of this preface to appraise the structure and functions of central government in Britain, but the emergence in recent years of a range of programmes and associated machinery concerned with urban deprivation, and the pattern of their development, are germane to a consideration of the aims, organization, and performance of the Urban Programme. It is for that reason that the other governmental measures are touched upon here and referred to in greater detail elsewhere in the book.

To revert to the Urban Programme itself, while it has been criticized for not being a co-ordinated or integrated programme, and for its miniscule scale relative to the problems it should be tackling, the Programme's defenders have argued that its ad hoc approach has the quality of flexibility. On the matter of adequacy of scale, the argument has to take into account:

(a) the aims of the Programme and its role in relation to the major programmes in housing, welfare, health, education, employment, income, and so on, as well as to the special smaller scale programmes such as EPA, CDP, GIAs, HAAs, and CCPs;

(b) the volume of resources — primarily financial — that government is prepared to allocate to the Urban Programme, which is certainly far less than the Civil Service and local authority administrators of the Programme and their colleagues in voluntary bodies consider necessary;

(c) the degree to which local government departments, voluntary agencies, and central departments are able to agree on priorities in Urban Programme spending;

(d) the extent to which local departments and agencies (statutory and voluntary) would be capable of managing effectively and economically a national programme many times its present size without major changes to their own organizations involving either expansion or redeployment of manpower, possibly on a considerable scale; and, related to these points,

(e) how a greatly enlarged Urban Programme should be organized and administered centrally and locally.

The reconciliation of divergent or contending views — where 'what is' differs so widely from 'what ought to be' — is frequently very difficult and sometimes impossible to bring about.

In their introduction the authors draw attention — as others have done — to the importance of subjective perceptions of 'need' and 'deprivation'. These perceptions, and the definitions which are derived from them, are influenced by the social and economic environment of the time — by, for example, the material standards of the day and by current expectations. Thus, in trying to establish the extent to which the Urban Programme has or has not been 'successful', observers must take into account the changing environment within which the Programme operates. It cannot be judged realistically solely by reference to some abstract or absolute standards.

John Edwards and Richard Batley have provided the most comprehensive and informed account to date of the Urban Programme. They trace the origins and development of the programme, place it in its historical context by examining its evolution from the rediscovery of poverty to positive discrimination, describe and appraise the organization and processes of the programme, and assess its effectiveness. Finally, the authors return to the question of 'what kind of programme', which has inevitably emerged at a number of places earlier in the book in recording and considering the views of central and local officials, examining the aims and administration of the Programme, and discussing the kinds of local project that have been accorded priority and financial support.

It is regrettable that the publication of this book has been so long delayed. Part of the price to be paid for access to the experience and judgements of Civil Servants and to documentary material is that the resultant report must be submitted for scrutiny before publication. The *Official Secrets Act* is a very wide blanket and is used to cover a multitude of sensitivities, many of which have nothing to do with the security of the realm. For instance, it might be deemed necessary to secure the views of a number of people in several departments on matters of fact, interpretation, and confidentiality. Such a procedure is time consuming.

For authors or research workers, therefore, the journey from the point at which a manuscript or report is delivered for comment and clearance may be slow, and the negotiations may be protracted before agreement is ultimately reached.

August 1977   John Greve
                                                          University of Leeds

Acknowledgements

We are indebted above all to Professor John Greve who directed the research team of which we were a part. Without his help, guidance, and diplomatic intervention in our support, it would have been impossible to undertake the research on which this book is based. We are also grateful to Professor J.B. Cullingworth who offered useful comments on an earlier draft of this book. Ultimately our work depended upon the co-operation of administrators in central and local government and in voluntary organizations. Conventions about public accountability prevent us from mentioning the names of government officials in the text but most of our data and many of our insights came from them. In particular, we are grateful to the staff of the Home Office for their friendly toleration of our presence over four years. Whatever criticisms we make of the Urban Aid Programme, we should not want to call into question the personal commitment of many of the individual Civil Servants responsible for its administration. It would be nice to think that they had gained as much from our evaluation as we have from our inside views of government. However, we are entirely responsible for the contents of the report and it does not necessarily reflect the views of the Home Office or of the other central or local government departments concerned.

J.E.   R.B.
1977

1 Introduction

One of the more intractable problems with which social policy has attempted to deal over the past decade has been the apparent persistence in some localized urban areas of social and physical conditions and patterns of behaviour that seem increasingly at odds with the general trend towards increased affluence and the greater security and social well-being bestowed by the Welfare State. The manifestations of these conditions and behaviours have been many and varied and they have been given the collective title of 'urban deprivation'.

It is to a fuller understanding of the interpretations of this phenomenon and of the social policy responses to it, and one response in particular — the Urban Programme — that this study is devoted. This is in part, then, the story of the Urban Programme, but it is also an examination, using the Programme as instrument and example, of area-based positive discrimination policies, of perceptions and definitions of 'urban deprivation', and of social policy formulation and implementation at central and local government levels. It is as much a study of the nature of governmental responses to ill-defined problems as of the successes and failures of one particular programme. The task of evaluating the Urban Programme from *within* government provided the opportunity of examining at first hand the nature of governmental reaction to urban deprivation, a reaction which consisted not only of the Urban Programme itself but also of a number of related programmes and initiatives. A number of these programmes and initiatives have now ended but each has, in some measure, contributed to the development of urban deprivation policies and to the synthesis of current views presented in the White Paper on Inner City Policy published in 1977. The Urban Programme itself continues as part of the new package of policies and programmes though in a modified and enlarged form. The story that is told here therefore is that of the Urban Programme up until 1977 in what might be called its first and modest stage. That it has been retained as one instrument of urban deprivation policy as outlined in the White Paper is one indication that, within government at least, it has been deemed a success. That is an assessment with which this evaluation does not wholly concur.

The UP is one of a number of area-specific positive discrimination programmes or studies, the aims of which, in general terms, have been to help alleviate some of the problems of 'urban deprivation' — though this label is so inclusive as to cover a whole range of the manifestations of urban problems. The move towards area-based positive discrimination programmes began in the United States in the early years of the last decade when the Headstart, Model Cities, and Community Action Programs and the Ford Foundation Area Projects were launched, and the extent to which these programmes influenced thinking about positive discrimination on this side of the Atlantic is discussed in Chapter 2. Whatever the paternity of the British programmes, they began to appear half a decade after their larger American counterparts, and during the second half of the 1960s General Improvement Areas, Education Priority Areas, Community Development Projects, and the Urban Programme itself were born, to be followed in the early 1970s by Housing Action Areas, Six Cities (or Total Approach) Studies, Comprehensive Community Programmes,[1] and Recreation Priority Areas. Though each of these differ in greater or lesser degree from the others, all have some features in common — their area specificity, their discrimination within a universalist framework, and their concern with some aspect of the complex of issues called 'urban deprivation'.

---

[1] It should be noted, however, that since their announcement the CCPs have moved away from an area-specific approach.

Research in and of government

In 1971, three years after the first grants had been approved under the Urban Programme, it was decided within the Home Office (the department responsible for administering it) that some attempt should be made to monitor and evaluate it. The reasons for the decision were probably threefold: first, that, after three years of operation, comment was beginning to be made among community and social workers, and in some interested journals and newspapers, that funds were being disbursed without any attempt at monitoring their impact; second, that the Community Development Projects (CDPs), administered by the same division in the Home Office and funded from UP sources, had a research element built into them thus providing the precedent; and, third, that the machinery for conducting some form of research on the Programme was conveniently at hand in the form of the CDP Central Research Unit, based at the Home Office and directed by Professor John Greve, then of Southampton University. This team could conveniently be expanded to take on the task of evaluating the Programme. A three-year, two-person research project was therefore commissioned of the Central Research Unit by the Home Office and the authors were appointed in 1971 and 1972. The research in fact spread over four years with a two-year overlap between the researchers. One aspect of the administrative arrangements for the work is of relevance to the research itself — and to this book. Although the researchers were appointees of Southampton (and later Leeds) University, a research grant having been made to that institution by the Home Office, they worked within the Community Programmes Division[2] of the Home Office alongside those Civil Servants responsible for administering the Programme. Their position was therefore that of 'outsiders in a closed institution'. The responsibilities of the researchers therefore were, first, the production of some form of report on the Programme for the Home Office, and, second (what should be the wider responsibility of all social researchers), to add to a corpus of information and knowledge and share it as widely as possible among interested colleagues in research and teaching or other relevant work. It was these administrative arrangements for carrying out the study, and

[2] Which later became the Urban Programme Section of the Urban Deprivation Unit, and subsequently moved to the Department of the Environment.

the close proximity to central government, that provided the opportunity to look closely at policy formulation and implementation.

Alternative approaches

Although the research was established to 'monitor and evaluate' the Urban Programme, no specific research brief was provided by the Home Office and neither was any asked for by the researchers. The first task, therefore, was to design a research programme, decide what form the evaluation should take, and establish a research role in the somewhat peculiar administrative arrangement. Broadly, two alternative approaches presented themselves (alternative to the extent that given the time and resources available it was not possible to do both). The first was to attempt to evaluate in some way the impact and effects of the large number and wide variety of projects which had been funded and which represented the Programme 'on the ground'. Such an approach involved seeking answers to such questions as 'to what extent have the projects succeeded in meeting the aims of the Programme?', 'what have they achieved?', and 'to what extent have they alleviated urban deprivation or served to meet the hitherto unmet social needs in the areas in which they operated?'. The second was to focus attention on the UP as a *programme*, to examine its growth and aims, the influences — from all quarters — that shaped it, the way in which it was administered at central government, local authority, and voluntary organization levels, and to try to establish why the distribution of projects and funds, both geographically and across the various project types, was as it was.

There were dominant reasons why the latter of these two courses was adopted. First, as is noted above, there seemed good reason to treat the Urban Programme in its wider context and to draw lessons that were of wider application than the Programme itself — for, with the lack of explicit commitment to a continuation of the Programme and the continued uncertainty over its future, there was always the possibility that it would not outlast the research. Any research that confined itself more narrowly to the Programme itself might then have been wasted effort. Second, it was felt that since the aims of the Programme had never been made clear — having been stated either in very general terms or in a multiplicity of terms — there was no adequate benchmark against which to measure the achievements or lack of achievements either of the Programme as a whole or of the projects it had initiated. Third, the range of types of project that had been funded under the Programme was so broad that no meaningful statement could be made in general terms about what overall achievements had been made, and to evaluate each type of project separately would have been a mammoth task beyond the capabilities of the researchers, requiring as it would experts in a wide variety of fields. Thus, educationalists and child psychologists would have been needed to assess the benefits of nursery education and other day-care schemes (and such benefits as did accrue might not have been observed for many years), housing experts would have been required to assess the achievements of housing-related schemes, legal experts of legal aid schemes, community workers of community centres and community action projects, health experts of health schemes, and so on. Add to this the lack of unanimity as to what constitutes urban deprivation and hence how measures of its reduction are to be established (even if such a task were meaningful — itself a matter of debate as Chapter 8 indicates) and the difficulties of this form of evaluation became forbidding. Fourth, and more positively, the administrative arrangements under which the research had been established provided the unusual opportunity (for social scientists at least) to look in rather more detail and from closer quarters at the machinery of social policy formulation and implementation at central government level, albeit within a finite and very narrow field. This opportunity it seemed was not one to be passed up.

Components, methodologies, and sources

The programme of research that was finally decided upon included a number of different components, a variety of techniques or methodologies, and a wide variety of sources. The research, like the book, was an entirely collaborative enterprise, but Richard Batley is primarily responsible for the writing of Chapters 2, 3, and 4 and John Edwards for Chapters 1, 5, 6, 7, and 8 and the Appendices. We begin with a documentation of the historical background to the Programme and the forces that brought it into being, and place it in the context of developing social policy and the emergence of area-specific positive discrimination. The bulk of this documentation draws upon published sources but, where relevant, unpublished departmental documents are used. Chapter 3 goes on to examine in more detail the birth, growth, and aims of the Programme, drawing upon contemporary documents and discussions with some of the administrators involved in formulating it. One of the major assumptions underlying this — as much else in the evaluation — has been that, since the Programme was born *in vacuo* as it were, with only the minimum of guidance from political leaders, the form that the Programme was to take, the problems at which it was to be directed, and the types of scheme that were to be promoted would be strongly influenced by the perceptions and values of those persons to whom the task of constructing it fell. In short, with a lack of clear political guidelines and direction, the Programme would in large measure be the product of the persons who formulated and administered it, given its organizational structures and the processes by which they were related to each other. It has to be said at once that this is a very difficult form of research to carry through in operational terms, requiring, as it does, modes of interviewing that are at the same time both subtle and, to the interviewee, apparently without much direct relevance to the immediate subject of the Urban Programme.

In Chapter 4 an account of how the Programme works in practice is given. Although the general procedural outlines involving administration and practice at central and local government levels and at the voluntary organization level are fairly simple, *in practice* the implementation of the Programme is a complex and varied affair involving many different facets and procedures as between different central and local departments, different local authorities, different voluntary agencies and their fluctuating relationships with local authorities, and, indeed, as between different individuals whose business it is to implement the spirit of one of the briefest Acts of Parliament.[3] This part of the research drew heavily upon documentary evidence, participant observation within the Home Office, interviews with central government officials, representatives of voluntary organizations, and officers and members in twelve selected local authorities that had made substantial use of the Programme.

Chapter 5 records the results of an attempt to identify the many

---

[3] The *Local Government Grants* (*Social Need*) *Act 1969*, which gives effect to the Programme.

factors that have influenced, and in some cases determined, the constantly shifting nature and direction of the Programme. Because the Programme has lacked clear policy lines, clear direction, and clear boundaries, its form and structure — in terms of (for example) the role of the voluntary sector, the relationships between central and local government, the types of project promoted, the Programme's financial scale, the relationships between the different departments involved both centrally and locally, the problems and areas at which it is directed, and the extent to which it is given a bias towards provision for ethnic minorities — have been constantly moulded and changed by events, by political and administrative expediencies, and by the perceptions and values of individual administrators and professionals within central and local government. Hopefully, it has been possible to show how the Programme, as it has developed, has been the result of these many latent and manifest influences. And hopefully, too, something of what is said in Chapter 5 will strike chords of relevance that go well beyond the Programme itself. As in the preceding chapter, our methods and sources chiefly drew upon interviews carried out within central and local departments and voluntary organizations and a large volume of documentary evidence culled mainly from government files.

In Chapter 6 attention is directed towards the projects themselves — the more tangible manifestations of the administrative procedures. Here, an attempt is made to give a picture of what the Programme means in terms of projects and funds by the use of selected statistical documentation. Thus details are given of the distributions of project types and funds, of the distributions of projects by type of sponsor (local authority or voluntary agency), by costs, and by approving department (the Home Office, Department of Health and Social Security, Department of the Environment, and the Department of Education and Science), and a comparison is made between the patterns of project applications and approvals. In order to produce this statistical material a punch-card index system was established whereby details of every one of the 3000 or so projects were recorded, one to a card.

Because of the lack of specific guidance given by politicians to those concerned with both constructing and implementing the Programme, the form that it took in design and in operation (as is argued above) was in large part determined by the ideas, views, value judgements, and perceptions both of the Programme itself and the problems it was designed to alleviate, on the part of its architects and implementors in central and local government. Chapter 7 examines — and records — the views and perceptions of a large number of relevant actors in the formulation and implementation processes, not only of the Programme itself but also of related issues: positive discrimination and urban deprivation.

The final chapter takes a wider look at the social policies and social context within which the Programme was born and developed, and examines some of the theoretical conceptions — and misconceptions — of social structure and social process upon which it and some of its sister programmes were based. The notions of urban deprivation and positive discrimination are critically considered, as are the tendencies to look for solutions in terms of the co-ordination of programmes and the development of specific and finite programmes as against broader-based social policies directed at socially-defined problems.

Finally, some of the more general implications for central and local government and voluntary agency involvement in area-based positive discrimination, as derived from the evaluation, are presented in *Appendix I*.

There is as much need for a programme of aid to urban areas today as there was in 1968 when the Urban Programme was initiated. The problems of 'urban deprivation' are as great, as widespread, and as topical today as they were then. And there was probably as much 'unmet social need' in 1977 as there was in 1968. These facts are less a reflection of any failure of the Urban Programme, however, as of the nature, definition, and conceptions of the problems it was designed to alleviate. The Programme — like any other social policy innovation — was a reaction to a conglomeration of social problems as they were defined at the time of its birth; it has been a child of its times, and if the times have changed — and with them society's definitions of social problems and the measures required to tackle them — it cannot be blamed for that, and, indeed, along with its sister programmes such as the Community Development Projects, Educational Priority Area Projects, and Comprehensive Community Programmes, it has in considerable measure contributed to that change. If in the late 1970s the Urban Programme is seen as an inappropriate response to the problems of deprivation, we must at least give it credit for being a part of that body of thinking — and action — without the benefit of which we might not have arrived so quickly at our present state of knowledge.

2 The emergence of positive discrimination

The Urban Programme is an example *par excellence* of area-specific positive discrimination and as such it can be allocated a position within the long-term development of social policy in Britain. The significance of positive discrimination programmes can only be fully understood within the context of the two principles of universalism and selectivity. Positive discrimination is a form of selectivity but one which requires as its pre-condition a universalist framework, for, as Titmuss has argued:

> 'The real challenge resides in the question: what particular infra-structure of universalist services is needed in order to provide a framework of values and opportunity bases within and around which can be developed socially acceptable selective services aiming to discriminate positively, with the minimum risk of stigma, in favour of those whose needs are greatest?'
>
> (Titmuss 1968: 135)

Indeed, as Pinker says, it 'is the only form of selectivity compatible with the idea of a welfare society because its ultimate goal is the achievement of optimal rather than minimal standards' (Pinker 1971: 190).

While the development of programmes of positive discrimination can be seen largely as a phenomenon of the 1960s and 1970s, and as a partial reaction to the feeling that universalistic principles had in part failed to eradicate the worst excesses of poverty and deprivation, their genesis can be traced back — albeit somewhat tenuously — as far as the early 1940s and the development of 'special area' policies based on the work of the Barlow (1940), Scott (1942), and Uthwatt (1942) committees.

The story of the development of social policy culminating in the principles of positive discrimination goes a long way further back than this, of course, and the main lines of development could be traced back as far as the *Poor Law* of 1834. For the purposes of the present sketch, however, it is necessary to break into the story at a more recent date, and the starting-point chosen for this examination of the social policy context of the development of area-based positive discrimination programmes is the 'rediscovery' of poverty during the 1960s.

The rediscovery of poverty

By 1960 the essentials of the Welfare State, constructed on the basis of the Beveridge Report (Beveridge 1942) during the unprecedented burst of legislative activity after the war, had been cushioning the majority of the population against economic and social misfortune for fifteen years, and it was not unreasonable to expect that during this period the worst excesses of poverty and social deprivation had been eradicated. 'Inequality, as a subject of political discourse, was less in evidence everywhere, and what remained of poverty in Britain was thought to be either eradicable through the natural process of growth or as constituting a permanent residue of the unfortunate and irresponsible' (Titmuss 1964: 11). Using a subsistence definition of poverty, Seebohm Rowntree had shown a reduction in the proportion of the population living in poverty in York from 17.7 per cent in 1936 to 1.7 per cent in 1950.

It was this feeling of optimism — even complacency — that was ruffled (shaken would be too strong a word) by a number of social reports that gave evidence that all was not as well as had been assumed. It was not so much that poverty was rediscovered (studies of the elderly had already revealed the persistence of low living standards) as that confidence in existing policy and practice was shown to have been misplaced. The optimistic assumption that economic growth and marginally-improved benefits would lift the 'residual' poor out of their situation was found to be false. Economic growth and inflation were leaving those on fixed incomes and those with weak bargaining power relatively further behind, and possibly even absolutely worse off. 'As-of-right' insurance benefits were allowed by governments to fall in real value, with the result that there was increasing resort by claimants to the means-tested national assistance benefits that Beveridge had seen as a residual and temporary adjunct to the main scheme. Moreover, poverty, it was revealed, was not restricted to those who had a 'right' to benefits but extended even to wage earners.

The new evidence mainly applied to concepts of relative deprivation on the basis that need could only be defined in relation to changing standards of living. Abel-Smith and Townsend (1965: 30) established such a movable definition on the basis of current rates of national assistance. It can be argued against this relative approach that in these terms 'a poor country can have a less troublesome problem of poverty than a rich country' (Seldon 1968: 263). However, it was in these relative terms that the rediscovery of poverty was made. Townsend and Abel-Smith found that the number of people living below national assistance rates, whether or not they were in employment, had increased from 600,000 in 1953/4 to 2,000,000 in 1960. The proportion of this group that lived in single-person and large-family households was increasing. More surprising was that of the 7½ million of the population living at less than 140 per cent of national assistance rates, '34.6 per cent were in households whose head was in full time work'. 'On the whole the data we have presented contradicts the commonly held view that a trend towards greater equality has accompanied the trend towards greater affluence' (Abel-Smith and Townsend 1965: 66).

Other studies in the early 1960s gave evidence of the inadequacies of a system that depended so much on the underpinning of the insurance schemes with means-tested benefits. Among the findings were that, in the fifteen years since 1948, pensioners' incomes had increased more slowly than average rates (Lynes 1963), that between a quarter and one third of the population had an inadequate dietary intake (Lambert 1964), and that 17 per cent of old-age pensioners were entitled to national assistance but not claiming it (Ministry of Pensions and National Insurance 1966).

The reports that are held to have constituted a 'rediscovery of poverty' were confined mainly to the area of income maintenance. But it is possible to discern the emergence at about the same time of a concern with other aspects of the Welfare State. The major social services — education, housing, health and social welfare (but especially the first two) — all came under criticism in the 1960s for a failure to reach some of those most in need. Most of the criticism emerged from official or semi-official reports. For example, the Crowther, Newsom, Robbins, and Plowden Reports on education 'have demonstrated that class inequalities still remain at every level of the system, and that social class still influences a child's chances of staying on at school after fifteen, and still more, of entering Higher Education' (Gaine 1971: 54). Indeed, the proportion of the sons of manual workers who reached university in 1964 (1.6 per cent) was if anything smaller than the proportion before World War II (Floud 1961). In housing, problems of homelessness were increasing:

> 'Official statistics on homelessness, collected by the Department of Health and Social Security, show that from the end of 1960 to the 30th September 1968 the number of persons in temporary accommodation rose by 190% in England and Wales as a whole.'
> (Greve, Page, and Greve 1971: xv)

Much of this homelessness was due to low wages, high rents, and insecurity of tenure in the private rented sector. Landlord harrassment and evictions contributed to the setting up of the Milner Holland Committee, 'To survey the housing situation in Greater London with particular reference to... rented accommodation'. This report (Committee on Housing in Greater London 1965) was to add official impetus to the growing demands for action in especially deprived areas.

Selectivism and positive discrimination

It would be simplistic to describe later developments as directly consequential on this 'rediscovery'. The social services and benefits are complex and have their own momentum. In spite of the scepticism seeping from the academic world, governments were still very much concerned with the abuse of the system, that is, with the problem of 'over'-use rather than 'under'-use of benefits and services. However, in bald terms, it could be said that a move towards greater selectivity (rather than a reassertion of universalistic principles) in the application of services and benefits was the governmental response to the awareness that the Welfare State was not reaching all the poor. Jordan has argued that the identification of the poor as a group has contributed to the reassertion of *Poor Law* principles: if the poor were still present in spite of a thorough-going welfare system it must be due to some inadequacy on their part which required selective State intervention:

'Thus the "rediscovery of poverty" in the latter half of the 1960s, while no doubt objectively justified, was not necessarily a step in the direction of improving services for the poor, for it has served as a ready excuse for concentrating all our social resources on the unfortunate sector for whom the old principles of poor relief are characteristically employed.'   (Jordan 1974: 31)

Others regard selectivism not as a step backwards but as marking a further stage in the refinement of the welfare system:

'the answer will probably lie in a solution which embodies universal benefits and greater selectivity. This would not be merely a compromise, it would be the application to our social security system of a process of refinement which has been found necessary in many other fields within the social services.'

(Rodgers 1969: 71)

To some extent such differences of opinion are based on different concepts of selectivity. Pinker has described one form of selectivism (the *Poor Law* variety) as 'exclusive', that is, as an attempt to deter potential applications by attaching social stigma (or even hardship) to the receipt of aid. It is characterized by the deterrent effect of an individually-applied means test. The other form of selectivism is 'inclusive' in the sense that it attempts to identify groups of people for favoured treatment by 'a process of diagnosis and selection free from stigmatisation' (Pinker 1968: 232). An arch-proponent of the latter approach was Titmuss: he argued that the rich had received more aid from the 'social services' than the poor in the shape, for example, of tax relief on mortgages, better health provision, more assured pensions, and tax-free fringe benefits (Titmuss 1964). The new challenge was: 'of positively discriminating on a territorial, group or "rights" basis in favour of the poor, the handicapped, the deprived, the coloured, the home-less and the social casualties of our society' (Titmuss 1968: 134).

The Labour Government of 1964-70 took steps in both direc-tions. Financially the more significant step was in the direction of making social security benefits both more differential and more 'exclusive'. The scope of earnings-related benefits was extended to cover sickness, unemployment, industrial injury, and widows' allowances by the *National Insurance Act 1966*. The Government also made effective efforts to increase the take-up of means-tested national assistance, later re-entitled supplementary benefit; in this case an 'exclusive' benefit was in a sense made less exclusive by the removal of certain stigmatic application processes, but in so doing its effective role was increased. Later, as unemployment figures grew higher, in 1968 the Government introduced measures to control voluntary unemployment by making supplementary benefit less accessible to the unemployed; a four-week limit on the payment of benefit was imposed on single men 'and in the 1971 Social Security Act provision was made for the automatic reduction of supplementary benefit of any claimant disqualified for unemployment benefit ... '. Meanwhile, on a pettier scale, during 1968 the provision of free school milk was restricted to primary schools and medical prescription charges were reintroduced (with relief by means test).

The 1970 election was fought and won by the Conservatives with selectivity as a major plank with respect to both the social services and government aid to industry. The new Government set out to extend selectivity in the application of benefits and also in the operation of the major services: 'Social spending will be concentrated on individual needs, group needs and area needs ... In breaking the circle of decay and decline we must move away from the indiscriminate, automatic subsidies paid on all projects whether they increase jobs or not' (Balniel 1970: 159). The Conservative Government's major developments in this direction were the introduction of Family Income Supplement (FIS) in 1971 and the 1972 *Housing Finance Act*. FIS was a new non-contributory benefit paid to low income families where the wage earner was in full-time employment. Its receipt automatically entitled the beneficiary's family to a range of other free benefits (e.g. welfare milk, school meals, prescriptions, optical and dental services).

This is part of the current policy to provide selective help to those in greatest need. Such an approach has serious drawbacks. In the first place though it ensures that assistance is:

'restricted to those in greatest need, it does not guarantee that all those in greatest need will, in fact, receive it ... It is costly in administration ... More important, it has severe "negative" effects particularly when other benefits are taken into account. This follows of course from its selective basis. An increase in income of £1 a week involves a reduction in FIS benefit of 50p ... [and] ... a reduction in other benefits, including the new rent allowance.'   (Cullingworth 1973: vol.2, 26)

The new rent allowance, contributing to this 'poverty trap', was itself a consequence of the *Housing Finance Act* (now rescinded, although the rebates and allowances remain). This altered the method of subsidizing local authority housing, raised rents in the public sector to an economic or 'fair rent' level, and, most importantly to this discussion, introduced a national scheme of means-tested rent rebates in the local authority sector and rent allowances in the private unfurnished sectors: 'Perhaps the major objection to the Act, however, is its massive extension of the selectivist approach. Rent rebates and allowances are means tested. Yet the weaknesses of means tested benefits are well known. They are a clumsy, divisive and ineffective way of assisting low income groups' (Lansley and Fiegehen 1973: 12).

The 1970 Conservative Government, with its commitment to selectivity, was ideologically prepared to adopt the earlier Labour Government's more novel advances in the field — the programmes of positive discrimination:

'On the whole ... the Conservatives in both Houses were more inclined to welcome the idea of positive discrimination as consistent with and expressing their own convictions about the need for selectivity throughout the public services generally and for distributing benefits according to some kind of need or means test.'   (Halsey 1972: 33)

These programmes followed a series of Government Reports (Crowther, Newsom, Robbins, and Plowden on aspects of education; Milner Holland on housing in London; and Seebohm on the social services) which both added evidence to the growing awareness that inequality and poverty were surviving in the Welfare State, and also proposed organizational and policy changes. These reports showed that the major services had not been successful in making themselves equally as available to all social groups in need of the services. Class, sex, location, and home environment remained influential variables in take-up even if in theory there was equality of access. The last three of the named reports went beyond suggestions for the improvement of the overall services to propose that the service should offer itself more readily and abundantly to groups in need. The aim was still equality of opportunity but the route was not through universalism: it could be argued that, in so far as universalism implies flat-rate, uniform provision for all *without* tests of need, it is itself essentially unequal in failing to take into account differences of need and resources. Rather, as expressed most powerfully by Plowden, the need was to weight the service in favour of the deprived so as to attempt to compensate for 'the handicaps imposed by the environment': 'We ask for positive discrimination in favour of such schools and the children in them, going well beyond an attempt to equalise resources' (Plowden 1967: vol.1, 57).

Of course, any of the existing spending programmes in favour of needy groups within the population — from standard education services to the provision of children's homes, from hostels for the mentally disordered to subsidized housing — could be called positively discriminatory in the sense that they set out to redistribute resources to these groups in need. What was new about the action proposed by these reports was that it was to concentrate attention and resources on geographical areas. An associated theme, as we shall see in the next section, has been that part of the failure of the services has been inadequate co-ordination and that it is at the local level that this can be developed.

The area approach has been criticized for omitting from consideration the high proportion of the deprived who do not live in the areas where problems are concentrated (Sinfield 1973: vol.3, 133; Glennerster and Hatch 1974). The related point has been made that 'deprivations are concentrated only to a limited extent' (Hatch and Sherrott 1973: 236). More fundamentally, it is argued (Jordan 1974) that a focus of services on a few specific areas of need cannot be successful in reversing the major distribution of resources that occurs through the operation of market forces — in the fields of income, employment, and housing — within but, more importantly, outside these geographical areas. From this point of view, the advent of positive discrimination programmes marks no break from the earlier over-optimistic view of poverty as a residual phenomenon: 'It is a view which was common in the 1960s. It can be called the "pocket of poverty" approach' (Jenkins 1972: 39). It is worth pointing out, however, that Titmuss, the major British proponent of positive discrimination, was arguing in the 1960s for a fundamental redistribution of resources and not just for a shift in direction at the periphery of the social services:

> 'What is certain is that the political alternative to separate, deprecating, programmes for the poor is to channel more resources to them through established, socially approved, "normal" institutions: social security, tax deductions, education and training, medical care, housing and other acceptable routes ... To recognise inequality as the problem involves recognising the need for structural change, for sacrifices by the majority.'
>
> (Titmuss 1972: 317-18)

The area-based positive discrimination programmes that emerged in the 1960s did not seem to imply this level of commitment.

Reports and special areas

The earlier reports were related to specific services. In education, the Newsom, Crowther, and Robbins Reports indicated in the late 1950s and early 1960s that working-class children often suffered environmental disadvantages which affected their performance at school. But, as Cullingworth points out (Cullingworth 1973: vol.2) area-based *solutions* were first proposed in the field of housing. Cullingworth traces the development of this area focus from the growing concern of house improvement policies with not only individual houses but also with areas of housing and later, through the General Improvement Area scheme, with the local environment as a whole. Next, the Milner Holland committee, which reported in 1965 on the problem of overcrowding and multi-occupation in housing stress areas, broadened the argument over areas beyond the question of physical improvement. The Report supported the case for intervention by a public authority in 'areas of special control', where it might not only require house improvement, demolition, and rebuilding but also take action to control sales and lettings and to buy property. Perhaps the nearest that public policy has come so far to the implementation of this suggestion is in the 'housing action area' proposals put forward in the 1974 *Housing Act* (initiated by the Conservatives and retained with amendments by the 1974 Labour Government) in which local authorities were empowered to require improvements and to purchase property for improvement.

While these proposals were service specific, the two reports — of the Plowden and Seebohm committees, which gave the major impetus to the development of a British poverty programme — broadened the argument to demonstrate that areas that were deprived in the field of one service were also often deprived across the board. The Plowden Report on primary education emphasized the relationship between school and home. Children in deprived areas were handicapped by virtue of their home conditions, which provided neither stimulus nor support for learning. The Report therefore argued for a policy of positive discrimination that would compensate these children by improving their schools and teaching.

The Seebohm committee a year later reported on its review of 'the organisation and responsibilities of the local authority personal social services in England and Wales'. The Report stressed that families in need found themselves commonly in need of a whole range of disparate and unco-ordinated social services. It advocated that these services should be brought together in a unified local authority social service department and that, in particular, 'designated areas of special need should receive extra resources comprehensively planned in co-operation with services both central and local, concerned with health, education, housing and other social needs' (Seebohm 1969: para.487). One way of achieving this without the stigma of a personal means test would be by a focus on community development.

While both the Plowden and Seebohm Reports pointed towards the interrelatedness of needs, they set, or were forced by their terms of reference to set, a limit to the range of services that were required to take action. Seebohm was followed by the reorganization of local authority personal social services into unitary departments. Plowden pointed to the important contribution of factors outside school in the neighbourhood to the life chances of a child, but in the ensuing Educational Priority Area (EPA) programme, although area information was examined to identify schools needing special help, the focus of action was still on the schools rather than the area. The reaction of the Department of Education and Science to the Plowden Report was couched simply in terms of educational provision; its focus was on schools needing special help, on primary school building, on a special allowance to teachers in 'schools of exceptional difficulty', on five EPA action research projects, and, under the following (1970-74) Conservative Government, on the nursery education programme.

The solutions that their respective government departments took up were therefore in a sense narrower than the analysis the reports provided. The first interservice response to the notion of *areas* of *multiple* deprivation was the Urban Aid Programme, announced in May 1968. It was followed in 1969 by the announcement of the Community Development Project also administered centrally by the Home Office and, indeed, financed out of earmarked Urban Programme funds. Compared with previous government action on deprived areas the Urban Programme and Community Development Project (CDP) offered the possibility of concentrated and interservice action. In the Urban Programme, central government was to subsidize a programme of local authority expenditure on additional services in deprived areas. CDP was to be an action research programme where teams of locally-based workers would explore the reasons for urban deprivation and test the scope for boosting self-help in communities and for improving the responsiveness of local services. They showed an ultimate concern with comprehensive action on multiply deprived areas: 'The basic aim of the Urban Programme is to alleviate deprivation in local areas of acute social need' (Home Office 1972: para.10). 'The purpose of the CDP may be summarised as: To improve the quality of individual, family and community life in areas with high levels of social need (multiple deprivation)' (Greve 1973: 7).

These programmes — General Improvement Areas, Housing Action Areas, Educational Priority Areas, the Urban Aid Programme, and the Community Development Project — had in common that they were (and are) a part of the same area-selective trend in the development of the 'Welfare State'. Through the struggle with unemployment, the State had slowly taken on responsibility for relief as of right. The range of universally-available benefits and services that were developed after the Second World War were not, however, proof against inflation, neither did they keep up with real increases in wages and material standards in the 1950s and 1960s. Moreover, the value of benefits had been set low initially because of Beveridge's over-pessimism in his predictions of post-war unemployment and hence the demand on benefits. Thus, means-tested benefits were progressively drawn in to make up the difference.

Even if 'our main concern is not now with the extremes of malnutrition' (Jenkins 1972: 42), it became increasingly clear that low take-up of selective benefits, available only on application and means test, was leaving a large number of relatively poor people unaided, and the social services were also not making themselves equally available to all social groups in need. The Labour Government of 1964-70 attempted to remedy these shortcomings by developing a series of programmes directly to favour poor areas: 'The aim was to provide extra help to some, within a framework of social services for all' (Jenkins 1972: 39). To this extent the positive discrimination programmes had some common origins. We will examine in the next chapter the complexity of influences that helped to shape the Urban Programme. But two of these influences merit a special outline at this stage as part of the context of the time. They were the anti-poverty programmes which had been developed a few years earlier in the United States, and the climate of race relations in Britain.

The American war on poverty

Whether or not the American programmes were directly influential, it is certainly true that much in their history and structure, many of their underlying assumptions, and some of the criticisms levelled at them were to be reflected in the later British effort.

The American 'War on Poverty', though generally ascribed (Sundquist 1969; Moynihan 1969) to a combination of President Kennedy's vision of 'a basic attack on the problems of poverty' (Harrington 1968: 156) and of the joint considerations of the President's Committee on Juvenile Delinquency, the Ford Foundation, and the New York-based Mobilization for Youth, was in large measure a response to a decline in confidence in the nation's capacity to eliminate poverty, which paralleled the 'rediscovery of poverty' in Britain. The message had been somewhat dramatically given in 1962 by Michael Harrington in his book *The Other America* which concluded grandiosely that: 'there must be a passion to end poverty ... I hope I can supply at least some of the material for such a vision'.

The first legislative strike in the war came two years later in 1964 with the signing of the *Economic Opportunity Act* which was to: 'eliminate the paradox of poverty in the midst of plenty in this Nation by opening to everyone the opportunity for education and training, the opportunity to work, and the opportunity to live in decency and dignity'. The Act was wide in the sweep of its attack. It included seven titles which ranged from a Job Corps, a Neighbourhood Youth Corps, rural loans, and support for small business to a 'Community Action Program' (CAP). It was the CAP that was the innovative and major feature of the Act. The Community Action Program was expected to help provide and co-ordinate services in poor urban areas with the collaboration of governmental and voluntary organizations and with the incentive of up to 90 per cent federal financing of approved projects. More importantly the programme was to mobilize the poor themselves. The 'maximum feasible participation' of the residents of the areas in the development and management of the projects would help to shake the inertia of the existing services and challenge the present distribution of resources with a new set of priorities fixed in partnership with those who were getting the rawest deal.

Marris and Rein (Marris and Rein 1971), and many others since, have shown how limited the participation of the poor actually was and how far from a real attack on institutional inertia the projects were. But the rhetoric of citizen participation and of challenge to the established power structure, linked later in the minds of politicians with the ghetto riots of the summer of 1967, led to complaints from big city mayors and to action by Congress to restrict funds after only one year of the CAP (Moynihan 1969: 132-43; Kramer 1969: 263-64). There were also complaints about the waste and mismanagement of funds. Senator Dirksen called the CAP 'the greatest boondoggle since bread and circuses in the days of the ancient Roman empire, when the republic fell' (Sellover 1969: 166). As a result of the growing criticism the White House cut back expenditure on community action and local discretion was increasingly reduced by the earmarking of funds, 'beginning with Project Headstart and expanding to include legal service programs and health programs' (Wafford 1969: 96).

The second main initiative under the poverty programme was the *Demonstration Cities and Metropolitan Development Act* (1966) which was the basis of the Model Cities Program. This was to be a 'demonstration programme' designed to show how 'the living environment and the general welfare of people living in slum and blighted neighbourhoods can be improved (Housing and Urban Development (US) 1965) by a concerted local attack on social, economic, and physical problems. Eligible cities were to be paid 80 per cent of the costs to prepare 'comprehensive development plans' within one year and further federal grants would be available in the five-year implementation period for 'new and innovative activities, the redirection of existing resources to better use, and the mobilization of additional resources'. Marris and Rein have shown that the drafters of the Model Cities Program had learned the lessons of the CAP. The Act advocated 'widespread' in place of 'maximum' participation and 'seemed deliberately designed to restore the initiative in reform to established authority in reaction against the radical tendencies of community action' (Marris and Rein 1971: 262). Money which under the *Economic Opportunity Act* had been channelled direct to neighbourhood organizations was under the programme to be distributed through the city administrations: 'A learning process is to be observed: When the Johnson Administration put forth its Model Cities Program, it was provided that the communities involved would participate in the planning process, but strictly in association with the institutions of local government' (Moynihan 1969: 185).

Whereas the earlier programmes had postulated the need to by-pass and reform existing agencies, Model Cities put much more emphasis on the need to develop co-ordination between services and to encourage their administrative competence (Taylor 1967). Amendments to the Model City Guidelines in 1970 further strengthened the mayor's powers in the administration of programmes and reduced the scope for federal intervention. The recognition of the authority of City Hall implied a decision to backtrack from the major reform of social service delivery mechanisms, not to mention the reform of the system of delivery of fundamental resources like income and housing. Instead money ($575 million a year in 1970, and in 1971 in 150 cities) was to be spent on the provision rather than the reform of services.

Certain criticisms of these two programmes — Community Action and Model Cities — were well established by the time their British equivalents were under way. The first criticism, made early on by mayors and Congressmen, was the one that lasted: the CAP had wasted funds, stirred up trouble in the ghettoes, and antagonized local government and services. As we shall see it was this lesson, if any, that British officials had learned from the American experience.

However, the opposite criticism, that the programme had failed to involve the poor and was in fact dominated by existing services, was the one that later emerged from detailed analysis. Sanford Kravitz, co-chairman of the President's Task Force which established the CAP Guidelines, has described the CAP as the victim of its own rhetoric: 'talk of black power and revolutionary violence in fact had little basis in real action but was enough to lead to the curtailment of the program' (Kravitz 1969: 64).

On this the critics agree — there was little involvement of the poor in the Community Action Program. Kramer argues that in the five CAP areas that he studied if there was any 'grassroots participation [it] would be sought *after* the planning or approval of programs' (Kramer 1969: 171), that 'few of the hard-core poor were touched, that the feared political insurgency of the poor did not really develop' (Kramer 1969: 235), and that there was 'more emphasis on the forms than on the substance of participation' (Kramer 1969: 267). Rose concludes that the established services that were supposed to be reformed by the CAP were able to contain the threat and transform the programme with the result that: 'Neither the groups intended in the rhetoric about participation, nor the action strategies planned to assist them, appear to have had much influence in the allocation of anti-poverty funds' (Rose 1972: 146). And Moynihan argues that middle-class community workers and social scientists seized on the participation clauses in the Act to engage in political activism, but without the support of the poor whom they claimed to represent: there did not 'appear to have been any very great deal of actual participation by the poor in the operation of the poverty agency' (Moynihan 1969: 132-33). With regard to the Model Cities Program, also, Warren argues that it 'was hardly a fair trial of citizen participation' (Warren 1971: 15) and that what residents were offered was a frustrating illusion of involvement in an underfunded programme, beset with deadlines that rendered the scope for influence marginal.

In spite of many failings, the poverty programmes are commonly attributed with certain small gains. Among these, three in particular recur:

a The development of minority group leadership: certain minority group (mainly black) individuals were given the opportunity to develop leadership skills even if the 'hard core' poor as a whole were scarcely involved either as organizers or beneficiaries (Moynihan 1969; Sundquist 1969; Kramer 1969). Federal support gave legitimacy to a new ethnic power base (Bachrach and Baratz 1970: 99).

b The promotion of new services: new developments in pre-school education, neighbourhood health and legal services, and job training were promoted through the CAP (Moynihan 1969).

c The advancement of new processes of government: the inclusion of the poor in a new political role is part of this 'gain'. Marris and Rein suggest that community action contributed to the development of a more open process of government by expanding the sources of information input to include more of the poor and black. Agencies were made more sensitive by contact with the poor and hidden issues were revealed (Kravitz 1969). Finally the US Department of Housing and Urban Development claimed that the very fact that cities participating in the Model Cities Program responded to the requirement to prepare comprehensive plans, negotiate with residents, and identify problem areas marked an advance in their technical capacity.

However, the trend of the American programmes towards firmer government control and the narrowing down of their purposes to the more effective delivery of services was already well-established by the time any equivalent British programmes of positive discrimination were initiated. A formal attempt to transmit the American experience was made in an Anglo-American conference of academics and government officials organized by both governments, but only after the British programmes were already under way.

Whether or not the lessons were directly learned — and Dr Halsey has described 'the ideas drifting casually across the Atlantic, soggy on arrival and of dubious utility' (Halsey 1973) — the British Government never let its 'poverty programmes' so far out of its grasp. The CDP local projects were centrally organized, modest in size, and very much related to service provision from the start.

The explanation is to be found perhaps less in the American experience than in the specifically British interpretation of need that was accumulating out of the government enquiries and reports referred to in the last section. These reflected a tradition of central government responsibility for welfare in Britain. However, they shared with the American anti-poverty legislation a concern to focus resources in deprived areas.

Race relations in Britain

There need be no doubt that the setting up of the Urban Aid Programme had something to do with problems of race relations. The Prime Minister, Mr Harold Wilson, put it firmly in that context when he announced its inception in Birmingham in May 1968. Mr Enoch Powell had, in a speech on 20 April 1968, forecast future problems from the concentration of coloured people in cities: 'Like the Romans, I seem to see the River Tiber foaming with much blood ... '.

Mr Wilson 'decided to challenge racialism directly' in a speech that he saw as a reply to Mr Powell. 'Whether it was politically wise or expedient, others can argue: but it was right' (Wilson 1971: 525). In his speech he announced 'new measures we had been working on to deal with the problems of areas where immigration had been at a high rate', in the context of which he:

> '... announced the "Urban Programme", which had been worked out interdepartmentally under the direction of the Home Secretary, to provide further help in housing, education and health in a number of big towns and cities where these problems were greatest, whether immigration was a factor or not.'
>
> (Wilson 1971: 526)

Even if immigration was only one among other factors that stimulated it, this sort of 'positive' government intervention in race relations was of recent origin. The 1960s have been characterized as a period of relatively benign neglect by official policy of both immigration and race relations.

Rose (Rose *et al* 1969) sees the Government's non-interventionist policy in race relations during the period as having two successive bases: the first was the commitment to the view that the law was colour blind and both guaranteed equality in civil rights and made government interference unacceptable; the second was that control of immigration (it was argued) ran counter to the principle of British citizenship within the Empire. Rose proposed that a delicate stage in the development of a multiracial Commonwealth out of the independence of African and Asian countries militated, for political reasons, against the introduction of controls. These were first rejected on grounds of administrative difficulty and then of the principle of free access for British citizens: 'After the Eden Government's decision not to introduce control, technicalities were erected into a principle, to which each party in turn adhered' (Rose *et al* 1969: 220).

This is not to say that there was no alternative view in favour of control. Rose shows that throughout the 1950s there was consideration of the possibility of control by government departments, and indeed that contingency plans were prepared. But these were suppressed in favour of broader foreign policy considerations to do with the development of relations with the New Commonwealth countries (Rose *et al* 1969: 209, 216). If there was to be any control it was to be by bilateral and informal arrangements with the migrant countries (Rose *et al* 1969: 213, 218), a policy built more on pious hopes than tangible results, but which lasted into 1964.

A succession of events between 1958 and 1961 transformed the situation. The fundamental and underlying development was that public concern about the volume and nature of the immigration was beginning to become both apparent and capable of mobilization by those who argued for control. Riots in Notting Hill and Nottingham in 1958 'were followed by sustained complaints in the correspondence columns, particularly of local newspapers, alleging that immigrants were making the housing shortage worse, were persistently unemployed and living off public assistance, and that they were turning the houses in which they lived into slums' (Rex 1973: 94). There was support for this view from the Conservative front bench: 'they come in by air and at once begin to draw National Assistance' (Hornsby-Smith 1958). But the Conservative leadership broadly resisted the ensuing demands for control at the 1958 Conservative Party Conference. This stand, based as it might have been on the exigencies of foreign policy as much as in principle, wilted further as the Government came under more concerted pressure from a grouping of Birmingham M.P.s and a newly-founded organization: the Birmingham Immigration Control Association. Furthermore the figures for immigration from the West Indies, India, and Pakistan in 1960 began to show a marked increase. After a decline in the net inflow from 46,850 in 1956 to

21,600 in 1959 they rose to 57,700 in 1960 and to 136,400 in 1961 (Davison 1966). The Conservative Conference in 1961 called again for control and this time met with a cautious affirmative from the Home Secretary, Mr Butler.

In the debate leading to the *Commonwealth Immigration Act 1962*, the Labour Party opposed the introduction of controls. The Labour leader, Hugh Gaitskill, referring to 'this miserable, shameful, shabby Bill', argued that the rate of immigration was already effectively controlled by its dependence on the level of employment in Britain (Hansard 5.12.1961: cols.1172-73). Both Rose (*et al* 1969: 218) and Foot (1969: 34) report that the responsiveness of immigration to the national need for labour persuaded the Treasury to press within the Government against control. Much of the early immigration had in fact been in direct response to public service recruitment drives. A much later Home Secretary, Mr Robert Carr, was in 1973 to refer back to this earlier justification for immigration and to remind the House of Commons why it could not have adequately staffed public services: ' ... there is the fact that unlike the situation that existed in the 1950's and the early 1960's, which was the last period during which we had this high level of employment, we are no longer permitting the entry into this country of large quantities of immigrant labour to take up jobs of this sort' (Hansard 1.11.1973: col.337).

The 1962 Act restricted entry to those issued with work vouchers but it is not clear that it had any effect in reducing immigration. Rose shows that in the eighteen months prior to the Act there was a large increase in the numbers arriving in an attempt to beat restriction (Rose *et al* 1969: 84). Even after control was in force, numbers did not drop much below those experienced in the mid-1950s (between 35,000 and 50,000 per annum). Moreover, immigrants who might, without control, have gone home, stayed, and those who stayed brought their families.

Once in government, events persuaded the Labour Party to switch its line, in spite of its commitment in the 1964 election, not to statutory restriction, but to informal bilateral controls, to aid for areas affected by immigration, and to the introduction of an anti-discrimination Bill (*Labour Party Manifesto* 1964: 19). Rex and Moore comment that the introduction of immigration restriction gave new 'opportunities for the open expression of resentment against immigrants, for the expression of this resentment now becomes a theme of legitimate politics' (Rex and Moore 1971: 281). Peter Griffiths embodied this legitimization by capturing the 'safe' Labour seat of Smethwick for the Conservatives in the 1964 election. He had campaigned for an almost complete ban on immigration, expressing prejudices and frustrations that were not permitted to surface in most other constituencies, on the grounds that: 'It would be hypocritical of anyone to ignore these problems or to try to pretend that they do not exist' (Griffiths 1966: 173).

In the face of the loss of Smethwick and later Leyton (on similar issues), the Labour Government, with a majority of only three, introduced proposals for an extension of statutory control in March 1965. An interim renewal of the *Commonwealth Immigration Act* in 1964 had now become a commitment in principle, restricting the issue of employment vouchers to 8,500 per annum and abolishing the entry of unskilled workers. There was considerable opposition to this reversal from Labour and Liberal parties as well as from immigrant organizations. Mr Wilson, referring to the 1965 Labour Party Conference, describes ' ... a major row over our immigration policies, about which a very wide section of party opinion understandably felt very strongly' (Wilson 1971: 141). The Government's official view was that integration was impossible without limitation (Rose *et al* 1969: 229), but Richard Crossman, the then Minister for Housing and Local Government, has exposed the electoral considerations: 'Politically, fear of immigration is the most powerful undertone today. We felt we had to out-trump the Tories by doing what they would have done and so transforming their policy into a bipartisan policy' (Crossman 1975: vol.1, 299).

However, the campaign for further control did not abate any more than the scale of immigration declined. The immigration question became a 'central issue in British politics' (Rex 1973: 107) and 'a willingness emerged to abandon restraints on the manner in which the debate was to be conducted' (Rose *et al* 1969: 606). The rise of Enoch Powell as a figurehead of the previously fragmented and unrespectable Right followed closely on the failure of the Conservative Party in the 1964 election. By May 1965, Mr Powell (Foot 1969: 79) was arguing that Commonwealth immigrants should be controlled in the same way as aliens, thus losing the automatic right to bring in their dependants. Through 1967 he, with Duncan Sandys, Sir Cyril Osborne, and other Conservative M.P.s, was speaking publicly in favour of further control and the introduction of measures of voluntary repatriation. According to Rose: 'The main motive force behind this renewed activity was the rapid growth in the number of British citizens of Asian origin entering this country from Kenya as a result of the Kenyanisation policy of the Kenyatta Government' (Rose *et al* 1969: 609-10).

As a result of independence legislation negotiated (ironically) by Mr Duncan Sandys as Commonwealth and Colonial Secretary in 1963, some 100,000 Kenyan Asians had been able to claim British citizenship. Under the threat of eviction from Kenya, they began to enter Britain in large numbers in 1967. In February 1968, the Labour Government introduced legislation that extended the operation of the *Commonwealth Immigration Act 1962* to British citizens whose passports were issued in the colonies, unless their parents or grandfathers had been born in this country. *The Times* declared that: 'The Labour Party now has a new ideology. It does not any longer profess to believe in the equality of man. It does not even believe in the equality of British citizens' (*The Times* 1968).

The Bill met considerable opposition from Labour and Conservative M.P.s, and Mr Wilson states: 'The Bill created agony for our backbenchers, as earlier it had for the Cabinet' (Wilson 1971: 505). This, and the earlier restrictive action, left the Government in need of some proof of its positive, integrationist intentions to be declared before the 1964 election. Through the 1950s and early 1960s the whole responsibility for the welfare of immigrants lay with the local authority social services from which coloured people received, at the best, equal, and certainly no special, help. Problems in the key areas of employment and housing were left untouched and evidence of discrimination was building up. Rex concludes that:

'... coloured people suffered discrimination in employment and housing, that the areas where they were settled were areas which were actually losing population and needed immigrants to man industries, and that housing deterioration followed from the closure of normal housing opportunities to coloured people.'

(Rex 1973: 95)

The conclusion of Daniel's study, carried out for Political and Economic Planning in 1967, was that: 'In the sectors we studied — different aspects of employment, housing and the provision of services — there is racial discrimination varying in extent from the massive to the substantial ... the major component in the discrimination is colour' (Daniel 1968: 209). Elizabeth Burney has shown that local authorities were not making up for the immigrants' weak position in the housing market by recognizing their needs (Burney 1967). Rex and Moore described how immigrants were forced into the multi-occupation of expensive inner-city housing by the discrimination of the private market and by local government selection procedures which limited the access of coloured people to public housing (Rex and Moore 1971).

Before 1965, almost the only intervention by central government in matters concerning the treatment of coloured people once they were in the country was in education. From 1963, the Ministry of Education recommended to local authorities a policy of dispersing immigrant children to schools outside their area. This policy was reiterated and sustained in the Labour Government's 1965 White Paper: 'The Circular 7/65 suggests that about one third of immigrant children is the maximum that is normally acceptable in a school if social strains are to be avoided and educational standards maintained' (Home Office 1965: para.42).

Cullingworth comments that 'it never was clear whether the objective of dispersal was to assist in the teaching of English or in the prevention of the formation of black schools — or both' (Cullingworth 1973: 100). But in Rex's view the significance of dispersal policies for *immigrants* was clear: 'For to declare that a child has to be moved to another school helps to emphasize, either that he is a problem, or that his neighbourhood is a problem, thus drawing attention to his inferior status' (Rex 1973: 85). This essential ambivalence became apparent on a broader scale when the Labour Government introduced anti-discriminatory legislation in 1965 and 1968, in both cases at the same time as the imposition of further controls. On the one hand, coloured people were sufficiently undesirable to be kept out of the country even if they were British citizens; on the other, once in the country they were to be treated as equals.

From the Labour backbenches, Fenner Brockway, M.P. had made several attempts to introduce an anti-discrimination Bill during the 1950s and early 1960s, when the Labour Party supported an 'open-door' policy. His Bill was adopted by the Labour Government and introduced in watered-down form in April 1965 shortly after the Government's conversion to a policy of immigration restriction. The 1965 *Race Relations Act* outlawed incitement to racial hatred and discrimination in public places but excluded the major areas of employment and housing. The Race Relations Board was set up to conciliate between aggrieved parties through local conciliation committees. With Roy Jenkins at the Home Office the Act was extended in 1968 to cover discrimination in employment and housing. The new Act gave the Race Relations Board limited enforcement powers though these 'left a good deal to be desired, especially in the field of employment where specific provision was made for voluntary action in advance of statutory consultation' (Rose *et al* 1969: 616).

The other wing of the Government's positive (rather than negative, controlling) reaction to problems of race relations was the development of the idea of special aid for immigrant areas. This had been promised by Labour before the 1964 election and was, indeed, one of the points that the successful Conservative candidate, Mr Peter Griffiths, had campaigned for in Smethwick. The first step in this direction was section 11 of the *Local Government Act* of 1966 which provided a 50 per cent specific grant out of Rate Support[1] in respect of staff costs incurred 'in dealing with some of the transitional problems caused by the presence of Commonwealth immigrants'. However positive the intent, the wording of the legislation seemed to confirm the view espoused by those who argued for yet more control that immigrants 'caused' problems rather than suffered from them.

The view that immigration and inner-city problems were causally related was given further support in the announcement of the Urban Aid Programme, two years later. As we have seen, the announcement by Mr Wilson was contained in his reply to Mr Enoch Powell's speech of 20 April 1968. Mr Powell's declaration arguing for further immigration control was made at a time when public agitation and discussion over the entry of British passport holders from Kenya had been given a new lease of life by the introduction of the 1968 *Race Relations Bill*. Like Griffiths before him, Powell argued that it was the responsibility of a politician to give expression to his constituents' feelings: 'All I know is that to

[1] Rate Support Grant is the means by which central government supplements the resources of local government. It is distributed as a block grant but specific grants for specific services are paid out of a general pool (Hepworth 1971; Committee of Inquiry on Local Government Finance 1976).

see and not to speak would be the great betrayal'. He therefore felt it incumbent upon him to relay stories transmitted to him about the misbehaviour of immigrants and about the pressure of their demands on the health and social services.

However vigorous though the Prime Minister's reply on 5 May 1968 in Birmingham was, it also was built on the view that inner-city problems were caused or exacerbated by the presence of immigrants:

> '...the load on our education system to say nothing of housing, health and welfare is such that the strictest control is now necessary... [This] social problem is presented for nearly sixty of our towns and cities, where the problem of immigrants and their families has made a great social impact.' (Rose *et al* 1969: 622)

The announcement of the Urban Programme, itself a small part of Mr Wilson's reply speech, was therefore set firmly in the context of the Government's immediate response, at a time of great political difficulty, to those who argued for more control and to those who pressed for a return to more liberal policies. The announcement seemed to offer a response to both sides in the argument — it was concerned with a programme to deal with the problems *experienced* by immigrants and at the same time it was a way of relieving the stress *caused by* immigrants.

However, if the inception of the Programme had its place in the immediate needs of the time it was also a product of the Government's longer term commitment (apparent since 1964) to introduce measures to aid areas affected by immigration. The Labour Government's retreat from an open-door policy left it now with a three-stranded immigration policy of which the Urban Programme formed part of the first:

> 'First, a positive programme of community action... Secondly, a clear determination by the Government to act administratively and by legislation to ensure equality of treatment. And thirdly, a decisive yet humane approach to immigration control.'
>
> (Rose *et al* 1969: 614)

Conclusion

The three contextual areas which we have described separately were of course overlapping in time. The reassertion of social welfare selectivism and its distortion into a principle of positive discrimination occurred at the same time as the Labour Government found itself pressed to manifest some positive concern for the alleviation of problems associated with the settlement, and not just the entry, of immigrants. The areas that government reports were identifying as deprived in the provision of services were also often those where coloured people were living. And, as a backdrop to this 'discovery' of poverty and racial stress in Britain, there was the violent black revolt in American cities and the struggle of the American authorities to contain it. Mr Wilson's reply to Mr Powell made the connection with the threat of violence:

> 'This century, with the loss of millions of lives, has underlined the fact that democracy survives as long as it is fought for. It is challenged today across the Atlantic. It is for us, living in the home of parliamentary democracy, to decide how we respond to the challenge here in Britain ... '   (Wilson 1971: 527)

The Urban Programme and, later, the Community Development Projects were products of this particular coincidence of political pressures and available models for action. They represented not only a response to the arguments about inner-city poverty and the failure of existing social services and benefits to deal with it, but also a reply to the argument that the Government had no positive race relations policy. The case for discriminating *in favour* of deprived groups had already been put in Britain, but the American programmes confirmed the possibility of focussing action on selected areas as a way of delimiting populations without stigmatizing them. They also appeared to confirm the arguments for operating through rather than against the service agencies.

3 Development and aims

The last chapter's *tour d'horizon* may seem a grand background to an initiative of the scale of the Urban Programme. It later emerged that the Government was to commit £20-25 million over an initial period of four years. In this chapter attention is focussed more precisely on the development and aims of the Urban Programme, by drawing on evidence from government records and from the memories of officials who took part in the background developments and in the transformation of the Prime Minister's statement into an operational programme.

There are three main elements in retracing the lines of development. The first is to sketch an outline of the events that immediately preceded the announcement by Mr Wilson on 5 May 1968 and to give a straightforward account of the governmental response in terms of the structures that were set up and of the bodies and people who were involved in getting the Programme under way. The second is to fill in this outline by determining how these structures and participant bodies and individuals defined the problem with which the Urban Programme was concerned, what issues they felt had to be resolved, and what influences were brought to bear on them. The third is to consider the outcome of the deliberations of these participants and to examine what aims had emerged and what means had been devised for their achievement.

What is of interest at this stage is not only to understand how, and how far, politicians' (and senior administrators') policies are transmuted into action and perhaps transformed in the process. It is also intended to offer some insight into the underlying assumptions about the nature of the problem and the available solutions, and into the policy alternatives that were considered. Later examination of what actually happened in the operation of the Programme will draw, for some of its explanations, on the influence of the formative assumptions and of the organizational means that were evolved and selected at this early stage. In this we share Marris and Rein's starting-point, that is, to explain the outcome of a programme in terms of the interplay between its underlying assumptions, its organizational structures, and the experience gained in its implementation (Marris and Rein 1971: 33-4). As an organization develops, it becomes subject to the exigencies of practice and to demands made on it from both within and without; but divergence is held in check by (or has to be rationalized in terms of) the recorded aims of the organization, and by the founders' assumptions and intentions as manifested in the organizations and processes that they established.

By the time this study began, the Urban Programme was already three years old; and by the time, even later, that the study was sufficiently far advanced to embark upon an informed discussion with respondents, many of the people who had been concerned with the Programme at the outset had moved on to other posts. The two sources of information had their separate defects. Of both it can be said that there is a tendency for personal opinions and influence to be lost or disguised behind the monolithic departmental view. The memories of officials had faded and were probably also inhibited by Civil Service decorum and by the tradition of consigning old posts to the past and leaving the present occupants unembarrassed by interference. File records, on the other hand, were often expressed in the blandest tones which concealed issues, differences of opinion, and rejected alternatives. There were inexplicable gaps and jumps in developments which may have been due to inspired advances in thinking but which may equally have indicated that papers had been lost, that there were unrecorded discussions, or that the topic had been consigned to unknown files. In any case, tracks were often broken and there can be no certainty that their end was always reached.

However, the files have proved to be a very rich source of

evidence as a result of the wealth and detail of the material recorded, stemming no doubt from the fact that — as R.G.S. Brown (1970) has pointed out — the possible need to justify decisions retrospectively in Parliament means that the processes of reaching them must be conscious and articulate and hence recorded. In consequence, a great deal of the minutiae of discussion and decision-taking are placed on file. What is not (and can never be) known, of course, is that which is never recorded on file and, while it is in general true that recorded information is in itself inadequate for the study of decision-making, the habit in the public service of filing so much detail does ameliorate some of the more serious shortcomings of this form of evidence. A thorough perusal of documentary material can sometimes enable the researcher to identify lacunae in the story (for example the sudden appearance of a final decision that appears to be at odds with the trend of foregoing events) and, though these must often remain as 'blanks' in the story, it is on occasion possible to fill them from the personal recollections of the actors involved — assuming of course that they are still alive, accessible, and willing respondents. A more serious drawback of file material is that it may *appear* to reveal the true and complete story when in fact the real forces at work remain hidden. To put it crudely, while the recorded evidence appears to reveal all, it is not possible to be sure what influence is brought to bear or what is decided over lunch in the Cabinet Office Mess or at Locket's Restaurant in Westminster.

Nevertheless, it is true that officials, and especially those concerned with the origin of the Urban Programme, showed a preparedness to be interviewed that seemed to reflect a high level of interest — and involvement — in the events and objectives they were describing. It can also be said that within the Home Office access was made available to all the files that were traceable, though there may have been others (and there were certainly some specific papers) that were not accessible. As for the other departments concerned with the Urban Aid Programme — the Treasury, the Department of Education and Science, the Department of Health and Social Security, and the Department of the Environment — interviews were conducted but their files were not made available. Since it is not possible to be certain, therefore, that the full range and depth of departmental views has been conveyed, the present account may be weighted towards the role of the Home Office. As co-ordinating department, however, the Home Office seems likely to have had on record most of the substantial views of other departments.

As was pointed out in Chapter 2, the Urban Programme was launched at a time of great public and parliamentary concern with race relations and immigration. There was a call for more control of immigration following partly upon the new arrival of Kenyan Asians. On the other hand, there was concern within and outside the Labour Party at the Government's movement towards control. Whether or not they accepted control, large sections of all parties supported the case for some more overtly-integrationist measures. The introduction of the *Commonwealth Immigration Bill* and the *Race Relations Bill* within a few months of each other in February and April 1968 expressed this ambivalence and dilemma on the part of the Labour Government.

Neither Bill succeeded in stemming the differing public expressions of concern. Indeed, Enoch Powell's speech of 20 April 1968 managed to capture, and add to, concern not only at the level of immigration but also at the possibility that the *Race Relations Bill* could contribute to: 'The sense of being a persecuted minority which is growing among ordinary English people' (Powell 1968). While Powell reflected a particular (and possibly widely-shared) point of view, however, others were equally concerned about what they saw to be growing discriminatory tendencies in some sections of society. In the midst of parliamentary and public discussion, the *Race Relations Bill* wended its way through a third reading in the House of Commons in July 1968, past official Conservative opposition and towards ultimate enactment in October. It thus provided a continuing background to the formative period of the Urban Programme.

Home Office organization for race relations and the Urban Programme

The Home Office was historically the department concerned with immigration. In 1965 race relations were, formally, a new subject of specific government responsibility that had to be found a home in the government administrative structure. It was not entirely clear where it would go. While the Home Office under Sir Frank Soskice had drafted and negotiated the 1965 *Race Relations Bill*, responsibility for co-ordinating Whitehall interests in race relations was allocated to Mr Maurice Foley, Parliamentary Under Secretary of State at the Department of Economic Affairs.

The position was clarified, shortly after Mr Roy Jenkins became Home Secretary, when in 1966 Mr Foley was moved to the Home Office with both his staff and his responsibility for race relations. This new division within the Home Office became responsible for the drafting of the 1968 *Race Relations Bill*. Jumping a step to which we will later return, this division was later joined in a new and enlarged Race Relations Department by a second division which was established in 1968 to co-ordinate work on the Urban Aid Programme. The Race Relations Department was subsequently renamed the Community Relations Department when administrative responsibility for the Urban Programme was extended to cover the Community Development Project, which was associated with it. Still later it became the Community Programmes Department and, most recently, the Urban Deprivation Unit.

In spite of changes in the names given to departments and divisions, the structure of Home Office responsibility for race relations and the Urban Programme has remained much the same since those early days. It is represented in *Figure 1*, which shows in simplified form how the Home Office itself is organized from the most senior official downwards.

First stirrings

Turning back from this brief outline of the official organization that existed before the Urban Programme and was then extended to receive it, attention is directed to the developments in thinking in the higher echelons of the Home Office, which were to contribute at least some of the impetus that led to the announcement of the Programme. It has been seen that there were other influences which provided their own contribution — the American poverty programme was possibly one — but, more importantly, there were developments in the social services towards positive discrimination and the commitment of the Labour Party to some positive response to race relations problems. Home Office official thinking was indeed very much a product of the need to develop government policy on race relations.

Before the end of 1967, as the pressure on the Government began

Figure 1   The Urban Programme in the Home Office organization

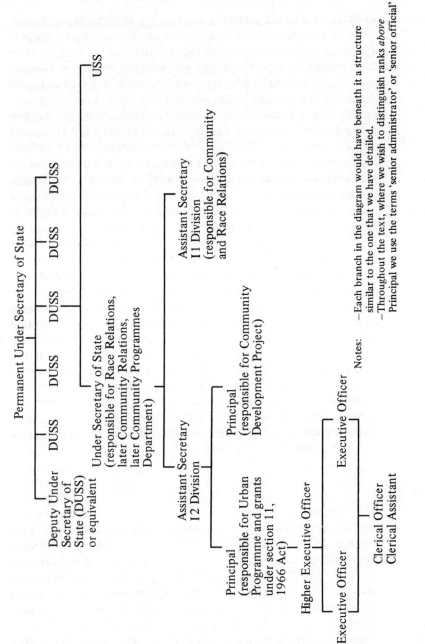

Permanent Under Secretary of State

Deputy Under Secretary of State (DUSS) or equivalent

DUSS DUSS DUSS DUSS DUSS DUSS USS

Under Secretary of State (responsible for Race Relations, later Community Relations, later Community Programmes Department)

Assistant Secretary I1 Division (responsible for Community and Race Relations)

Assistant Secretary I2 Division

Principal (responsible for Community Development Project)

Principal (responsible for Urban Programme and grants under section 11, 1966 Act)

Higher Executive Officer

Executive Officer

Executive Officer

Clerical Officer
Clerical Assistant

Notes: –Each branch in the diagram would have beneath it a structure similar to the one that we have detailed.
–Throughout the text, where we wish to distinguish ranks *above* Principal we use the terms 'senior administrator' or 'senior official'

to build up with the arrival in the country of the Kenyan Asians, officials were becoming increasingly concerned at the absence of a systematic government view on race relations questions. Except on immigration control, there was no basis on which the Government's critics could be answered, and there was not even any solid statistical information with which to counter Enoch Powell's immigration population projections. Questions about government policy towards those who had entered the country fell even more into a vacuum. Should the focus of government policy be wholly on immigration control or should it extend to the promotion of toleration and adjustment? What number of immigrants and their descendents could be expected? Should the Government promote the absorption of immigrant groups into the native culture or encourage them to maintain their separate identity?

From the beginning of 1968, when Mr Roy Jenkins became Home Secretary, officials across several departments, chaired by the Home Office, began the task of reviewing immigration and community relations policy. According to one senior administrator (see footnote to *Figure 1*), the idea of some sort of programme of expenditure to help immigrants and to smooth their relations with the native community began here: 'That was, I think, the very first spark.' But the Government's concern with integrationist policies had, at least temporarily, been overtaken by the growing furore over the immigration of the Kenyan Asians. The *Commonwealth Immigration Bill*, aimed to restrict the influx, was immediately presented to the House of Commons on 22 February 1968. Attention was deflected towards questions relating to the provisions and administration of the Act.

The Prime Minister's speech

The 'first spark' was slow to show any signs of spreading any further, but when it did so it seems to have taken officials by surprise. In his speech of 5 May 1968 in reply to Enoch Powell, the Prime Minister annouced that ' ... we have decided to embark on a new and expanded Urban Programme ... ' (Wilson 1968). While the idea (without the programme title) had broadly occurred in the official review of policy, it seems that the Prime Minister catalyzed developments by making the announcement at this stage. Officials' memories differ on whether they had any prior notice, but it does seem that a few days before the speech officials were called upon to prepare sketch proposals.

Other Home Office officials, working in the Children's Department on early proposals for the Community Development Project, were similarly taken aback and were left wondering whether their ideas had come to fruition or been pre-empted. Nevertheless, according to the most senior administrator involved in the construction of the Urban Programme, the Prime Minister had read the official proposals and was likely to have been influenced by them.

Though brief, the Prime Minister's announcement contained several phrases which were to become underlying principles of the Urban Programme, as officials took what guidance they could from his speech:

a This was an *urban* programme: the Prime Minister's reference was to the problems of towns;

b the problems referred to embraced education, housing, health, and welfare;

c the Programme was announced in the context of problems of immigration, but 'Expenditure should be on the basis of need and the immigration problem is only one factor, but a very important factor in the assessment of social need';

d the Programme was to have a 'particular emphasis on education ... ';

e 'the Home Secretary will be in charge of working out the details of this programme';

f ' ... this cost will have to be met within the ceiling of expenditure laid down in the announcement I made to Parliament in January'.[1] Favoured areas would therefore have to contribute to deprived areas.

It would be a mistake to read too much into the inclusions and omissions in such a brief statement, but even at this stage it is possible to discuss some major assumptions about the problems the Programme was to tackle and the way it should deal with them.

First, as has been noted, the announcement of a Programme linked explicitly with the problems of immigration assumed that to a significant degree, the strain on services was a consequence of immigration even if this was 'only one factor' — in other words, not only did the immigrants have needs but also their presence highlighted or created needs. The statement was, however, equivocal about the

[1] The announcement referred to here concerned general economy measures.

nature of the relationship between social needs and immigration.

Second, the Prime Minister defined the problems in broad terms reflecting the view of the Seebohm and Plowden Committees that in the more disadvantaged places needs tended to occur in inter-related bundles. Although education was described as a priority, the speech opened the way for action on 'multiple deprivation'; a manifestation of the broader intentions (and also of the racial context) was the location of responsibility for the development of the Programme with the Home Secretary, who had direct responsibility for none of the service areas mentioned.

Third, the solution seems to have been envisaged in terms of the service areas for which government, central or local, was already responsible: education was named explicitly and the other services were named as problem areas to which solutions had to be found. Non-service features relating more to the economic and social structure, like income distribution, employment, and the allocation of resources to housing sectors, went unmentioned. Nevertheless, though the solution was couched in terms of the application of *supplementary* services, these were to be financed by moneys found from 'savings in the general management of the economy'.

Fourth, the statement did not indicate any feeling that the fault and remedy might lie — at least in part — in the decision-making processes of central and local government and other service agencies. By contrast, the US programmes had been much concerned, as we have seen, with co-ordinating services, planning, inducing local participation, and by-passing entrenched bureaucracy, which seemed to be obstructing the flow of resources to poorer areas. At least, as far as can be gauged from the Prime Minister's speech, no such inadequacies in the existing organizational processes seem to have been assumed. More evident was the presumption that the problems arose from the lack of resources available to the existing services in particular stress areas.

A fifth assumption was that what was required or possible, given economic exigencies, could be met within existing national budgets. In practice, however, unless other spending agencies of central government were to be seriously deprived, the Programme could not, within these constraints, become a big spender. If there was to be redistribution it was, at the least, unlikely that the existing services and the wealthier local authorities would be prepared to make politically embarrassing sacrifices.

Sixth, it is interesting to note that the Prime Minister did not make any reference to the idea that need might be concentrated in small areas within local authorities. The notion that there were 'pockets of deprivation' was later to become an integral part of the Programme, but Mr Wilson expressed his concern with the problems of whole towns.

The structure of the response

In this section we shall describe the immediate organizational response made by the Civil Service to this unexpected, if not 'surprise', announcement. Later we shall examine the issues which this organization considered in the period of less than three months before the Urban Programme was launched in operational form.

The Prime Minister had put responsibility for developing the Programme into the Home Secretary's hands, but had also suggested that it should deal with a range of problems falling outside the Home Office's field. The Home Office could not make decisions that would affect other government departments without consulting them. There already existed the interdepartmental structure chaired by the Home Office which had contributed the 'first spark' to the Prime Minister's announcement, but this was at too high a level to be directly occupied with the detailed sifting of ideas and possibilities which was required to set up the Programme. A body had to be created, as the senior administrator responsible observed: 'We didn't have any interdepartmental network to prepare papers ... but that we created quite easily. It's a thing Whitehall is used to doing. We got like-minded chaps round the table.'

On 7 May 1968, two days after the Prime Minister's speech, a new interdepartmental Working Party met at the Home Office with representation at assistant secretary level from the Ministry of Health and Social Security, the Department of Education and Science, the Department of Employment and Productivity, the Ministry of Housing and Local Government, the Treasury, and the Home Office. It had the following terms of reference:

'to consider implementation of the "new and expanded Urban Programme" mentioned in the Prime Minister's speech ... but it would *in addition* serve the interdepartmental committee of officials who were to meet for the first time on 9 May to consider

a wide range of subjects affecting areas of immigrant population.'   (Working Party Meeting Minutes 5.1968)

The Working Party was thus at its first meeting given a wide
brief which could be broken down into three categories:

i   information on immigrants especially in the field of employ-
    ment;
ii information on existing programmes of help;
iii an assessment of the correspondence between areas of need
    and areas of immigration, and of the sort and amount of
    further aid which was needed.

The Home Office official who found himself chairman of the
Working Party had been drafted to his new post only two days
before the Prime Minister's speech. As the forerunner of the
administration of the Programme he was more or less without a
division to support him, and there was in effect no Under Secretary
between him and higher ranks. His previous post had been in the
Children's Department of the Home Office where he had been
working on proposals for the Community Development Project,
which, though separately conceived, was later to be financed out of
an Urban Programme earmarked fund and to be administered
jointly with the Urban Programme.

The interdepartmental structure which has been outlined was, at
each level, chaired and led by a Home Office senior administrator
or minister. The leading role of the Home Office allowed the
formality of the hierarchical structure to be bridged by a close
working relationship between the chairmen. On the one hand there
was the formal progression of instructions, observations, or views
down and proposals up the ladder of interdepartmental bodies and,
on the other, there was the day-to-day exchange of ideas and
drafts within the Home Office, which, if it did not by-pass, at least
speeded up the formal procedures.

Though other departments' views were influential, as we shall
see, the two official chairmen were the main architects of the
detailed decisions and compromises which allowed the Home
Secretary (Mr Callaghan) to inaugurate the Urban Programme less
than three months after the Prime Minister's brief statement.
Nevertheless the formal interdepartmental meetings established the
framework and deadlines within which the Home Office produced
background papers, guidelines, and drafts for discussion.

The Working Party had largely executed its initial part by the end of May 1968; criteria for the selection of areas, existing aid, possible future aid, and systems of payment had all been considered and reported back. The remaining two months before the Home Secretary's announcement was taken up mainly with decisions about the scale of the Programme. The Prime Minister's statement had anticipated that the Programme would be financed within existing ceilings of expenditure. However, government departments were unwilling to make sacrifices out of their own budgets, and ministers were unwilling to go far in the direction of raising extra funds. Ministers, on the other hand, were anxious to get the Programme started quickly to meet the expectations created by the Prime Minister's statement and to demonstrate some governmental response to urban needs and the state of race relations.

These exigencies forced a re-examination by officials of the scale and nature of the Urban Programme just two weeks before Mr Callaghan's statement to Parliament. The Programme that was made public by the Home Secretary on 22 July was much slighter than the Working Party had hoped to reveal.

The issues

The Home Secretary's statement was the tip of the iceberg of the discussions that had taken place between officials. By then, much of the future form of the Programme had been determined, though three important questions remained to be resolved: 'how many local authorities should or could be assisted?', 'how large should the grant be?', and 'what types of project should be funded?' The main issues considered by officials arose directly from the need to translate into concrete reality significant but vague phrases in the Prime Minister's speech. Was this a programme for immigrants? What was 'social need'? What were the 'solutions', and where would the money be found? What machinery should be set up to operate the Programme, and in what ways might central government departments work together?

The immigrant focus

Initial discussion reflected the role which the Prime Minister had thrust upon the Programme by launching it in the context of the debate on immigration. We have seen that the Working Party's terms of reference, and its first meeting, were very much directed at the subject of immigration and at the collection of information on associated problems. The official discussions were taking place within machinery concerned with immigration. The focus on areas where immigrants settled was, however, to be progressively weakened with the growing recognition by officials that positive discrimination in favour of immigrants carried with it its own political difficulties.

In the three weeks after the Prime Minister's announcement on 5 May, officials questioned, for instance, whether it might be possible to disguise the focus on immigrant areas by describing them as 'urban areas of general social need'. The starting-point, then, was that the Programme was indeed designed to help immigrants though the fact might have to be disguised. The next step was to question the case for a simple focus on immigrant areas and problems. It was noted that the Prime Minister had emphasized that the Programme would apply to *all* the deprived urban areas: 'The Government do not look at this in terms purely of the immigrant areas ... '

The Race Relations Division of the Home Office supported this view by arguing against suggestions, in early drafts of the Working Party's report, that the presence of immigrants was somehow itself a measure of deprivation. They were the victims rather than the cause of the deprivation of the areas they might live in. Arguments like these supported the political case for overriding a programme strictly devoted to immigrants, and ministers agreed in their meeting of 30 May that the Programme should deal with needs in general as well as with the particular problems presented by immigration. The Working Party, drawing on a paper prepared by the Department of Education and Science, which was apparently influenced by the work of the Plowden committee, then outlined the possible existence of two sorts of need: one associated with problems of immigration and the strain on social services; the other relating to questions of urban environment and multiple deprivation. The adoption of this view led to the conclusion (much as the Prime Minister had originally proposed) that numbers of immigrants should be counted as only one among other factors in the assessment of social need.

The Home Secretary's statement to the House of Commons on

22 July 1968 was thus able to give the topic of immigration a sort of passing reference which should have satisfied those who did not believe that immigrants needed special help. The Programme had been carefully steered into a middle course. Nevertheless, it was clear from the debate (Hansard 22.7.1968: cols.237-53) which followed in the House that, on both sides, it was the UP's relevance to race relations and immigration that was of considerable interest. There was little debate about the nature of the Urban Programme itself. Most of the questions from the Opposition Party centred on the issue of restricting further immigration of Commonwealth immigrants and aliens.

Existing programmes

From its first meeting the Working Party was concerned with other and earlier programmes of help to urban areas. It was intended to establish not only what was already being done and what gaps were left for the UP to fill, but also to derive from these Programmes ready-made criteria for the definition of priority areas. The Working Party had been asked to report within a fortnight on the implementation of the Programme. It decided that this did not leave enough time to wait for the derivation of the new and 'scientific' area criteria that were expected to come out of the deliberations in the Home Office that were, quite separately, leading towards the establishment of the Community Development Project. Instead, departments were asked to submit lists of the areas which benefited from existing priority programmes and to set out the criteria by which they qualified for inclusion.

The most important of these programmes was the Department of Education and Science scheme offering special aid to 'educational priority areas' (EPAs) for which the Plowden Report had provided an authoritative set of criteria. Less 'scientific' (in the sense that their criteria were more nebulous) were the Ministry of Housing and Local Government's 'housing priority areas' (mainly relating to slum clearance) and the Home Office's 50 per cent grant for extra staff in areas of immigration under section 11 of the 1966 *Local Government Act*.

By the time of the second meeting of the Working Party, the Home Office had put together lists showing those areas that were identified by all three programmes and those that appeared in only one or two of them. Because of the difficulty of comparing programmes which operated at different geographical levels (section 11 at local authority and the other two at sub-authority levels) the Home Office list was based on the largest of these: the local authority. With the intention of restricting the list to *urban* areas, only county boroughs and London boroughs were included in what was regarded by the Working Party as 'a useful working list of "areas of social need"' (Working Party Meeting Minutes 5.1968).

The list which went with the Working Party's report showed a wide range of authorities affected. Of a total of 114 county boroughs and London boroughs, ninety were identified: twenty-three of these were 'priority areas' for all three purposes, forty for two of them, and twenty-seven for one only. The Ministry of Health was able to offer additional figures relating to perinatal mortality and TB notification which showed that, of seventy-eight county boroughs and London boroughs where, on these grounds, the health services were in need of improvement, sixty-seven occurred among the ninety county boroughs already identified. This left a further eleven county boroughs that were priority areas in terms of health if not otherwise.

The Working Party had thus arrived at a list that excluded only thirteen county boroughs from one or other of these priority categories! Consequently, ministers were advised that areas should not be identified in this way, but the exercise had been influential in evolving the sort of selection criteria that were to be used and in involving other departments in the course of doing so.

Criteria

The Prime Minister's initial speech, which named a range of services and made it clear that several departments would be involved, set the Programme in pursuit of 'multiple deprivation'. There had been earlier impetuses (for example in the Plowden and Seebohm Reports) for the notion that needs were related and should be treated together: this idea was at the root of thinking on the Community Development Project which was being developed within the Children's Department of the Home Office. The Chairman of the Working Party had been active in the Community Development Project and brought with him a strong sense of the artificial disparity of government departments' programmes and the geographical areas they covered.

The examination of existing programmes and their overlap was the first step towards the identification of the areas of multiple deprivation that the Working Party assumed existed. The Department of Education and Science's Educational Priority Area programme (EPA) was the most influential. Its allocation of expenditure was based on the criteria of need proposed by the Plowden Report:

a occupation
b size of families
c supplements in cash or kind from the State
d overcrowding and sharing of houses
e poor attendance and truancy from school
f proportion of retarded, disturbed, or handicapped pupils
g incomplete families
h children unable to speak English.

This list was eventually drawn on heavily in the guidance that went out to local authorities, but in these early stages it seemed that another more sophisticated approach could be adopted. Birmingham County Borough had carried out an exercise in response to the EPA programme which entailed the use of census statistics to identify those deprived areas that seemed broadly compatible with Plowden's intentions:

i persons born elsewhere than England, Scotland, or Wales
ii social class of economically-active males
iii households and persons by occupation density
iv households without exclusive use of a fixed bath
v persons unemployed for a year or more
vi children aged 0-14 in the total population
vii households sharing a dwelling.

These criteria, with their ready availability from the census, had the advantages that they would include areas of immigrant concentration, that it would be possible to compare areas systematically, and that central government would not be dependent for the collection of data on returns from local authorities. The approach had a concomitant disadvantage, however: any set of criteria that resulted in the designation of specific areas for inclusion in or exclusion from special benefits would be in constant dispute from potential recipients or non-recipients and could be administratively and politically embarrassing. Its very clarity was a disadvantage because it left no room for manoeuvre.

Officials rejected the use of census criteria for immediate application on the grounds (or pretext) that social planning had not yet reached the stage where there were agreed techniques for assessment of needs. Further study of the possibilities was urged and in fact did continue, though its results were inconclusive for the next two years. In the meantime, it was agreed that a looser approach should be adopted whereby local authorities should measure their own needs as far as possible on the basis of stated factors of need which government departments would take into account in making a final assessment. This was the approach that, in fact, became the formal pattern, though, as we shall see, the stated factors of need never acquired a clear place in the operation of the Urban Programme.

The circular issued in October 1968 listed a set of sample manifestations of deprivation: large families, overcrowding, unemployment, poor environment, concentration of immigrants, children in trouble or need of care. The list owed much to the Plowden experience but no cut-off points were established and no definitions offered for each of these conditions. It was very much up to local authorities to decide how to respond.

Areas of deprivation

Mr Wilson's statement made no mention of areas smaller than local authorities, but it quickly became apparent to the Working Party that, whether local authorities were identified on the basis of earlier programmes or from census criteria, too many were thrown up for any foreseeable programme to deal with. One third of the United Kingdom's population was implicated in the first definition of deprived areas! Whether or not areas were to be formally designated it was obvious to officials that the Government had not conceived a programme to be run on this scale. Some formula had to be found to permit greater selectivity for a programme that was intended to touch *priority* areas.

Two of the existing programmes on which the list of county and London boroughs had been drawn up were in fact concerned with small areas within local authorities. We saw in the previous chapter that EPAs and the housing priority areas were manifestations of a tendency in many areas of the social services towards small-area positive discrimination. The idea that need occurred in concentrated blackspots seemed to be confirmed by the Birmingham exercise: overlay on overlay of shaded maps (showing the incidence of the various factors) built up an attractively clear picture of the distinctiveness of the areas of multiple need. The possibility was not considered that the stark clarity of these 'needle points' (as they were described) might have been a feature of the cut-off points that happened to be chosen for the criteria in Birmingham rather than the objective statement of the distribution of deprivation that they were taken to be.

Areas were not designated but the idea that there were distinct urban blackspots which could be identified corresponded with the exigencies imposed by the shortage of funds and with the minister's urging that resources should not be spread so thinly in an attempt to cover all possible needs that no real effect on the problem was achieved. On 22 July the Home Secretary was able to announce a programme that did not sound as if it would be too obviously overwhelmed by the remaining 'areas of severe deprivation in a number of our cities and towns — often scattered in relatively small pockets'.

Community Development Areas

At about the same time as the Working Party was developing the details of the Urban Programme, another interdepartmental working party under Home Office chairmanship had presented proposals for an experiment in community development. This owed its origins much more than the Urban Programme to official rather than ministerial initiative and consequently had a less ready claim on funds. For a full account of its origins see Lees and Smith 1975, but the most immediate outside stimuli were the 1963 *Children and Young Persons Act*, the Seebohm Report, and the American poverty programme, which had all stressed the failure of bureaucratic services to make themselves accessible to the needy. The proposal was to set up experimental action research projects in up to twelve defined areas to assess the community's needs, to improve the responsiveness of the social services to those needs, and to promote the community's self help.

Though the idea of community development areas had been conceived separately from the Urban Programme, they had in common both concern with multiple deprivation and priority areas, and the solutions which they envisaged in terms of cross-service action. They were linked in the flesh by the adoption as chairman of the UP Working Party of a Home Office official who had previously been a member of the interdepartmental body concerned with community development. Though officials were at first unsure whether the Urban Programme spelled the pre-emption of the community development areas, they were quick to take the opportunity to associate the latter with the fortunes of the former. It was argued that there would be presentational[2] advantage in announcing the two programmes together. The Community Development Area scheme (as it was then called) could be seen as the research wing of the Urban Programme, seeking information and solutions which would be ploughed back into the Programme.

In fact the Home Secretary restricted his announcement to the Urban Programme, but the conceptual link between the two schemes had been made. In the following year, 1969, the Community Development Project was launched and funded out of the UP. In 1970 the two schemes were brought together administratively when the Community Development Project's parent, the Children's Department, was transferred from the Home Office to the Department of Health and Social Security as part of the reorganization of central government departments following the 1970 General Election and the installation of a Conservative administration led by Mr Edward Heath.

Multiple schemes

From its first meeting the Working Party talked in terms of 'multiple need'. The Prime Minister's speech set the discussion on a course that seemed to be confirmed by the evidence that the various government departments represented on the Working Party produced about their different priority programmes. The first question was whether areas of multiple need were somehow worse off than those with acute individual needs and demanded a more generous response. The second question was whether the response should be in the same terms (that is, whether the aid should also be 'multiple' and concentrated on areas) or, on the other hand, widely scattered between areas.

The proposal for 'multiple schemes' was pursued and given strong support in official reports. It was seen partly as a response to

---

[2] A commonly-used Civil Service word implying a concern with the appearance or 'image' of a public statement.

ministers' requirements that resources should not be spread so thinly in an attempt to cover all deficiencies that no real effect on the problem was achieved. It was argued that multiple schemes would be suited to areas where there were multiple needs while single projects would be reserved for lower priority areas. The multiple schemes would be integrated projects including, for example, a school, new housing, day nurseries, family advice centres, health centres, and playgroups. The belief was that integrated projects would be the best way of making an impact locally and on the public as a whole.

While officials recognized that these schemes might take longer to plan and agree with local authorities, it was clear that they were seen as an important (if not the major) aspect of the Urban Programme. This view was accepted by ministers. However, it appears that the financial stringency of the time ruled out their immediate implementation. In the short term at least, the UP was to be a programme characterized by single scattered projects. Of course, there was nothing to stop the use of even limited resources in a concentrated way; the assumption can only be made that ministers felt that the virtues of the multiple approach were outweighed by the need to reach a larger number of areas than such an approach would permit and to do so quickly.[3]

Projects

The Prime Minister's statement had given some indication about what the new Programme was to do. The problems he outlined were wide-ranging but, in terms of solutions, the Urban Programme was to have a particular emphasis on education. Nevertheless, from the start, discussions in the Working Party about possible expenditure embraced the whole field of the government departments which were represented — Health and Social Security, Housing and Local Government, Education and Science, Employment and Productivity, and the Home Office. It appears that an initial list of ideas for possible projects was culled from the representatives of these departments assembled for the first Working Party meeting. With little change these proposals recurred through the interdepartmental discussions that followed and were in fact to form the basis of the future Urban Programme:

[3] In 1971 'multiple schemes' were initiated in Liverpool and Teesside (Batley 1976).

Building   i new schools, and improvements and enlargements of school buildings;

        ii nursery schools and classes;

        iii day nurseries;

        iv pre-school playgroups;

        v health centres;

        vi children's homes;

        vii family advice centres;

        viii limited further promotion of new house building and housing area rehabilitation (though probably through existing programmes);

Staff   ix grants for salaries of additional teachers, further to those available under section 11 of the *Local Government Act 1966*;

        x additional education staff: welfare assistants, liaison officers, nursery assistants, further education lecturers, and youth workers;

        xi grants for in-service training of teachers;

        xii staff for housing improvement projects;

        xiii health and welfare staff;

Other   xiv equipment and materials for schools;

        xv transport costs for immigrant pupil dispersal;

        xvi increased help for the appointment of local authority staff needed as a result of the presence of immigrants (section 11 of the 1966 Act);

        xvii grants for the appointment of interservice social work teams and university researchers for the proposed Community Development Area scheme.

In so far as the logic of this choice was related to any sense of the Urban Programme as a distinctive programme, two features of the Prime Minister's statement seem to have informed it or were seized on as arguments for the projects proposed:

a the immigrant focus of the Urban Programme was employed in relation to projects i-iv, ix, xiv, and xv; and

b the Prime Minister's focus on children and education was reflected in the majority of the proposals.

One or other of these two characteristics applies directly to every project type, except the health centres, the family advice centres, the Community Development Areas, and the housing improvement and house building (which were never in fact promoted through the Urban Programme). Beyond these simple leads taken from the Prime Minister's speech, the choice seems to have depended more on the individual department's views about gaps in their particular services than on a collective view about the purpose of the new programme. Given the haste with which the Urban Programme was conceived, and given the involvement of the whole range of government departments with their separate commitments, it is perhaps not surprising that what emerged was an all-inclusive list without any priority ordering.

This 'shopping list' of projects, as it was known to officials, was at first approved by ministers with the qualification that it might be extended to include other suitable schemes. But, a week before the Home Secretary's announcement, officials were asked to rethink the scope of the Programme to adjust it to the reduced scale of available funds. As a result, the Prime Minister's immigrant and education emphasis was sharpened: the reduced Programme would focus on assistance for staffing immigrant areas and on pre-school education. The Home Secretary's announcement was in fact even more limited, referring only to nursery education and child care at least for the first year of the Urban Programme.

Finance

The Working Party's initial brief contained no suggestion about the scale of the funds available. Officials were expected to find departmental savings to finance the Urban Programme and to make proposals for expenditure without knowing what they had to find and what they had to spend. Perhaps it was hoped that the savings made would determine the level of expenditure. But how were departments to volunteer to contribute savings in the absence of any agreed view about the types of existing expenditure which were to assume lower priority than the as yet unspecified Urban Programme? The proposals that departments made for savings were either vague or, in the case of the Home Office itself, non-existent.

It was a bad time to ask for further savings when departments were already being asked to prune their expenditure as part of the

Government's deflationary measures (Crossman 1975: vol.2, 619-21).

The questions which presented themselves to officials were:

i at what level to fix expenditure?
ii through what channels to spend it?

The figure of £30 million to be spent over two years emerged early in the Working Party discussions for no reason that is now easily discernible. It was roughly on the scale of the savings that had been talked about and it sounded like a serious figure even if it was not massive. However, financial controls and the absence of savings forced the figure down first to £22 million over two years and eventually to the same sum over four years — £1 million in 1968/69, £5 million in 1969/70, and £8 million each for 1970/71 and 1971/72. This was the scale of the Programme that was announced by the Home Secretary on 22 July. At this stage the expenditure was seen as being overwhelmingly devoted to 'capital', that is, to construction costs; staffing and running costs of projects were regarded as 'current' expenditure, ancillary to the main 'capital' project. This early focus on buildings (which was to be modified) reflected the initial project proposals made by departments. However, the first circular left open the question of the balance between capital and current expenditure.

It was never in question through which agency the expenditure was to be made. Officials never doubted that use should be made of the existing channels for the distribution of social services, i.e. the local authorities. The question was: through which of the possible channels of central government funding to local government was the UP to operate? Central government supports local authority finance through the general Rate Support Grant system (see Hepworth 1971; Committee of Inquiry on Local Government Finance 1976; North West Interprofessional Group 1975) and through specific grants which are paid as a first call on the RSG general pool. The former is a general payment to all local authorities with some compensation for a lack of local resources and the presence of special needs; the latter offers grants for expenditure on specific types of service which the Government wishes to promote.

The salient difference between the two methods of funding was that if the UP had been operated through the general RSG system it would have been for recipient local authorities to spend

UP funds at their own discretion, whereas the specific grant system allowed much more direction by central government. If it had operated through the general RSG the UP would not have functioned as a programme with its own budget, but rather as a means of redistributing RSG between local authorities by adjusting the distributive formula to give further aid to those authorities with special needs. This would mean that the 'Needs Element' of the formula would have to be revised.

Though there was advantage in operating through the RSG, which gave a fixed limit of funds to authorities, officials recommended ministers to adopt the specific grant model. It presented advantages in terms of the possibility of central government 'discrimination' in favour of types of project and types of recipient areas within authorities; the RSG, on the other hand, was designed to follow the lines of existing local government expenditure and, as the Ministry of Housing and Local Government pointed out, negotiations for the formula to be adopted in the following year had already advanced too far for modification.

The new specific grant, which ministers approved, did present some difficulties. First, it required enabling legislation; second, a certain resistance was expected from local authorities who were known to be hostile in principle to the scope for central government intervention which was inherent in the specific grant system. However, it was anticipated that support for the principle of positive discrimination would give the Bill easy passage through Parliament and that, even if local authorities did object that they should control the Programme, the answer was clear: the Working Party's remit was to get a central government programme going.

Involvement of government departments

We have already seen that an interdepartmental organizational framework was established immediately after the Prime Minister's speech. The idea that there were small areas of deprivation, the criteria that would define them, and the projects that would serve them owed a lot to accepted opinion and practice among the various departments represented, even if it was primarily Home Office officials who tried to group the opinion into a coherent whole. The setting up of a tiered interdepartmental structure is the standard Civil Service means of avoiding the infringement of departmental sovereignty in any policy that runs beyond the scope of a particular department. The case for doing so was no more questioned by Home Office officials than there was any dispute among officials about which government department should have prime responsibility for running the programme that was being created.[4] The Home Office already chaired the relevant interdepartmental bodies for the establishment of the UP; nobody suggested that this state of affairs should change in its implementation.

The Home Office led the deliberations and was to co-ordinate the UP, though with deference to other departments' established responsibilities and expertise. The Department of Education and Science was the most responsive to the invitation to participate. The DES had experience of the main predecessor of the UP, the Educational Priority Area scheme, which had been mentioned in the Prime Minister's speech. The Department was able to offer the Plowden criteria and the Birmingham experiment as aids in the selection of deprived areas. It recommended against the *designation* of priority areas on the grounds of practicability, but also, one suspects, because designation could lead to dispute with local authorities against exclusion from the Programme. For the DES, the UP offered the opportunity to advance towards the Plowden Report's proposal for universal nursery education. It also offered escape from the embarrassing provision of Circular 8/60 which ordered local authorities to restrict nursery education to the level pertaining in 1957 (for fear of absorbing scarce teachers).

The Department of Health and Social Security was hardly yet formed (1968) out of the amalgamation of the separate Ministries of Health and Social Security. At this stage only two project proposals related to this new Department: the health and welfare staff and the health centres. The other child-oriented social service projects were still the responsibility of the Home Office although they were to be transferred with the Children's Department to the DHSS in the following year.

It is not easy to explain why the Department of Employment and Productivity dropped out of effective participation. According to Home Office officials, the question of employment was touched on largely in response to the request that the Working Party should

---

[4] The evidence seems to be against Rose *et al's* assertion of conflict: 'After a sharp internal struggle, Callaghan had succeeded in retaining the responsibility for the Programme at the Home Office' (Rose *et al* 1969: 623).

examine the scope for a programme of immigrant dispersal, which never came to fruition. The possibility of establishing industrial training projects through the Urban Programme was discussed a year later, but also died an unseen death.

The place of the Ministry of Housing and Local Government (MHLG) in the Programme was debated more hotly. At one stage Home Office officials were hoping that about £8 million out of £30 million per annum would be devoted to basic building projects. However, there were certain reservations about their inclusion in the Programme, on the following grounds:

i the allocation of funds for house-building already took account of special need, and priority-area authorities had already been permitted to build to capacity;

ii any increased grant for housing in Urban Programme areas could lead to pressure from local authorities for an increase in grants for all council house-building;

iii if the Urban Programme was to be financed as a specific grant out of the Rate Support Grant, housing already had its own separate support scheme in the *Housing Subsidies Act 1967*.

The omission of house-building from the UP was confirmed when it emerged, as a result of ministerial decision, that the Programme would be much smaller than officials had anticipated. Even if the entire funds were used, the boost to the housing programme would be minute. Nevertheless, it was only two years later (Home Office 1970) that a public statement finally ruled out house-building.

From the initiation of the Programme, house-building and employment-related projects were thus excluded not in principle but by default, and to the regret of the Home Office officials most closely concerned. In terms of expenditure, the Department of Employment never had a share in the UP, but the MHLG (later Department of the Environment) slowly acquired a modest place.

The Treasury's formal role in the setting up of the Urban Programme was to ensure that the financial aspects of the proposals were consistent with the policy statements made by ministers and that, where necessary, collective ministerial approval was obtained to any modification or filling in of financial details as the proposals developed. Once the UP got under way, the Treasury had responsibility for examining financial provisions in the course of the annual surveys of all public expenditure programmes:

> 'The Treasury stands sentinel over all public expenditure, controlling every departmental request to Parliament for funds and deciding what new or additional expenditure would be necessary. Treasury control is a continuous process working through well established conventions.'   (Self 1972: 133)

This formal role and responsibility had to be interpreted in practice and in discussion with other departments, as far as possible in accordance with established principles.

One example of the working out of this role was the interpretation of the requirement that the UP should be financed within the current ceiling of public expenditure. At first this seemed to depend on specific departmental savings being found. However, when it became clear that departments could not, or would not, make the necessary adjustments, room for the UP had to be found in a more general interpretation of the public expenditure ceiling. As one senior official said: 'If a Prime Minister says he is going to have a programme, he is going to have a programme.' Similarly, in the discussion over the level of the central government grant, the Treasury's starting point was to question the case for deviating from the normal practice of offering 50 per cent specific grants.

By its very nature, the Urban Programme to some extent represented an offence to established practice. It was intended, to some extent, to by-pass the usual departmental channels; it was intended to focus resources geographically; and it was even intended, at a time of financial stringency, selectively to promote additional expenditure.

Towards the first circular

By the time of Mr Callaghan's 22 July statement to the House of Commons, the main operational features of the Programme had been decided. Soon after the statement, the chairman of the Working Party became Assistant Secretary of a new division for the UP, though he was not to be joined by a Principal until September. The main initial tasks of the new division were three-fold:

1 To settle outstanding features of the UP;

2 to prepare for its immediate launching;

3 to prepare enabling legislation.

Although the new specific grant would require legislation, the Government was prepared to commit itself to sanctioning expenditure of £20-25 million over the next four years.

Before inviting local authorities to bid for these funds the Government had to clarify two points which had been touched on but so far left undecided: what was to be the level of the grant, and to which authorities was it to be open? It had already been decided that to give the Programme a quick and visible impact, for the first year at least, expenditure would be restricted to nursery education and child-care projects. Both could be initiated quickly, within existing legislation, and both had been given the backing of the Plowden and Seebohm committees.

On the level of the central government grant to local authorities incurring expenditure under the Urban Programme, one view was firmly that the UP should not exceed the 50 per cent of expenditure that was the normal level of specific grants. To do so would constitute a breach of the restraints on public expenditure. The alternative view was that, as a central government programme conceived on the basis that normal measures had failed, the UP should offer a larger than usual grant so as to ensure a greater amount of government direction. There was also a hope that local authorities, which were generally opposed in principle to the intervention implied by specific grants, might be more inclined to co-operate if the grant were larger.

Meetings were held with the Local Authority Associations (the County Councils Association and the Association of Municipal Corporations) during the period before and after the first UP Circular, which was sent out on 4 October 1968. The Associations, under special pressure from a group of West Midlands authorities, campaigned not against the proposed specific grant, as had been expected, but in favour of a *100 per cent* central government grant. They also argued that the new grant should not be drawn, like other specific grants, from the amount already available for distribution on general Rate Support Grant but that it should be drawn from a fund added to the general pool (see Chapter 5 for a fuller discussion of the funding issues).

The discussion about the size of the specific grant was maintained well into the following year, and, although a 75 per cent compromise was eventually approved by ministers and became an established feature of the UP, the decision was postponed until after the issue of the first circular. There was also only delayed success for those most concerned with financial control in resisting the local authority organizations' demand that the UP grant should be stated to be *additional* to the existing RSG total. In fact, for the period to April 1971, it *was* additional since the total RSG for the year 1970/71 had been fixed before decisions on the Urban Programme specific grant had been made, with the result that further funds had to be allocated. The Home Secretary was thus able to claim, in the debate in the House following his statement, that 'Bournemouth would not be robbed to pay Birmingham'. In any year from 1971 this would not have been true since all future RSGs were negotiated with the UP as a specific grant component.

The second question — that of which local authorities were to receive the funds in the first 'crash' phase of the UP — was settled partly by reference to the earlier discussion of criteria; but at least as important were other factors, which had entered into the discussion at that early stage: the accessibility of data, the political/administrative embarrassment of selectivity, and the scale of the available funds. The criteria had previously been in terms of selection of areas within authorities; now some means had to be found of restricting the opening phase of the Programme to a few authorities, for the sake of a speedy launching.

The reduced scale of the Programme emphasized the need for extreme selectivity. The dilemma was whether to achieve the selection by overt, 'objective' criteria, which could always be criticized by those with different assumptions about the symptoms of need, or by hand-picking (whether or not on the basis of covert criteria), which could always be criticized for being arbitrary. Consultation between Home Office and Department of Education and Science officials concluded that an 'objective' list would be more defensible.

The criteria selected were among those already mentioned. They had the advantage of being able to draw on information from the 1966 Census and DES statistics, but it is not possible to dignify them with roots in any articulated view of the nature of deprivation. They were: the proportion of immigrant children on the school roll, and the proportion of households in an authority having more than one and a half persons per room. The cut-off proportions were eventually settled respectively at 2 per cent and 6 per cent, but only after they had been 'juggled' to produce different lists of between thirty and forty authorities (a number that was regarded as unlikely to lead to complaint for its undue exclusivity or inclusivity). Ministers accepted a list of thirty-four authorities that met one criterion or the other. The list was restricted to county boroughs and London boroughs (thus excluding county councils and second-tier authorities within them) on the grounds that most of the deprived *urban* areas were within these county or metropolitan boroughs.

The first circular issued on 4 October 1968 alluded to the sorts of manifestation of deprivation that the selected local authorities should watch for in bidding for funds. They were told that in the first phase the funds would go to nursery education, day nurseries, and children's homes. But within the Home Office there were no illusions about the depth of thinking which underlay either the criteria or the projects. The main aim was to get the Programme launched as quickly as possible within the budget allowed by ministers. Added to the political case for some demonstration of concern for the problems of the inner cities, there was now an open commitment to urgent action. There was every reason to rush the circular out so that it appeared during the Labour Party Conference where Mr Wilson called for an answer to violence and racialism, ' ... by asserting our faith that social grievances require social solutions — by positive social action by the State' (Wilson 1971: 564).

The legislation

The drafting of the legislation, the passage of the Bill, and its Royal enactment as the *Local Government Grants (Social Need) Act 1969* were achieved, unusually quickly, by January 1969. There was no opposition to the Bill at its second reading (Hansard 2.12.1968: cols.1107-66) although several Conservative Members of Parliament sought to revive the UP's link with the issue of immigration by introducing questions of immigration policy into the debate. More significantly for the future, the adequacy of the proposed funding and of the criteria for its allocation were questioned. During the Bill's parliamentary course, discussions were held by

Home Office officials with the Local Authority Associations, especially the County Council's Association and the Association of Municipal Corporations. The local authorities' main concern was with the level of the grant and with its 'additionality' to the RSG; both these factors were treated administratively and were not covered in the legislation.

The main participants in the development of the legislation were the officials of the new, specially-established division (see page 38) and the Home Office's parliamentary draftsmen. The Treasury was constantly in the wings in view of: ' ... the need for all legislative proposals to receive Treasury comments before presentation to the Cabinet' (Self 1972: 133).

The new *Urban Programme Bill* was modelled on section 11 of the 1966 *Local Government Act* which offered a 50 per cent specific grant. This was administered by the Home Office and it was related to the Urban Programme in its concern for costs arising from immigration. At one stage it was thought that the two might be combined in one Act, with the section 11 grant retained for immigrant areas and the UP grant established for all 'areas of special social need'. By this time, Home Office officials and ministers (Mr Callaghan and his junior minister, first Mr David Ennals and then, from October 1968, Mr Merlyn Rees) were convinced that the Programme should not have a narrow immigrant designation.

There was pressure on the Home Office to include the Urban Programme legislation in another Bill which already had a place in the legislative programme. The Lord Privy Seal proposed that the Urban Programme should be included either in a *Home Office Immigration Bill* (relating to appeals procedures and points of entry) or in the MHLG's then current *Housing Bill*. This proposal was resisted strongly by the Home Office, in the first case on the grounds that the UP should not be identified as an immigrant programme; in the second case one can suspect a certain amount of departmental jealousy, but there was also the prospect that the long and complex *Housing Bill* was not likely to receive Royal Assent before mid-1969.

The urgent need to provide the UP with a legislative framework, which would allow the Home Secretary to make the grants to which he was committed, dictated that there should be a separate and short Bill. Many questions remained to be resolved by discussion and experience — the size of the grant, the proportions of capital and current expenditure, the qualifying criteria, the nature of future forms of expenditure — and this uncertainty added to the case for a brief and open-ended statement. The legislation left a vast area to ministerial and official discretion. The key subclause (1(i)) read: 'The Secretary of State may out of moneys provided by Parliament pay grants, of such amounts as he may with the consent of the Treasury determine, to local authorities who in his opinion are required in the exercise of any of their functions to incur expenditure by reason of the existence in any urban areas of special social need' (see *Appendix II*).

This vagueness embraced three further areas of expenditure: payments to voluntary organizations, to the proposed Community Development Project, and to the research associated with the CDP. It was decided in each case that such expenditure was covered by the combination of existing powers with the new authority given to the Home Secretary to make payments to local authorities with 'areas of special social need'. The idea that voluntary organizations should be capable of receiving UP funds had emerged in the course of discussions between officials and ministers although it had been the Working Party's view that the proper channel for aid to voluntary organizations would be through the Community Relations Commission set up under the 1968 *Race Relations Act*, rather than through the UP.

The desire to keep the Bill simple, to rest on existing powers, and also to respect the territorial preserves of local government meant that the decision was taken to fund voluntary organizations *through* local authorities, a decision which some voluntary organizations were later to resent. Power to do so was found under section 136 of the 1948 *Local Government Act* which gave local authorities, with ministerial consent, the power to contribute to bodies promoting trade, industry, and commerce, or giving 'advice, information or other assistance'. A Treasury attempt to close this new floodgate by requiring ministers to give consent to each specific claim was successfully ignored.

Conclusion

The Bill was published on 20 November 1968 and had received the Royal Assent by 30 January 1969. Its brevity assisted its quick passage through Parliament: there was little to debate and less to object to in the Bill.

It is not surprising, given its origins, that the Urban Programme is often said to lack clear objectives. It was very much the political product of its time, with its roots in broad issues like race relations and the development of selectivity in social welfare, most recently expressed by the Plowden and Seebohm Reports. At another level it was a useful addition to the armoury of Mr Wilson's response to Enoch Powell and to his own critical 'liberal' wing; at yet another level it sprung from official attempts to evolve a race relations policy for the Government.

It was for officials to work out a programme that would meet these political needs, would also be practicable to operate, and would respect the constraints by which officials felt bound. The overriding constraints which ministers imposed on the Programme were the financial stringency and the sense of urgency, which was partly attached to the political necessity of being seen to be doing something about race relations.

The other major set of constraints which officials respected were those related to departmental sovereignty: the need to base the UP on past experience, thus giving it a 'small-area' focus, to incorporate other departments in the project proposals for the UP, and the need (ultimately, as we shall see) to set up a decision-making structure for the selection of projects that respected departmental integrity. Predominant in all decisions was the Treasury's authority in financial matters; but it was an authority tempered by the close interest of ministers, the initiation of the Programme by the Prime Minister, and the expectation of the Local Authority Associations. Though the UP was smaller than the Home Office officials hoped for, it was not financed out of departmental savings; it was additional to the Rate Support Grant (RSG) allocation in the first year; it offered a new specific grant and not just a redistribution of the RSG; and it offered a 75 per cent grant, which was more than standard practice.

The special task of the interdepartmental bodies was to knit out of these strands a programme that met the Prime Minister's intentions. This was not a mere cynical exercise of adaptation and compromise. Officials did not depend for their motivation on ministers' requirements but were inspired by the idea that they could contribute to the attack on 'rediscovered' poverty. Titmuss was read and provided high authority for the academic case for positive discrimination (especially Titmuss 1968). The Plowden and Seebohm Reports (especially the former) confirmed not only that concentrations of need existed but also that the problem and the *solution* lay partly with the organization of governmental action. Somewhat in the background, seeping into the Urban Programme mainly through the connection with the CDP, was the experience of the American poverty programme. Officials concerned with the UP attribute little direct influence to the US experience, except that it was taken as a warning that to attempt to by-pass local government was to court failure.

The Programme was not built up from any *clearly-stated* set of aims. The starting-point was the Prime Minister's statement, which said little more about aims than that the Programme was to help urban authorities suffering from strains on services which partly arose from the presence of immigrants. Both here and later the objectives of the Urban Programme tend to have been stated in terms that make it difficult to distinguish this from any other programme and are so unspecific as to make it very difficult to establish criteria for the selection of areas and projects. 'The purpose,' said the Home Secretary in his statement of 22 July, 'is to supplement the Government's other social and legislative measures to ensure as far as we can that our citizens have an equal opportunity'. It was not, however, going to do the work of the existing services but to supplement them and to encourage projects that went quickly to the roots of 'special social need'. The UP seemed here to be identifying for itself a sort of gap-filling role, but the line between supplementing and doing the work of existing services is difficult to trace.

Even more doubtful is the meaning of 'areas of special social need'. These have never been defined except in terms of the sample manifestations that were proposed in the first circular: large families, overcrowding, unemployment, poor environment, concentration of immigrants, children in trouble or need of care — a potentially endless list of problems and of groups thought to have problems. If it was a list of examples of need, it offered no particular view of priorities; if it was a list of indicators of deprivation, it did not reveal the underlying conception of deprivation and how the indicators were related to it (see Chapter 8).

Because of its connection with the immigration issue, the

Programme was launched with a haste that militated against the development of any clear objectives or strategy. It was politically imperative to be doing something and to be seen to be doing it, and this was associated with hopes for a quick and visible impact. Its rushed and uncertain background imposed an ad hoc nature on the UP from the outset: the lack of specific terms of reference launched the Programme on a course that was characterized by flexibility and responsiveness. Indeed, officials framing the legislation wished to preserve the Urban Programme from any rigid definition of purpose that might inhibit its future development.

At least as much as any sense of purpose, it was the exigencies of budget and time and the constraints of departmental and local authority influence that gave the Urban Programme its small-area focus, its interdepartmental structure (though we shall discuss later whether this was departmentalism in disguise), its major concern with child-related projects, its wide distribution of funds through local authority channels, and its clear service orientation.

4 Administrative organization and process

It is the concern of this chapter to describe the procedures that were followed in administering the Urban Programme. By fixing the pattern of the relationships between organizations, these procedures helped to decide which interests should be incorporated into the Programme and what views should mould its development.

While the operating principles of the new programme — the size of the grant, the nature of the grant, the balance of capital and non-capital funds, the types of project to be promoted — were decided after considerable and urgent discussion (as we saw in the last chapter), the *procedures* by which the money was to be allocated were allowed to grow on the basis of tradition and in response to events. There were already-established patterns in the relationships within and between central government departments, between central and local government, and within and between local authority departments. The newer area where there was little or no tradition to call upon, especially in the Home Office, was in the relationship between central government and voluntary organizations; this, in its turn affecting the established and sometimes paternalistic relationship between local authorities and voluntary organizations, was to be one of the UP's main areas of embarrassment built on incompatible expectations.

Officially, the Urban Programme is seen as a 'programme of local government expenditure'. This is an accurate description in the sense that, apart from the first distribution of funds in 1969, the

Programme has been funded out of the Rate Support Grant. What apparently gave an extraordinary degree of potential central government control over these 'local government funds' was the fact that the UP was to be offered as a specific grant. This was against the whole trend of central-local government relations, which had been increasingly to move towards block grants of general spending capacity to local authorities (although most of the block grant is pre-empted by central government requirements on local government to provide particular services). As one interviewee, who had had charge of the UP, said: 'Where the UP does differ is in so far as it earmarks a tiny part of the Rate Support Grant Fund and says to local authorities: "you can only have this money to spend in certain areas with our agreement and at a certain time"' (former Home Office official, later Director, Centre for Studies in Social Policy).

The budget that was allocated to the Programme at the outset for five years, and later renewed, acted as the basis for deciding the annual availability of funds. Each year, at the time of the Rate Support Grant negotiations with Local Authority Associations, the year's budget for the Urban Programme was decided in the light of past years' expenditures and of the maximum allowed for the whole period of the Urban Programme.

Within this financial framework, relationships between participating organizations are governed by an annual cycle, known in central government as a 'Phase'. Within each major annual phase, there is a smaller phase which we can for the present ignore. The annual phase contains three main stages: the issue by central government of a circular to local authorities inviting applications for funds; the submission by local authorities of 'bids' which propose specific projects for financial support; and the issue by the Home Office of its 'approvals'. In more detail and with an approximate idea of the time scale, the bare bones of the process are:

i November: a meeting is held between all of the government departments concerned (Department of the Environment, Department of Education and Science, Department of Health and Social Security, and the Home Office) to decide the level of the budget, the rough division of the budget between departments, and the projects which departments wish to promote;

ii November-January: the Home Office draws up a circular in consultation with other departments. The circular describes the intention of the Urban Programme to serve deprived areas, outlines the types of project that it is hoped local authorities will propose in their applications, and describes the sort of information that it is hoped will accompany them;

iii the circular is shown to ministers in draft and then to the Local Authority Associations in finalized form;

iv January-February: the circular is issued to all local authority Chief Executive's or Town Clerk's departments and to certain voluntary organizations with national headquarters;

v the local authorities decide how to distribute the circular among their departments (Social Services and Education, and usually Housing) and among voluntary organizations;

vi the local government departments and voluntary organizations generate proposals for projects. These are usually brought together, selected, and given a priority rating which may or may not run across departmental responsibilities;

vii July: the Town Clerk's or Chief Executive's departments of local authorities send proposals to the Home Office;

viii the Home Office distributes project proposals to the central government departments with relevant responsibility;

ix departments consult within their own organizations and then make recommendations to the Home Office for project approvals up to the limit of their respective budgets;

x the Home Office co-ordinates the results of these recommendations, suggesting minor changes to departments so as to achieve a rough 'balance' between local authorities;

xi the Minister of State at the Home Office is shown the co-ordinated results and may suggest small alterations;

xii September-October: the local authorities are informed which of their 'bids' have been successful;

xiii where necessary, local authorities transmit this information to voluntary organizations.

It can readily be seen that this is a procedure resting heavily on the official machine and also that, while it is co-ordinated by the Home Office and, usually, at local level by the Town Clerk's or Chief Executive's departments, it fans out to include a wide range of government departments at both levels, as well as certain voluntary organizations. This reflects not only the original intention to make the Urban Programme a cross-departmental operation, but also, as is argued in this chapter, a strong resistance (especially at central government level) against anything that seems to imply the intrusion by one department into another's territory. This sense of 'departmental sovereignty' was found to have a fundamental effect on the management of the Urban Programme and, consequently, on the objectives and manner of the distribution of its resources.

In this chapter, the operation of the Programme is examined first at central government and then at local government level to show how the relationships and procedures, which were built up around the simple process outlined above, contributed to decisions about the allocation of UP resources. The analysis at central government level is based on participant observation at the Home Office and on interviews with officials of the Department of Education and Science, the Department of Health and Social Security, the Department of the Environment, and the Treasury. At local government level, twelve local authorities were selected for close study on the basis of the criteria listed in *Appendix V*. Our intention, for each local authority, was to trace the course of decision-making about Urban Programme applications, to see who was included and excluded, and to identify the perceptions of the problems of urban deprivation and of the role of the Urban Programme that informed decisions. Interviews also included officials of one Local Authority Association and officials of the headquarters of a wide range of voluntary organizations (see *Appendix VI*) to identify the parts they played in decision-making.

The twelve local authorities selected were not, in any statistical sense, a representative sample of the more than 300 local authorities that have received funds from the UP. Rather, the local authority research was in the form of case studies which illustrate the effects of a range of possible working relationships and procedures (see *Appendix V*).

The next chapter shows how these operating procedures and working relationships influenced the course of the Programme.

Central government management

The participants and their relationships

It has already been shown that from the outset the UP was to be an interdepartmental programme, at least in the sense that it was to involve several departments. This essential (and, in terms of central government, novel) feature of the UP can be traced back to the official body set up to consider immigration policy, which was cross-departmental in its membership, as was the subordinate working party on the establishment of the Urban Programme. Once the Home Office had found itself in the chairs of these two bodies it was clear that, if it was to continue in a co-ordinating role, then other departments would have to be involved in the execution of the Programme. The Home Office alone had no programme of service provision or expenditure through local authorities, since the Children's Department had been transferred to the Department of Health and Social Security (DHSS) in the course of central government reorganization in 1970/71.

Even if the Home Office had wished, or had been able, to by-pass other departments and local authorities, there was a determination to launch the UP rapidly and therefore 'to use the machinery that was available [for which] the natural funnels were the local authorities' (Senior Home Office administrator).[1]

Besides the Home Office, the departments most concerned with the UP were the Department of Education and Science (DES) and the DHSS. Some of the cross-departmentalism was lost when the Department of Employment was diverted in a different direction to investigations into immigration policy (a study of the scope for 'immigrant dispersal'). Similarly, the Ministry of Housing and Local Government (MHLG), after the initial meetings of the Working Party, backed out of a full involvement in the programme, probably because house-building, their main relevant local government service, could hardly benefit significantly from a programme of the order of £30 million over five years. There was the added problem that local government housing is financed separately and not from the Rate Support Grant which was to be the UP's source of funds.

Although the Department of the Environment (DOE), which incorporated the MHLG, was later to take a slightly more active part, these early 'self-exclusions' affected the future of the UP. The exclusions were never on grounds of principle and yet the tradition became established that the Programme did not include house-building or employment-related projects.

[1] Except where otherwise stated, quotes are from interviews with the authors.

The Home Office's co-ordinating role apparently gave it an authoritative position. However, in its management of the finances, it was almost wholly governed by the five-yearly budget determined by the annual suballocation from the Rate Support Grant. The Home Office was scarcely more independent in its twice-yearly drafting of the joint-departmental circulars issued to local authorities: here it was dependent on the reiteration of the basic principles of the Programme, on the advice of other departments about the projects to be recommended to authorities, and on the drafting by the DES of the section concerning education.

It is true that, in its apparently most important role of approving local authority bids, it was the Home Office that issued letters of approval; but it almost always respected other departments' recommendations: 'At the moment each department does its own selection of approvals independently in the light of its own policies and priorities' (Home Office official). The Home Office restricted its attempts to influence other departments almost wholly to what it called matters of 'balance' — that is, to ensure that no particular authority did startlingly well or badly in the number of approvals it received.

In spite of appearances, then, the UP was highly fragmented between departments and it could be said that it was only in appearance that the UP existed as a coherent programme. While several officials connected with the Home Office professed to be in favour of more co-ordination, the difficulties appeared to be insuperable: 'The UP had no corporate strategy and it was decided that we must trust the competence of the other departments. The only possible level of co-ordination was at local authority level' (senior Home Office administrator); 'The assumption was that each department's area of work was equally important, or at least that the Home Office was not in a position to establish priorities between them' (Senior DES administrator).

The question was not only that of departmental competence, but also, and more fundamentally, of ministerial responsibility:

'It would be quite unacceptable for the Home Office to intervene in the selection of projects. This runs through government: the Department of Education and Science can only allocate funds according to its own ministers' feelings; it cannot be made responsible to another department or its ministers.'   (DES official)

A Home Office official made the same point in reverse, that, if there were to be co-ordination, it implied joint accountability and a joint budget: 'I would advise government to insist on some form of co-ordination in which those being co-ordinated would in some way be (jointly) accountable' (senior Home Office administrator).

In the view of officials, then, a move towards a programme with a corporate strategy such as was reflected in the decisions about the distribution of funds implied a common accountability to a minister.

Given these limitations, the Home Office's 'co-ordinating role' was primarily in the routine servicing that it provided for the Programme: writing and distributing the circulars, receiving bids from local authorities and distributing them to departments, receiving recommendations from departments and issuing them as approvals to local authorities, and keeping a check on the available budget. It was able to make some changes in the UP's budgetary categories, gradually increasing the proportion of funds going to non-capital (that is, non-building) and to voluntary organizations' projects. It also transmitted to other departments the occasional pressures of its ministers to focus on areas of immigration or immigrant-related projects. However, the Home Office's policy-directing role was apparently limited to the promotion of incremental changes which did not seriously affect other departments' authority (see Chapter 5).

In a sense what is being discussed here is the maintenance of *ministerial* sovereignty in the face of a programme that purported to extend across the boundaries of that sovereignty. It was the issue of ministerial accountability that was the ultimate obstacle to joint planning and implementation. And yet, an examination of the way in which decisions about project recommendations and approvals were made throughout the life of the Urban Programme revealed that at least as much departmental (or official) sovereignty was involved as ministerial.

After the formative period of the Programme, ministers of the departments involved were formally concerned with policy changes and the approval of the list of projects proposed by departments for funding within each phase. Their influence in these areas, as the next chapter argues, was more an ad hoc than an integral part of the operational procedure. In general, the approval by ministers of the circular and of the proposed projects was a matter of ratification of their officials' decisions. Indeed, officials would not have expected ministers to take a detailed part in the procedures: ' ... it is not a sensible operation if, after much painstaking effort by officials, a scheme is altered by a minister perhaps not according to the same criteria officials have used and perhaps not necessarily with a full understanding on his part of the total scheme' (senior Home Office administrator).

With three changes of the party in power and five changes of the minister responsible for the UP between 1968 and 1974, it would indeed have been difficult for ministers to acquire deep knowledge of the Programme. But to officials it appeared that the ministerial role was properly limited to policy decisions, not just for practical reasons but also on grounds of principle — that it was the officials' responsibility to manage the operation. Nevertheless, ministers did influence a very small proportion of the decisions on local authority bids, usually as a result of a commitment entered into on a ministerial visit or of some other particular concern with a project or place.

Once its nature and momentum were established, then, the Programme was, in fact, without a firm centre for the direction of policy. Home Office officials were, by their tradition of maintaining a respectful distance from other departments, inhibited from being too directive, and the Programme was not so big as to warrant the sort of major ministerial input that could have pushed it in new directions.

Within central government departments, the involvement of branches (or sections, or divisions, depending on departmental terminology) and of regional offshoots reflected the existing organization in these departments. The Home Office, without responsibility for other local authority services, placed responsibility for the Programme on I2 Division (see Chapter 2), with the Voluntary Services Section (VSS) and Finance Division in secondary advisory roles. Perhaps because the VSS was removed to the Civil Service Department between 1971 and 1974 (and then returned to the Home Office), it never acquired a central role in the management of the UP in spite of the Programme's growing concern with the voluntary sector.

The structure of the Department of Health and Social Security's operation was the most diffused, involving:

1 the Local Authority Social Services Division as co-ordinator;
2 up to ten client-group branches (e.g. elderly, physically handicapped, mentally ill) as the main decision-makers;
3 regional social work service officers as advisers.

The Department of Education and Science's operation included:

1 the Schools II branch, which had broad responsibility for
  positive discrimination programmes within the DES, as co-
  ordinator and decision-maker;
2 as advisers, district inspectors of further education and schools
  who had direct professional contact with local authorities;
3 as advisers, staff inspectors who were located in the central
  office of the DES;
4 from 1974, the Youth and Community branch for comments
  on relevant projects.

The Department of the Environment transferred co-ordinating
responsibility for the Urban Programme from the Housing Division to the Planning Urban Policy (PUP I) Division, which from
1973 had responsibility for the DOE's concern with deprivation.
From the time of this transfer in 1973, the DOE began to consult its
regional offices for advice on local authority bids, but the responsibility for decisions rested with the PUP I. In this way, the
Programme was not only fragmented between departments and
subject to separate policy considerations but was also, within
departments (especially the DHSS), subject to a wide variety of
intepretations, priorities, and pressures. The Urban Programme
could thus hardly be expected to have its own clear and simple view
of the nature of the problem of urban deprivation or the ways in
which it should be confronted.

Central government constraints

As has been shown, certain constraints were imposed on the
Programme from the start as an essential aspect of its origins and
objectives; others grew out of the organizational structure that had
been established and the traditions of relations between the incorporated bodies. The more tangible constraints on the operational
procedures are here briefly stated, beginning with the more rigid
and shading off into the more flexible limitations.

(a) *Available funds:* Phase 7 (approved in October 1972) can be taken as an example of the sort of overriding financial limitations imposed on each main yearly phase.

Budget sectors	Terms of funding	Sum
capital	with five years' running costs	£2,213,000
	with no running costs	£ 833,000
	— special allocation by the DHSS for pre-school children	
		£3,046,000
non-capital	for five years	£ 252,000
	for four years, to voluntary organizations only	£ 155,000
	for two years, special allocation by DHSS for family planning	£ 80,000
	for three years, special allocation by DHSS for pre-school children	£ 111,000
		£ 598,000
once-only	1 year, capital or non-capital	£ 157,000

The above figures show the amount of the grant in the first year and the period over which, for capital projects,[2] running costs will be met and, for non-capital projects, the period over which the sum will be paid at the same rate. The 'once-only' budget is derived from savings out of previous budgets: for example, where local authorities do not undertake expenditure as quickly as they could, or at all.

(b) *Balance between capital and revenue:* The balance between capital and revenue (or non-capital) budgets was fixed in the

---

[2] A *capital* project is broadly defined as a capital works project financed by local authority direct expenditure, which is usually met from loans. In the case of the UP, 75 per cent of the cost of the loan is paid out of the Programme. Capital projects almost always involve buildings — payment for the purchase of site, for equipment, for furnishing, and for construction. Revenue or *non-capital* projects are financed out of local authorities' revenue accounts (i.e. rates and Rate Support Grant, and in this case by the UP out of Rate Support Grant at 75 per cent of expenditure). They include items such as rents, rates, employees' salaries, and payments to other organizations.

early stages of the UP and is not easily alterable. In terms of the original allocation of funds to projects, the balance has been heavily in favour of capital (accumulatively a ratio of about 6:1 for phases up to Phase 9, though the ratio has fluctuated over the phases).[3] But it should be remembered that the UP normally meets five years' running costs on capital projects and that these will often include the staffing of buildings, as well, for example, as costs of heating and rates. It is estimated that on average a capital project implies running costs per year of about one-third of the original capital expenditure.

(c) *Special budgets*: UP funds have occasionally, from phase to phase, been swollen by the 'special promotions' of particular departments. In the Phase 7 figures above, it can be seen that the DHSS added funds out of its departmental budget to be allocated through the UP machinery for family planning projects and for social service projects (e.g. playgroups) for children aged up to five years old. Another 'special budget' was the allocation of £155,000 reserved for voluntary organizations as part of the Conservative Government's attempt to promote voluntary activity.

(d) *Balance between voluntary organizations and local authorities*: Voluntary organizations have won a growing proportion of UP non-capital funds (about one-third up to Phase 4 and 48 per cent from there to Phase 9: see Chapter 6) but have received a very small proportion of capital funds (about 7 per cent). In effect, voluntary organizations up to Phase 7 only had access to the non-capital budget.

(e) *Balance between departments*: Although the Home Office is responsible for administering the Programme, in fact it generally accepts the advice of other departments on the selection of those projects that are not regarded as Home Office responsibilities. In practice, therefore, departments are allocated 'budgets' which reflect past practice and the proportion of current bids which fall within their responsibility. The Home Office,

---

[3] The February 1976 revisions in public expenditure estimates indicated a reduction in the capital allocation to the Home Office 'Community Services' budget — the capital element of which consisted almost entirely of Urban Programme expenditure — from £12.1 million in 1970/71 (at 1975 prices), to £8.2 million in 1973/74, and then to only £1.0 million in 1979/80. These financial revisions have, however, been overtaken by the 1977 recasting of the UP (see p.235 onwards).

DHSS, and DES have always been the main participants, though in varying proportions. The figures for Phase 7 were as follows:

	HO	*DHSS*	*DES*	*DOE*	*All*
	%	%	%	%	
capital	21	48	30	1	100
non-capital	37	52	9	2	100
total	25	49	25	1	100

(f) *Balance between areas*: The Urban Programme is not operated on a regional basis and there has been no attempt to allocate funds on the basis of any scale of area priorities. Nevertheless, there exists a tacit constraint which would, for example, make it highly unlikely that any government would allocate all the funds in one phase to one region, or to only a few local authorities. There is an underlying and 'instinctive' view that there should be a 'fair' national distribution that does not weight the Programme heavily in any authority's or region's favour, except where, as in the case of the south and south-west regions, it is felt to be self-evident that little 'urban deprivation' exists. Thus, the north-west region, for example, has received a fairly consistent 20 per cent of the total funds per phase without this figure ever having been consciously calculated.

The first three of these conditions — the level of funds, their division between capital and revenue, and the separateness of special budgets — can be properly thought of as rigid constraints on the use of funds. The others — the balance between voluntary organizations and local authorities, between government departments, and between geographical areas — are in varying degrees more matters of established practice. The constraints on inter-organizational and inter-area 'balance' and access to resources can be seen as practical results of the fragmented organizational structure that has already been described.

Decision-making criteria in central government

The selection criteria, or rules governing the access by applicants to central government funds, operate at three main stages: at the point where decisions are made about who is, in principle, eligible to receive funds; at the time where applications are ordered and allocated to different queues; and when judgement is made about the applications to be approved (Schaffer and Huang Wen-hsien

1975: 13-36). The local government operation (discussed later) contributes to the first two stages, but central government sets the framework.

(i) *Eligibility*: In Chapter 3 we explained that only in the first phase launched in 1968 was eligibility strictly limited to local authorities meeting certain specific criteria. Thereafter, the Programme was open to all local authorities in England to submit proposals for projects which it is within their power to promote. A separate circular was issued for Wales and a separate, but related, programme applied to Scotland.

Voluntary organizations were not directly eligible to apply to the Home Office but, after Phase 2, local authorities were encouraged to pass on applications which they received from voluntary bodies. The circular, requesting applications, went to the Town Clerk's or Chief Executive's department of local authorities, and while they were encouraged to distribute it 'as widely as possible' it was (as we shall see) for them to decide which local authority departments and which voluntary organizations were informed. One inherent condition of eligibility was therefore access to information about the circular and, for voluntary organizations, not only the goodwill of the local authority, but also their own willingness to tolerate local authority supervision. Other eligibility conditions expressed, though often only tacitly and unsystematically, in the Home Office circulars were:

a the local authority should be prepared and able to meet 25 per cent of the cost of the proposed project, whether its own or voluntary;

b the project should be within the local authority's power to promote. For example, hospital and university building projects would be excluded as central government responsibilities;

c the areas chosen for projects within local authorities should show the characteristics regarded as suitable, loosely defined in the first circular as being: 'Notable deficiencies in the physical environment, particularly in housing; overcrowding of houses; family sizes above the average; persistent unemployment; a high proportion of children in trouble or need of care' (Home Office 1968: para.2);

d proposed projects should be new and, preferably, not already in the local authority's programme;

e projects should be of the types considered suitable for inclusion in the Programme, listed in the circulars. These were for projects to which government departments would give particularly favourable attention, but they did not exclude other ideas. Typically the recommendations included, as capital projects: nursery schools and classes, day nurseries, social and community centres, old peoples' homes and day centres, and adventure playgrounds; and, as non-capital projects: adventure playground leaders, playgroups and playgroup advisers, neighbourhood information centres, housing aid centres, legal advice centres, family welfare and family planning services, and voluntary service bureaux.

The last three points hardly merit the term 'conditions' since, as we shall see, local authorities were able to interpret them so broadly, or omitted to supply the information on which central government could make a judgement. While reiterating 'conditions' c and d, central government itself did not attempt to apply them rigorously. More important were three hidden conditions:

f the recipient should be able to understand and appreciate the relevance of the Home Office circular inviting bids;[4]

g the putative applicant should have the organizational capacity to give the information requested. This presented little difficulty for local authorities, but voluntary organizations often depended on the help of local government in compiling financial information for their bids;

h the putative applicant should have the capacity to make his application within the three to six months variably allowed by the circulars.

Thus while the eligibility conditions were theoretically very open, it can be seen that tacitly they favoured the better-organized authorities and the more established and integrated voluntary organizations. The very fact that the formal conditions were so open meant that a great deal depended on the initiative of the applicant in presenting and pressing his claim.

---

[4] One Town Clerk is known to have filed five years of UP circulars under 'Court Buildings'. Another county borough did not apply for several years on the grounds that 'it doesn't apply to us because we have few immigrants', although the proportion of immigrants had been dropped as a condition after the first phase.

(ii) *Ordering*: The chances of a bid by a local authority department or voluntary organization were affected by the channel through which it was processed. Bids were not judged simply on a 'first come, first served' basis, nor were the merits of each bid assessed against those of all others. Bids were, in principle, treated on their own merit, but, in effect, the channels to which they were allocated decided both what their proportionate chances were and on what grounds they were to be evaluated.

We have seen that the departments each received a proportion of the UP budget to allocate. The overall budget was divided not only in proportion to the number of bids received but also on the basis of tradition (or 'fiscal inertia' as one official put it). There were special earmarked budgets, e.g. in Phase 7 for children's, family planning, and voluntary projects. Furthermore, departments, and in particular the DHSS, allocated most of the responsibility for the making of decisions concerning particular project types to the competent branch within the department. (Until 1975 the DHSS allocated its UP 'budget' to the different client-group branches in much the same way as the overall budget was split between departments.)

Thus, a bid's chances were influenced by the ratio of applicants to funds in its particular budget sector and by the attitudes of the officials responsible for that budget sector. The results of this discrimination as it applied to the north-west region in Phase 7 have been assessed in a separate study (Batley and Edwards 1974) which showed that while applications were overwhelmingly weighted towards capital and local authority projects (in terms of the ratios of both funds and projects, but especially the former), central government procedures and constraints reduced or reversed this weighting by tending to favour non-capital and voluntary projects, though with great variations between departments.

Apart from the matter of the queue in which they found themselves, the other important question was related to the placing of bids in an order of priority by the official applicants (the local authorities). Since 1969, but with much increased emphasis from Phase 7, ' ... authorities are asked to indicate an order of priority for the projects which they submit ... Where more than one project is submitted by an authority, and these are sponsored by different committees, authorities are asked to give their own priority order' (Home Office 1972: para.6; Annex C para.4). While the Home

Office added a disclaimer to the effect that 'it is not always possible to adhere to the priorities indicated', the local authority's priority rating, which also covered voluntary projects, was of considerable importance in the final decision. Thus, in yet another sense, the bids were placed within queues in categories having greater or lesser chances of success.

The other question that distinguished between the chances of bids even before they were examined by central government departments was the capacity of their applicant to wait the seven to eight months that the whole process required. Voluntary organizations with limited funds could not afford to depend only on the chance of getting UP finance, and many made parallel applications to other funds. More fundamentally, applicants with an urgent need of resources to implement a project were in a sense excluded by the anticipated time lag from even applying.

(iii) *Selection*: By the time applications (or bids) reached the stage of decision they found themselves classified under different budgetary subheadings and in separate government departments. If the Programme's decision-making was to retain any unity one might have expected that, at least, government departments would agree on the criteria they were to apply. However, not only was there no discussion of the criteria to be applied but also, even within departments, the criteria were for the most part unstated.[5] Nevertheless, the selection process which did take place was severe: in Phase 7, for example, 2063 bids were distributed for selection between departments and only one fifth were successful.

All departments, at some stage, experimented with the use of standard stated criteria to be applied rigorously to bids;[6] in every case the experiment fell into disuse after its application in one or two phases, and the department resorted to the use of tacit and flexible criteria.

The Department of Education and Science led the field during Phases 1 and 2 with the use of criteria related to the level of deprivation in the *areas* with which the bids were concerned. The criteria were drawn from the Plowden Report and had recently

[5] The Home Office allowed the researchers to observe their selection process through several phases. In the cases of the other departments, we must rely almost wholly on the accounts of officials.

[6] They were particularly influenced in this by the exercise carried out and reported by the authors (Batley and Edwards 1974).

been used to identify Educational Priority Areas (EPAs: see Chapter 2 p.18). The DES did not at this stage need to use criteria to distinguish between the merits of *projects* (rather than the area covered) since in the early phases all DES money was being used on nursery education. The DES soon found, however, that it was one thing to use the criteria — relating to an area's population age structure, proportion of substandard housing, demand for free school meals, and proportion of people in lower socio-economic groups — in a final identification of the EPAs, but a very much more complicated matter to get access to the relevant information for each UP bid as it arrived.

The Department of Health and Social Security experimented from Phase 9 with the issue of score sheets to the regional social work service officers and the client-group divisions. The effect of this scoring system was, however, not to make comparisons *between* project types but to compare like projects. The pattern in the DHSS continued to be that client-group branches received a budgetary allocation, which, in effect, added Urban Programme resources to the department's existing policy orientation.

The Department of the Environment also drew up a set of criteria, which were used in Phase 9 to identify the level of deprivation in an area but not to assess the relative merits of different projects or different types of project.

The Home Office attempted in Phase 7 to introduce three sets of criteria for the assessment of both the merits of the project and of the area it served:

1 *Minimal tests of UP suitability*
    a degree of area deprivation;
    b amount of community participation;
    c rapidity of benefit.

2 *Consideration of local authority priorities and special emphases*
    d local authority priority ratings;
    e special policy emphases — e.g. in favour of voluntary organizations or particular age groups.

3 *Administrative tests*
    f costs;
    g viability;
    h innovative or traditional nature of projects;
    i national priorities overriding local authority ratings.

The universal experience of government departments was, however, that they lacked the information on which to apply these criteria, and local authorities had a variable concern and capacity to collate data on small districts within their areas.

Second, departments had difficulty in applying their criteria as a result of confusion over their meanings, '...because they were vague in conception' (DOE sociologist). An evaluative report on the Home Office's attempt illustrates this:

> 'However, the criteria were not applied in a rigorous way, and some difficulty was found in applying them — particularly that of community participation. In the session attended by [one researcher], he was several times asked for his advice on the meaning and application of "community participation". In practice, the interpretation of this criterion resulted in higher scores for any voluntary organisation project that did not involve professional workers.'   (Batley and Edwards 1974: 16)

No more did the Home Office have any clearly worked-out understanding of the meaning of 'deprivation' (see Chapter 5 for a fuller discussion of this concept), 'innovation', or 'viability', let alone the information to apply these concepts.

The development of stated criteria was part of an attempt to relate the decisions of administrators to the original aims of the Urban Programme or, at least, to the administrators' current interpretation of those aims. The key criteria, however, which survived these attempts to rationalize the selection procedures of the Programme, were ones that related more to the pressures on the UP than to any original aims. In all departments it was found that the most important criteria were:

a the local authority's priority ranking of their bids;
b a concept of 'balance' or spread between geographical areas which was applied both by the Home Office and by other departments in drawing up a final list out of departmental recommendations:
  — 'there is a natural tendency to get as broad a spread as possible';
  — 'to a certain extent we try to spread the jam evenly ... ';
c the cost of the project: the goal of spreading resources itself contributed to a tendency to favour cheaper projects;
d the relationship of projects to departments' current policy

emphases, partly expressed as project recommendations in the circulars;

e an unstated notion of deprivation which tended to exclude the least 'deprived' authorities.

The necessary selection came to rely more on the sifting effect of the administrative procedure than on any point of judgement where clear criteria were consciously applied. The inputs to this process ranged, for one government department, from the local authorities' priority ranking, through the district advisers' comments, to the recommendation of headquarter advisers. Combined with departmental officials' interpretation of this advice and their own views of eligibility, these contributions acted as the gates through which applications were passed, gaining or losing credit on the way. Thus, the point of decision and the basis on which the decisions were made were lost in a complex process of consultation. Decisions emerged from a network of officials, many of whom were more concerned, and familiar, with other services than the Urban Programme. One view was that, in such vague territory as urban deprivation, 'common sense' was the only realistic basis for decision-making: 'We knew that if a project came forward from Liverpool 8, there was a good case for it' (senior DES administrator). Indeed, the rejection of the early use in the Home Office of social indicators to identify areas of need was partly on the basis that 'as soon as they failed to meet a common sense view of what a deprived area was, it would have caused dispute, and I could not reject a bid from one area on the basis of my maps' (senior Home Office administrator).

The advantage of *not* using stated criteria (except in the first phase when they were helpful in launching the UP quickly in a few areas) was that their absence allowed administrators to respond flexibly to pressures to include a wider range of projects and areas. It would have been politically difficult to justify any set of exclusive criteria and might have plunged administrators and their ministers into the need to provide a public justification for the criteria. By comparison, there was much less risk of embarrassment in a programme that had no overt or clear decision-making criteria.

For all the coherence implied by the word 'programme', and for all the unity implied by the joint issue of circulars and approvals, we see that central government decision-making in the Urban Programme was diffused and fragmented. The chances of an application's success depended on the route into which it was channelled. Put one way, the Urban Programme was a flexible operation open to new ideas; put another way, without any clear policy direction, it was constantly open to the further dissipation of its central powers of decision-making.

Local government management

Much of the initiative lay with local authorities. As we have seen, they played an essential role in decisions about the eligibility and ordering of bids, and, although central government made recommendations, they had the prime responsibility for the generation of bids. At this level, it is therefore important to ask which bodies were so incorporated into the machinery that they had access to information about the Programme and could influence the priorities established locally.

The participants and their relationships — who gets the circular?

Briefly stated, the typical pattern among the twelve sample local authorities was that the Town Clerk or his equivalent would receive the circular from the Home Office and pass it out to the chief officers of at least the social services and education departments. Usually a limited number of voluntary organizations would hear of the circular through contact with these departments. Departments and voluntary organizations would generate applications and pass them to the relevant service committee (e.g. social services and education) for approval. They would then be grouped into an overall order of priority by a cross-departmental meeting whose decision would be ratified by a non-departmental council committee. The applications in order of priority would then be sent to the Home Office by the Town Clerk.

The form was nearly always similar to this but the practice varied. The main elements of the variation can be grouped as follows:

1 the degree to which councillors were involved in decision-making;
2 the degree of the diffusion or co-ordination of political decision-making;

3 the degree of the diffusion or co-ordination of administrative decision-making;

4 the level at which decisions were made in the administrative structure;

5 the degree to which voluntary organizations were encouraged to submit applications.

In every case the Home Office sent the circular to the local authority's senior or co-ordinating officer: the Town Clerk or Chief Executive in municipal or county boroughs; the County Clerk in county councils; or the Town Clerk, Chief Executive, or Borough Secretary in the three corporately managed London boroughs.[7] These officials were urged by the circular to see 'that distribution will be made as widely as possible' (Home Office 1972: para.1). It was found that the distribution by the Chief Executive always included the social services and education departments and usually housing — the three services normally referred to in UP circulars. There were necessary exceptions in the case of Kensington and Chelsea and Tower Hamlets which, like all central London Boroughs, had lost their educational function to the Inner London Education Authority. Similarly, Lancashire, Yorkshire West Riding, and Northumberland, like all county councils, had no responsibility for housing, which was left to the second-tier authorities, municipal boroughs and urban and rural districts.

In two of the three London Boroughs where corporate management systems had been established, the Housing Officer had lost his directoral role and title. In Tower Hamlets the housing department received a copy of the circular through its senior officer — the Director of Community Services. In Kensington and Chelsea he had been placed in a subordinate position to the Director of Technical Services who received the circular but did not pass information about it to the housing department. In Kensington and Chelsea the Programme had thus, in local authority terms, become an entirely 'social service' operation.

Other departments in local authorities also received the circular, but in their cases for information rather than action. In particular, finance (or treasury) departments needed to be prepared to offer advice to other departments on the costing of projects, and to

---

[7] The types of local authority (except for the London boroughs) referred to have been replaced since 1974 by a new local government structure.

incorporate the Urban Programme allocations into the annual budget; Architects' departments needed to be warned of the possibility that they would have to produce designs for projects within the deadlines imposed by the Programme.

In only one local authority, Sheffield, was it found that members of the social services and education committees received copies of the circular as a matter of course and at the same time as officers of their departments. Sheffield, as we shall see, was also one of the authorities where politicians had greatest influence on what went up to the Home Office.

The more general question relating to the distribution of the circulars concerned how far they were passed down to the junior levels of departments and whether the local authority made any effort to pass them on to voluntary organizations. Only if they were informed of the announcement and conditions of a phase of the UP could voluntary organizations propose applications. The local authority was not, however, the only source of such information to voluntary organizations. We have seen that the Home Office distributed the circular to certain voluntary bodies with headquarter organizations. These in their turn distributed information to their local branches; but this network reached by no means all voluntary organizations.

The other important source of information for voluntary organizations was their contact with officials in departments. 'Seepage' was likely to be increased the more the information on the UP's phases was spread to junior members of staff.

The distribution of the circulars, or a formal note about them, is illustrated in *Table 1*. It is not easy to be sure to what degree news about circulars permeated departments, but there were certain local authorities in which it is clear that the circulars were dealt with only at a high level. In the Warley education department they concerned almost only the Chief Education Officer, the deputy, and the chief adviser; similarly in the social services department they went to the director, the deputy, and the principal assistant. In Northumberland County Council's social services department, the matter was dealt with by the director with his assistant directors and administrative staff; area field office staff had no real possibility of contributing to the discussion. Northumberland Education Department had no local area divisions, so that its operations were highly centralized, not only in matters concerning the UP.

Table 1 The distribution of Urban Programme circulars as of 1974: twelve selected local authorities

| Local authority | First recipient from Home Office | | Recipient from Chief Executive (or equivalent) and subsequent distribution within departments and to voluntary organizations | | | | | | | | |
| | | | Social Services Department | | | Education Department | | | Housing Department | | |
	Town Clerk or chief officer	Direct distribution to voluntary organizations	Recipient	Distribution within departments	Distribution to voluntary organizations	Recipient	Distribution within departments	Distribution to voluntary organizations	Recipient	Distribution within departments	Distribution to voluntary organizations
London boroughs											
Haringey	✓	×	✓	Limited	×	✓	Limited	×	✓	×	×
Kensington and Chelsea	✓	Press advertisement	✓	Limited	×	No education function	No education function		Director of Technical Services	×	×
Tower Hamlets	✓	×	✓	✓	×	No education function	No education function	×	Director of Community Services	Housing Manager	×
County councils											
Lancashire	✓	×	✓	✓	×	✓	To 12 out of 30 divisions	×	No housing function		
Northumberland	✓	×	✓	×	×	✓	✓	×	No housing function		
Yorkshire West Riding	✓	×	✓	✓	To CVS and AC after Phase 9	✓	✓	×	No housing function		
County boroughs											
Hartlepool	✓	To CCR	✓	×	×	✓	×	×	✓	×	×
Leeds	✓	To CCR	✓	✓	×	✓	✓	Newsletter	✓	×	×
Leicester	✓	To CCR and CVS	✓	✓	×	✓	✓	×	✓	×	×
Sheffield	✓	×	✓	✓	×	✓	✓	×	✓	×	×
Walsall	✓	×	✓	×	All known voluntary organizations from 1974	✓	✓	×	✓	×	×
Warley	✓	To CCR, CVS, and APA	✓	×	×	✓	×	×	✓	×	×

Notes:
CVS — Council of Voluntary Service
CCR — Council for Community Relations
APA — Adventure Playground Association
AC — Age Concern
✓ — included in distribution
× — not included in distribution

At the other extreme, in Tower Hamlets the Director of Social Services said that he distributed the circulars to his entire staff. The same seemed to be true in Leicester's education department and in its social services department; indeed, it was found generally that centralization or decentralization in one department was reflected in others.

The *typical* pattern was for chief officers to pass the circular to deputy and assistant directors; from there, in social service departments, area officers and senior social workers were usually informed; in education departments, information would typically reach assistant education officers and senior inspectors of education. It was at these levels that applications were typically formulated and discussed. In the two county councils other than Northumberland, there was also the question of distribution to the divisional (i.e. local area) offices of the social service and education departments. Lancashire, unlike the West Riding of Yorkshire, operated a selective distribution system in an attempt to fulfil what they took to be the UP's objective of discriminating in favour of deprived areas. The county's social services department initially distributed the circular to five of its fourteen divisions, and the education department to twelve divisions out of thirty. On the grounds that the Home Office seemed to them to have a declining interest in selectivity, the social services department had later extended its distribution to all divisions and education was planning to do the same.

The table shows that in six of the twelve authorities, an attempt was made to reach voluntary organizations either by a formal distribution of the circular or by some sort of publicity. In only three of those six authorities, Leeds, Kensington and Chelsea, and Walsall, was an attempt made to reach directly more than a select few voluntary organizations — in the first case by a newsletter published by the education department; in the second case, starting in 1973, by a press advertisement; and in the third by direct mailing to 'all known voluntary organizations' by the social services department. Walsall's commitment arose in 1974 from pressures from one councillor and constituted a reluctant conversion on the part of the department: 'In the past, we have been able to base our contacts with voluntary organizations on our knowledge of them. This time we will be inundated with submissions' (Assistant Director (Administration), Social Services Department, Walsall C.B. 1974).

Most local authority departments preferred what had been Walsall's approach in the past: the passing of information by direct contact between officials and voluntary organizations. This allowed a certain selectivity on the part of the local authority. Lancashire divisional directors were specifically requested by the social service and education departments to consult with local voluntary organizations and this was also the pattern in the West Riding of Yorkshire. In Sheffield Education Department, and in Kensington and Chelsea, it was assumed that informal contact between officials, councillors, and voluntary organizations would be the main transmitter of information: 'Voluntary organizations which have existing associations with the department are likely to hear from one of us when a circular comes out' (Assistant Director, Education Department, Sheffield C.B.).

In other local authorities or departments — Tower Hamlets, Haringey, Northumberland, Hartlepool, Sheffield Social Services Department, and Walsall's education department — it was assumed (wrongly) that 'the Home Office writes to all voluntary organizations — we assume the Home Office does this' (Director, Social Services Department, Sheffield C.B.), or that 'they have their own ways of learning about the Urban Programme' (Chief Executive's Department, Tower Hamlets L.B.), or it was concluded that there were too many voluntary organizations to contact (Senior Administrative Officer, Social Services Department, Haringey L.B.) and no co-ordinating machinery by which to do so.

The 'natural' co-ordinating machinery most often depended upon by local authorities was the local Council for Voluntary Service (CVS). The national headquarters of the CVS, the National Council of Social Service (NCSS) in London, received the circular from the Home Office which regarded it as the main organization for the tapping of local voluntary organizations. Although branches received the circular from the headquarters organization, in three cases — Yorkshire West Riding, Leicester, and Warley — the local authority also sent copies to the local CVS branch.

In five authorities — Leeds, Leicester, Warley, Northumberland, and Lancashire — where there were local branches of the CVS, these branches took on the responsibility for informing some, if not all, of their associated organizations. This distribution took many forms. In Leeds the CVS:

'sent copies to about twenty-seven voluntary organizations, but this would not be a complete list. Really, I send out a note or copies of the circular to all our affiliated bodies and to other voluntary organizations that I know might be interested. Taking together all affiliated bodies and the other also-rans I reckon I send out between 80 and 100 copies of the circular or a note.'

(General Secretary, Leeds CVS)

In Lancashire the equivalent organization put out copies of the circular, more selectively, to 'interested organizations'.

In three authority areas — Walsall, Sheffield, and Yorkshire West Riding — the local branch of the CVS received copies of the circular but made no systematic attempt to distribute the information. In Yorkshire West Riding the CVS had confidence in the social services department's system for informing voluntary organizations through contact with officials of the department. In Walsall, the Council of Voluntary Service and also the local Council for Community Relations felt that there was no scope for them to take on any sort of co-ordinating role in such a situation, where relations between voluntary organizations were characterized by competition for resources from the local authority. In Sheffield, the CVS seemed as antipathetic as some local authorities to the consequences of spreading the circular widely: 'We do not put it out because otherwise you get a spate [of applications]'.

Although there is a Council of Social Service that serves the whole of London, and several London boroughs have their own branch, in Kensington and Chelsea, Tower Hamlets, and Haringey there was no CVS co-ordinating machinery and other bodies had stepped into the breach. In Haringey, the role of distributing information about the Urban Programme circulars to voluntary organizations had been taken on by the Community Relations Officer of the Council for Community Relations (CCR). In Kensington and Chelsea, the council-sponsored North Kensington Amenity Trust had taken on something of the same role.

In several other authorities, the Council for Community Relations assumed a wide co-ordinating role even where there was an effective distribution network established by the CVS. In Leeds and Leicester there seemed to be some competition between the two organizations for the role of co-ordinator. The Leeds CVS thought it reached about 100 voluntary bodies and the CCR in its turn passed the circular on to about sixty, many of them overlapping.

The CCR in Leicester had been encouraged by the CVS and the social services department to make its own applications through the CVS (the regular co-ordinating channel for the voluntary sector) but preferred to make submissions directly to the local authority where it was thought that the CCR had the best chance of wielding its influence.

In spite of these occasional cases of overlap and even competition to fulfil the co-ordinating role, the picture for voluntary organizations generally was of restricted access to information and therefore to the possibility of submitting applications to central government. Access was not restricted in an absolute sense and usually not deliberately, but it depended upon connections with the local authority and with the voluntary co-ordinating agencies. The scope for such connections was increased the more the local authority spread information among more junior and, especially, field staff, and the more the local authorities and organizations such as the CVS and CCR made an effort to distribute the information.

It is true that voluntary organizations were not totally reliant on the initiative of the local authorities, the CVS, or the CCR. The Home Office was prepared to distribute copies of the circular to voluntary bodies on request; but proportionately few knew of the possibility of this unadvertised facility. It was also possible for them to approach the local authority for information; but this depended on some minimal knowledge that a circular had been issued.

Processes for the selection and ranking of bids

From 1969 the Urban Programme circular had asked local authorities 'to indicate an order of priority for the projects which they submit'. From 1972, in as neutral a tone as possible (wishing to avoid offence to the authorities), the circular added: ' ... some authorities have found it useful to discuss priorities with the voluntary organisations before submitting applications for their areas' (Home Office 1972: para.8). However, in only one authority, Leicester, was the voluntary sector involved in any way in the 'prioritizing' of applications. Here a CVS committee worked with the social services department to rank the voluntary organizations' applications which were then submitted separately from the local authority's own proposals to the Home Office. In other authorities, it was rare for the voluntary organization to be informed even in what order of rank its application was being passed on to the Home Office.

While the incorporation of voluntary organizations into the process of selection and ranking of bids was in general slight, there was considerable variation between authorities on the other elements (see pp.88-9 under *Local government management*): the degree of councillor involvement, the diffusion/co-ordination of decision-making, and the level in the hierarchy at which decisions were made.

The typical simple pattern (of which Leicester and Northumberland are examples) for the processing of bids could be described as follows:

a generation of bids in local authority departments and voluntary organizations;

b passing of voluntary bids to the relevant local authority department;

c selection and ranking of bids within departments by the directorate (chief officer, deputy, and assistants) of each department;

d reporting of separate departmental lists to service (e.g. education and social service) committees for formal approval;

e passing of separate lists to a meeting of chief officers of all relevant departments to arrive at a cross-departmental ranking;

f reporting of these overall rankings for formal approval to a cross-service committee such as the 'General Purposes Committee' or 'Policy and Resources Committee';

g passing of ranked bids through the Chief Executive's department to the Home Office.

The variations on this theme were immense but are shown briefly and diagramatically in *Table 2* which indicates the location of the responsibility for the main functions of generation and selection of bids, ranking within departments, and ranking across departments.

The wide variations in the levels of complexity of this processing can be illustrated from the accounts given by officials in two local authorities.[8] At its most simple, in Walsall projects were

---

[8] Paraphrased except for sections within quotation marks.

Table 2 *Schematic representation of application processing in twelve local authorities*

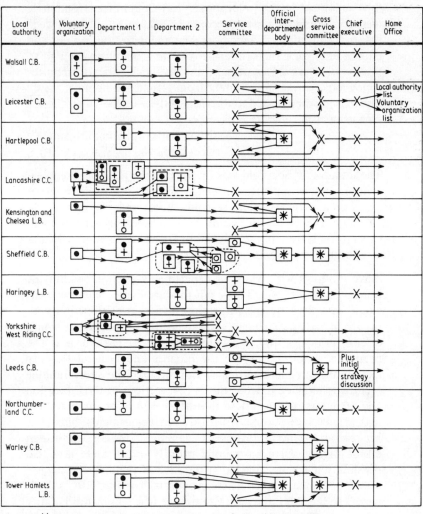

Key: X No significant function — information only
      ● Generation of bids
      + Selection of bids

      O Ranking within departments
      ✳ Ranking between departments
      [...] District committees/departments, subcommittees/departments

formulated and ranked at a senior level in departments and then:

> Bids are costed with the support of the Finance Department and then submitted to the [relevant service] Committee. Committee members would see a list of recommended projects about a week before the meeting: 'Councillors take an interest but do not add bids or alter their rank order'. From the Committee they go to the Town Clerk's Department and to the Finance Committee which looks at the bids 'purely from a financial point of view'. The bids are then passed to the Home Office by the Town Clerk's Department in separate rank order per committee.
>
> (Assistant Director (Administrator),
Social Services Department, Walsall C.B.)

The situation in Sheffield was by comparison far more complex, presenting opportunity for influence both by a greater range of departmental officials, and by councillors, and yet in the end achieving a level of co-ordination both between departments and between committees. In the Education Office, the Senior Assistant Education Officer would:

> 'have meetings with heads of departments [sections within the Education Office] which have put forward ideas'. The proposals would be costed by the Education Office in conjunction with the Architect's Department and the heads of departments would discuss priorities and draw up a suggested rank order. The proposals would then go to the Finance and General Purpose Committee (a subcommittee of Education). The subcommittee relating to individual departments [i.e. sections of the Education Office such as 'Youth and Adult Further Education' or 'Schools'] may at this stage put in a word for their departments' bids. The Finance and General Purposes Committee (F & GPC) will then decide the overall departmental priority order: there is a real possibility that they will change the rank of the officers' suggestions and they may even delete proposals. The F & GPC's list is passed to the full Education Committee where approval is fairly automatic. The Senior Assistant Education Officer would then pass the proposals on to the Town Clerk, who submits them to a chief officer's meeting to establish a priority order across local authority departments. The joint list goes to the Policy Committee on the full Council. The Policy Committee is very likely to adjust the priority order and 'in fact this year altered Education's

ordering'. The Policy Committee's proposals are ratified by the full Council and passed to the Town Clerk for forwarding to the Home Office.

Sheffield councillors thus played an important part in ranking bids both departmentally and for the whole range of council submissions: 'The Policy Committee [consisting of chairman and deputies of council committees] is very conscious of its role in establishing priorities across departments' (Education Committee Chairman, Sheffield C.B.).

Councillors were influential on the priority ranking of bids in four other authorities — Tower Hamlets, Haringey, Leeds, and Warley. In all these cases, however, the process was more 'streamlined' than in Sheffield; Warley and Tower Hamlets had effectively eliminated the influence of service committees, which seemed to serve merely as 'constitutionally necessary' but ineffective steps on the way to submission, and had vested councillor influence solely in co-ordinating committees. In the case of Tower Hamlets, the Policy Committee, advised by a chief officers' management team, established priorities between departments.

Warley had established a special Urban Programme subcommittee of the full council to establish cross-departmental priorities. There was here no administrative (i.e. official) framework for co-ordinating the submissions of departments.

Leeds and Haringey had adopted systems that allowed chief officers of departments to by-pass the services committee itself and to consult with committee chairmen about the rankings of departmental bids. Leeds maintained this selective involvement of councillors (where the chairmen, deputies, and shadow chairmen of committees made decisions) to a co-ordinating level, where a pruned-down finance committee made decisions, on chief officers' advice, about cross-departmental ratings. Haringey left final decisions about rank order to a joint meeting of the chairmen, vice-chairmen, and shadow chairmen of the civic amenities, education, general purposes, and social services committees.

In Haringey and Warley co-ordination between departments seemed to rest entirely on these meetings of elected representatives. In Sheffield, Leeds, and Tower Hamlets, political decisions were taken after the advice of a joint meeting of chief officers had been received.

However, the real possibility that councillors would override the priority ranking proposed by their chief officers had led in at least one of these authorities to collusion between officials at local and central government level. Upon receiving the authority's bids, one central government department was said normally to have contacted the equivalent department in that authority to ask the chief officer what *his* real priorities were. (This was the situation as described by a Director of Social Services in one authority.)

In the other authorities, elected representatives seemed, with regard to decisions about the Urban Programme, to have a nominal role which entailed the ratification of their officials' decisions at service committee and council level. Typical comments about councillor influence on the selection and ranking of bids in Walsall, Leicester, Hartlepool, Lancashire, Yorkshire West Riding, Kensington and Chelsea, and Northumberland were: 'We are not an authority which leaves things to the council'; 'Councillors do not add bids or alter their rank order'; 'The Committee is a rubber stamp'; and, 'Councillors always accept the bids and the recommended order'.

In three of these authorities — Walsall, Lancashire, and Yorkshire — the process was dealt with entirely at departmental level without any attempt to produce an overall 'council list' of recommended and ranked project proposals. Officials here found it difficult to conceive how quite different areas of expenditure could be compared and priorities arrived at. Yorkshire West Riding Education Department found it difficult enough to imagine how to establish priorities even among its own departmental proposals from widely differing geographical areas: 'how can I decide between a mining village, a cotton town, and an area of Batley full of immigrants? If I am forced to make that sort of decision I know I shall choose areas which I know about' (Administrative Officer for Social Education, Education Department, Yorkshire WR C.C.). The result was that: ' ... usually someone from the Home Office or DES phones up and says: "You have put up twenty-five, we can give you three, which three?".'

In Leicester, Hartlepool, Kensington and Chelsea, and Northumberland, on the other hand, the job of selecting and ranking was carried out by officials not only at departmental level but also between departments. Each had a framework for cross-departmental meetings, usually at chief officer level (e.g. in Hartlepool, Kensington and Chelsea, and Northumberland); but in

Leicester meetings were held at assistant director level between the social service and education departments.

If we were briefly to characterize these processes according to the degree of councillor (or 'political')[9] influence and cross-service co-ordination that they incorporated, we could categorize the authorities as follows:

1 apolitical with co-ordination undertaken by administrators: Leicester, Hartlepool, Kensington and Chesea, and Northumberland;

2 apolitical without co-ordination: Walsall, Lancashire, and Yorkshire;

3 political with co-ordination primarily by politicians: Warley, Haringey;

4 political with co-ordination achieved by politicians and administrators: Tower Hamlets, Leeds, and Sheffield.

Decision-making criteria in local government

From the point of view of the Urban Programme as a whole the main contributions of local government were related to the eligibility of bids and their ordering; decisions concerning their eventual success or failure were left to central government. But local government was also making what might be called a 'sub-selection' about the project proposals it would pass on.

Eligibility criteria   A condition which underlay all the eligibility criteria that central government intended local authorities to employ was that the putative generator of a bid, whether within the local authority or among voluntary organizations, should be sufficiently informed to make his proposal at the right time in the right way. We have already seen how restricted was the spread of information about the UP in most local authorities, and especially with regard to voluntary organizations. Voluntary organizations depended very much on the contacts and goodwill that they maintained with local authority departments or on their membership of the local co-ordinating voluntary organization (where one existed).

---

9 In using the terms 'political' and 'apolitical' we are describing the presence or absence of political representatives in decision-making; this is not to suggest that politics can be absent from government decision-making.

Eligibility for a voluntary organization's proposal was thus a matter to be decided by not only the local authority but also by the capacity of the voluntary organization to discover information, to decide which local authority department its application most closely suited, and then to make the application in the terms demanded by the circular. Without the aid of a co-ordinating voluntary organization, like the CVS in Leeds or Leicester, many voluntary organizations were unofficially excluded.

There was a further excluding factor for voluntary organizations. Although the Home Office formally allowed six months between the issue of the circular and the receipt of submissions, by the time the circular had passed through the local authorities and then out to the voluntary organizations there was often little time left to formulate applications. 'You do not know what a circular will cover until it arrives, so you have to do all the background work and hold all the consultations after it has arrived. This often cannot be done with voluntary organizations in the time' (Chief Administration Officer, Education Department, Haringey L.B.).

More fundamentally, the eligibility rules which local authorities applied to their own and to voluntary applications depended on what the local authority thought the Programme was about. Opinion could be far removed from that in the Home Office, as is shown in Chapter 7. Nevertheless there were, as we saw earlier in this chapter, certain eligibility criteria which the Home Office made explicit.

Areas of need: Only Lancashire County Council specifically ruled out certain areas as ineligible for the Urban Programme. Both the Education and Social Services Departments excluded certain geographical areas and concentrated UP funds on the areas around the Manchester/Liverpool conurbation. However, under pressure from councillors and the area subsections of departments to spread the funds more widely, and with declining confidence in the Home Office's interest in selectivity, from 1974 both departments had decided no longer to confine bids to these 'classically defined areas'. Like most other local authorities, they decided that they should examine each proposal, wherever it came from, on its own merits: 'even in affluent areas, there are pockets of deprivation.'

Project recommendations: The guidance in each circular about the types of project that might be proposed was never intended by central government to restrict the range of projects proposed by local government. It was indeed only in this loose sense that the guidance was generally understood by authorities and voluntary organizations. Only two authorities' departments, in Warley and Tower Hamlets, asserted their strong adherence to the circular recommendations. Most others treated the advice as useful information for the tailoring of projects into a shape which was likely to appeal to central government: (a) it helped them to modify already-conceived projects into conformity with central government priorities; and (b) it offered them some guidance for the selection and ranking of bids.

New projects: Few local authorities gave any serious recognition to the Urban Programme circular advice that: 'One of the main purposes of the Programme is to encourage the provision of facilities which would not otherwise be provided in the area concerned ... Local authorities are therefore asked to say whether a particular project has previously been considered by them outside the Urban Programme' (Home Office 1972: para.5).

In general, local authorities saw this advice as contradictory with the other circular advice that projects should alleviate deprivation in areas of acute need. How could it be that acutely-necessary projects were not already in a department's existing programme unless that department had failed to observe the need? If it had previously failed to observe the need, why should it do so now?

Selection and ranking criteria In effect, the above factors were less important in deciding the *eligibility* of projects than in deciding:

 a how they should be presented to the Home Office; and
 b how they should be ranked.

In essence, if a local authority department was predisposed to accept an application, because it fitted well with the department's view of current needs or had the support of elected representatives, the eligibility criteria were sufficiently flexible to allow the department to put the application up to the Home Office.

The influences that shaped local authorities' methods in selecting and ranking bids for submission to central government can be classified into five main types:

 a conceptions about the areas that should be served;

b conceptions about the special character of the Urban Programme;

c conceptions (related to (b)) about what would appeal to central government;

d departmental priorities;

e relations of mutual respect between departments.

Areas of need: Local authorities were generally unable to state the criteria that they applied in identifying areas of need, and preferred to attribute their judgements to a shared, local common sense view. 'Common knowledge' and 'evident need' were generally quoted as being sufficient to define the areas. Even where, as in Leeds, the Planning Department had mapped the geographical distribution of need according to social indicators, this information was tempered by a common sense view of where the deprived areas were. Yorkshire West Riding Education Department was one of the few to have employed stated criteria — relating to 'the incidence of free school meals, one-parent families and supplementary benefits' — to decide between submissions. Generally if there was any selection according to area it was done on a more ad hoc basis that implied no clear view about the nature of priority areas: 'When we are considering bids, we knock out the least deserving areas and then try to spread the funds around the most deserving areas' (Assistant Director (Special Education), Education Department, Lancashire C.C. 1974).

Special character of the UP: Two main characteristics of the Urban Programme were frequently cited by local authorities and voluntary organizations as affecting their selection and ranking of submissions. One was a view, which was never however expressly stated by the Home Office, that the Urban Programme was concerned with innovation. The 'requirement' that projects should not already be in local authority programmes encouraged this view, and the 75 per cent grant (as is shown in Chapter 7) had the effect of easing innovative projects through committees.

The other 'feature' of the Urban Programme that was often quoted as a basis for selecting projects for submission to the Home Office was the flexibility it offered to respond to new pressures where departmental budgets were already committed: 'Priority ranking mainly reflects a responsiveness to current pressures' (Assistant Director (Research and Development), Lancashire C.C.);

'It depends what special pressures are being applied to the department by councillors, for example "to help the gypsies"' (Assistant Director (Schools), Education Department, Leicester C.B.).

In Leicester, the Programme was used in particular to support projects in immigrant areas, both because the local authority was aware of newly-arisen needs (especially with the arrival of the Ugandan refugees), and also because the UP provided a useful instrument of selective help for projects that it would have been politically difficult for the local authority to promote out of regular departmental budgets.

The Director of Social Services in Kensington and Chelsea saw the UP projects in similar terms, as 'inhabiting a different, more immediate world ... [the UP] allows an immediate unprogrammed response to need'.

The characteristics of innovativeness, flexibility, and immediacy which applicants tended to attribute to the UP arose not so much from a view that the Programme had different *objectives* from those of regular local authority programmes as from the fact that the different *conditions* surrounding its budgeting allowed them to use the UP in this way.

Departmental priorities: As we saw in considering eligibility criteria, in spite of the circular's advice most local authorities put forward projects that were already a part of their planned programmes. This applied less to voluntary organizations, but only because few had sufficient resources to justify a spending programme; but, even here, voluntary organizations generally regarded the Urban Programme as just one (though often the main) source of funds for projects they intended to implement.

The degree to which the UP was incorporated into local authorities' existing programmes varied, but the selection and ranking of bids might be typified as follows: projects would be proposed that had already been conceived within a department; from among these proposals would be selected:

a those that seemed to relate most strongly to the circular's recommended projects; and

b those that the department might have most difficulty in financing otherwise, either because the project was unusual, or because it implied selective help to a group or area.

'Home Office appeal': In ranking projects local authority

departments were not only responding to their own view of priorities but also trying to guess at what 'the Home Office is looking for'. They knew that central government judgements were not based only on the priority rating provided by local government and that in the circular there was a vague reference to the UP's having ' … a national as well as a local purpose, and it is not always possible to adhere to the priorities indicated' (Home Office 1972: para.6). The guess about what this national purpose might be was based on the circular's recommended projects, on a reading of past approvals, and on a sense of the special characteristics of the Urban Programme. One authority argued that, in putting local government into a situation where it had to make priority listings on this indefinite basis, 'the Home Office is shelving its responsibilities'.

However vague, the idea of 'Home Office appeal' was present in most authorities: 'It's really done on this basis of realism rather than criteria. The subcommittee has some idea of what the Home Office is looking for and will try and push projects that fit in with that' (Town Clerk, Warley C.B.); ' … it is more often based on what is thought will appeal to the Home Office rather than on real criteria of priority' (Assistant Education Officer, Education Department, Northumberland C.C.); 'Well, we already have ideas for projects, but when we get the circular we do look at what sorts of project are suggested and only send on those which fit in with this list' (Divisional Education Officer, Education Department, Yorkshire West Riding C.C.).

Mutual respect between departments: Within departments the question of priorities, if it was not based on shared understandings, could be concluded by resort to the authority of the official hierarchy. Between departments, this hierarchy did not exist except in the shape of the Chief Executive, who in only one authority took a serious part in the UP decision-making. There were four types of solution to the problem quoted by local authorities:

   i prioritizing on the basis of a strategy common to different departments;
  ii referring to political authority;
 iii resorting to bargaining for position between departments through the administrative machine;
  iv achieving a consensus between departments, though without any stated and shared strategy.

We shall briefly consider which of these four possible solutions were adopted by the authorities.

In only one local authority, Leeds, was there any attempt (in this case through the Town Clerk) to establish a cross-departmental strategy at the outset of each phase. The generation of bids, departmental, and then interdepartmental ranking were based at least partly on this initial strategy. The problem of interdepartmental ranking was further eased by the avoidance of any attempt to give each proposal an order of rank; instead they were grouped in ranked categories.

Nevertheless, in Leeds as in the other four more 'political' authorities — Sheffield, Haringey, Tower Hamlets, and Warley — final decisions about ranking were referred to cross-service council committees (e.g. 'General Purposes' or 'Policy and Resources'). In this way, the need was eliminated for *officials* to establish cross-departmental criteria which might favour one department over others. The avoidance was greatest in Haringey and Warley where there were no separate interdepartmental meetings to consider bids. The basis for decision-making in the council committee was generally attributed by councillors to strategy and mutual understanding. In Warley the major ranking decisions seemed to be taken in the controlling Labour Party group and then carried through the later meeting of the Urban Programme subcommittee. In Tower Hamlets and Sheffield, effectively single-party (Labour) rule had a similar effect of taking discussion outside the realm of departmental views about priorities into one resting on the party hierarchy and on political strategies (which it was not possible to discover). In Haringey, where it was possible to observe the ranking process in committee, decisions about priorities seemed to stem from:

a an attempt to satisfy both major committees (or departments), social services and education; and

b the authority of the leader of the council who proposed the order of rank.

The meetings between officials of different departments that established final priorities in four local authorities — Leicester, Kensington and Chelsea, Northumberland, and Hartlepool — seem to have been based not on any clearly-stated cross-departmental strategy but on a common understanding that each department's priorities should be respected and that no particular department's projects should have a regularly higher rating than any of the others'. Usually projects were said to have fallen into place without discussion; the basis of this agreement seems to have been not only a shared understanding about the geographical areas which should receive attention but also a sense of fair shares for all or 'back-scratching', as it was described by one chief officer.

The remaining authorities, Walsall, Lancashire, and Yorkshire West Riding, solved the problem of cross-departmental decisions about priorities by ignoring it. This disclosed not only the general separation of departments in these authorities but also a view that there were no specific characteristics of the Urban Programme that would provide a basis for comparing applications from different services: 'We really do not understand what the UP is supposed to be doing' (Director, Fieldwork Services, Social Services Department, Yorkshire West Riding C.C.); '[it is] difficult to imagine how unlike projects could be compared and rated ... it could only be by a process of interdepartmental bargaining ... ' (Assistant Director, Education Department, Walsall C.B.).

Conclusion

This chapter has considered the structural and procedural form of the Urban Programme, broadly in terms of the chances which it gave to different applications from various sources to surface and receive funding, and of the factors which influenced these chances.

It has been shown that, in central government, decisions were diffused between departments and that the Home Office's co-ordinating role was highly circumscribed both by the structure which was given to the Programme at the outset and by the well-established traditions of departmental sovereignty. In the absence of any consistent policy directing by the Home Office, or by any interdepartmental body, or by ministers, the UP tended to lose itself in regular, established, and separate departmental machinery. The fortunes of an application depended very much on the department to which it was allocated and on the budgetary and other categories in which it found itself. Certainly, an attempt was made in all departments to apply criteria relating to the needs of particular areas and the relevance of projects to Urban Programme objectives; but they were applied only flexibly and unsystematically.

The more rigorously-applied eligibility and selection criteria were incidental to the main purposes of the Programme and arose partly out of the UP's structural and procedural characteristics; they related to such factors as the level of the applicant's information and competence, the local authority's priority ranking, a concept of 'balance' between areas, the cost of projects, and their relation to departmental policy.

This might have been consistent with the Urban Programme's original highly-selective intentions if, at local authority level, the distribution of information had been sufficiently general and the selection and ranking criteria systematically related to UP goals. In general, as in central government, there was a wide dispersal of information and of decision-making at local authority level, but this dispersal was primarily within the governmental machine and to those voluntary organizations that either already had good contacts with it or had their own distributive framework.

Except where there was a specific category of project that was peculiar to the Programme — for example, nursery classes — applications were rarely generated in response to the Urban Programme itself. The criteria which local authorities drew from their understanding of the Programme were more often used to make selections from among already-planned projects and to present them to central government in terms that were likely to have 'Home Office appeal'. Local authorities saw the Programme as having not so much different objectives from their regular programmes as different operational conditions which permitted the promotion of some projects otherwise perhaps difficult to finance.

At both local authority and central government level, decision-making was highly diffused and the co-ordination that took place tended to respect departmental authority; this was less true in the more political local councils where a degree of centralized decision-making took place, a feature that was almost entirely absent in central government.

5 Influences on policy formulation and implementation

Though opinion about the Urban Programme continues to be divided, about the following facts there need be no dispute: certain monies have been allocated in different budget types (capital, non-capital, once-only), for certain periods of time (five years, three years, one-off payments), to certain local authorities, and through them to certain voluntary agencies, to enable them to establish a wide and shifting variety of projects for the assumed good and benefit of a large and fluid body of the population. The means by which such assumed goods or benefits are delivered, however — the sums of money, the rate of grant, the types of budget, the agencies involved, and the types of project funded — have not all remained fixed and immutable over the life of the Programme. Most have been the subject of continuing debate and some — such as the types of project, the overall scale, and the relative proportion of each budget type — have constantly shifted, with the result that the beneficiaries of Programme funds and the ways in which they have benefited have continually undergone change. The central concern of this chapter is to examine why such shifts in the means of benefit delivery (and hence of recipients) have occurred, what has occasioned them, and who or what has determined them. This must entail the study not only of the details of the allocation procedures (which projects to fund for which 'clients' in which areas) but also of the general structure and confines of the Programme within which these allocations are made.

The following elements of the UP have been selected as those that provide an important structural context for the allocation of funds, but which have remained under varying degrees of fluctuation over the life of the Programme:

— its scale and financial arrangements;
— the relative importance of central and local government as the instruments of implementing the Programme;
— the involvement of voluntary agencies;
— the main types of project promoted; and
— the provision for ethnic minorities as special recipients of aid from the Urban Programme.

Further examination of the factors that have influenced or determined shifts in these important aspects of the UP cannot proceed without some consideration of that perennial — and difficult — issue of the distinction between policy formulation on the one hand and administration on the other, and an examination of the respective roles of politicians and administrators or officials and the interrelation between them.

The UP is a device for the disbursement of public funds on a discriminatory basis. Some people will 'benefit'; others whose need is equally great will not. Are the decisions which influence the choice of beneficiaries in this context political decisions or administrative decisions? *Should* they be political or administrative decisions or can they safely and legitimately be left to 'administrative discretion'? (On this subject see Hill 1972: Chap.4.) At what point does policy formulation become policy implementation and where does (or should) the role of the politician give way to that of the administrator in policy decisions? Such questions, in a more general context, have long taxed the minds of political and social scientists, and it is not our intention here to pursue the theoretical substance of these issues. To do so would not very far advance our analysis of the UP. Rather it seems more sensible for present purposes to agree with Hill when he says that since in practice it is difficult to draw any clear lines between politics and administration — though a number of attempts have been made (Simon, Smithburg, and Thompson 1950; Brown 1970) — it is more logical to avoid making such a distinction (Hill 1972: 200). Nonetheless, in practice the social analyst should bear in mind the relative roles of politician and official (and the controversy surrounding the boundaries of

their interdependence) in his examination of government programmes. The debate should, if possible, be illuminated by examples from actual procedures — the more so since there is a dearth of
evidence about the practices of the middle and senior Civil Service.

Such work as has been conducted on administrative discretion in
Britain has either concentrated on the activities of low-ranking
Civil Servants with direct interface with the public (Hill 1969:
75-90), or concerned itself with the influence of professionals on
policy formulation (Donnison and Chapman 1965; Smith 1976;
Hall 1975; Heclo and Wildavsky 1974; Hall 1974). In addition,
there have been a number of accounts of the work of particular
departments or of the Civil Service as a whole (Kelsall 1956;
Critchley 1951), but these have often been written by ministers or
Civil Servants who, though writing with the benefit of first-hand
knowledge, have on the whole been circumscribed not only by the
Official Secrets Act (which of course applies to everyone) but also
by the conventions of Whitehall, with the result that description
has usually taken precedence over analysis. The role played by Civil
Servants themselves in the formulation and implementation of
policy has remained largely unstudied. As Gordon says,

> 'Almost without exception text book writers on British politics
> reaffirmed the orthodox view: civil servants had no partisan
> opinions, were efficient and loyal administrators, and served
> dutifully whichever party triumphed at the polls. All the same,
> the underlying nagging question that remained was whether the
> executive machine was so structured that ministers had many
> informed ideas of their own, could count on their being rigor-
> ously analysed ... by officials sympathetic to them and could be
> sure of getting a wide range of divergent views frames ... '.
>
> (Gordon 1971: 31)

Only relatively recently have the activities of senior officials been
the subject of more rigorous examination — and that ironically as
the result of incidents that reflect behaviour less exemplary than
that ideally expected of British Civil Servants.[1]

In this investigation of influencing or determining factors on
shifts in the structure and process of the Urban Programme,
evidence has been drawn largely from three sources: interviews with

---

[1] The incidents were the Vehicle and General Affair and the repercussions within
the public service of the activities of Mr John Poulson (Chapman 1973: 273-90;
Wright 1973: 1-15).

officials in central government departments and officials and politicians in local authorities, participant observation on the part of the researchers, and material from Home Office files. The wealth of documentary records available in government departments and their adequacy as sources of evidence have already been discussed in the introduction to Chapter 3 (see pages 35-6). There may be many contributions to (and hence influences on) the discussion of policy, including, as R.G.S. Brown notes (Brown 1970: 160), professional experts, Civil Servants, ministers, and Members of Parliament as well as, on occasion, researchers, pressure groups, and the media. No attempt has been made to identify the role of each of these groups in the formulation and modification of UP policy — indeed the evidence is that some of these, especially professional experts, academics, or researchers, have had little influence except in the cases that we have already cited (the work of Titmuss and the Seebohm and Plowden Reports).

Instead it has proved more useful to focus attention on the ways in which influence has been brought to bear by a smaller range of participants. Thus, in analysing contributions made and influences affected, particular attention has been paid to the following:

— the perceptions of the problems, on the part of Civil Servants and politicians, that the UP sets out to tackle;
— the perceptions of the aims and functions of the UP on the part of Civil Servants and politicians;
— ministerial and other political influences;
— the influence of local authorities and Local Authority Associations;
— the influence of voluntary agencies and other public or media comment;
— the influence exerted by each government department involved *vis-à-vis* other departments.

Thus, wherever possible we have attempted not only to identify the relevant actors — Civil Servants, politicians — but also to see whether and to what extent their contributions have depended on their perceptions of important components in the cause-and-effect chain of deprivation, and possible 'solutions'.[2] At the same time,

---

[2] For, as Townsend says: 'A "plan" may be adopted and put into effect as policy, but it is normally distorted in the process by the subjective interpretations and emphases of Government and officials, concessions to interest groups and limitations imposed by external forces' (Townsend 1975:6).

where decisions about shifts in structure have been taken or influenced by ministers or other politicians, these have been identified as such, as have the influences of other parties closely involved in the Programme (local authorities and their Associations and voluntary agencies) and those not involved (the media). Finally, on the assumption that in a multidepartmental programme some decisions must be influenced by the actions or wishes of departments other than the Home Office, whether at official or ministerial level, these also are investigated as a possible input to the continual shaping of the Programme.

It should be remarked, however, that because of the provisions of the *Official Secrets Act*, and (more importantly) Whitehall conventions of confidentiality and secrecy, much of the detail of these decision-making processes, including the identification (even if only by rank) of individual actors, the influences bearing upon those in positions to make decisions, disagreements between departments, and reference to substantiating documentation, cannot be recorded here. The authors can only ask to be excused if the narrative in places appears to become somewhat coy and if evidence supporting the assertions is less full and explicit than either they or the reader might have wished.

The scale and financial arrangements of the Urban Programme

Chapter 3 described the deliberations surrounding the establishment of the UP and the definition of its initial financial limits. The financial scale of the Programme has not however remained static since 1968/69; there have been periodic injections of funds from the DHSS and other sources — such as the disbursement through the UP of £6 million of aid originally destined for Uganda but diverted from thence subsequent to the expulsion of the Ugandan Asians in 1973. In 1970, the Government of the day extended the life of the Programme from four years (1968-72) to eight years (1968-76) and approved expenditure of £40 million over and above the initial £20 million. A further £10 million were added in 1971 and 1972, consisting of £6.5 million of capital funds (with no running costs attached) for infrastructure works in special development areas, £1.3 million earmarked for the extension of family planning services (a DHSS injection), £1.0 million (with no running costs for capital schemes) for the stepping up of day nursery and pre-school playgroup provision (another DHSS injection), and £1.1 million as additional aid to voluntary agencies as part of the Government's promised extra encouragement for the voluntary social services. Then, in the autumn of 1973, a further £2 million for each of two years were voted to the Programme, largely in anticipation of a decrease in the level of approvals between 1973 and 1976 made necessary by the high level of approvals up to 1972 and the heavy inroads that the running costs of these projects would make into the total Programme allocation up to 1976. In 1977 the UP was recast as part of the new inner cities programme and its budget for 1979/80 increased to £125 million at 1977/78 out-turn prices. Thus, the financial scale of the Programme — and hence the number of the beneficiaries — has been a matter of continual debate and amendment. Where has the impetus for these shifts come from and who has determined the size of the increases and the conditions attached to them?

Officials made the initial estimates for the cost of a new programme (see Chapter 3) in the context of the Prime Minister's stipulation that: 'This cost will have to be met within the ceilings of expenditure laid down in the announcement I made to Parliament in January. Every extra penny spent will have to be met by corresponding economies' (Wilson 5.5.1968). They suggested a sum of £22-£23 million spread over 1969/70 (Interdepartmental document 1968). This figure, however, proved unacceptable to ministers for two reasons: first, it seemed too high in the light of the then required cuts in public expenditure of £400 million — a view that can be interpreted either as economic common sense or political expedience; and, second, because, whereas departments had been asked to seek for areas in their expenditure which could be cut in order to release funds that could be used for the Programme, it had not proved possible to do so and monies had therefore to be found within a review of the 'general management of the economy'. It can be argued therefore that the initial scale of the Programme might have been greater if the relevant central departments had been able to introduce the necessary economies to provide some £22 million over two years.

In this context it is significant to note that in a later (1970) discussion between officials about how to find the funds for a further increase in the Programme it was argued that savings should not be sought from existing departmental votes since relevant departments had made it clear that this was not a possibility and: 'the fact that extra money was found to launch the original programme and compensatory savings were not imposed on departmental votes was an important factor in securing the co-operation of other departments' (Working Party on Immigration and Community Relations 1970: internal Home Office document). In the event, therefore, the Home Secretary of the day had to settle for a smaller programme than that devised by officials. Concerned as he was, however, that something be done quickly, he suggested reducing the immediate cost by phasing the Programme over four years instead of two. Subsequent to this, officials produced the formula that was finally adopted of £1 million in the first year, £5 million in the second, £8 million in the third, and £8 million in the fourth as outlined in Chapter 3 (see page 56).

The diversity of thinking that went into the early deliberations of the Working Party set up to design the UP and the variety of perceptions of the problem which they brought to their task have already been described (see Chapter 3), but it should be noted here that a significant factor in the determination of the initial scale of the Programme was the assumption made by the officials concerned, *without seeking expert or professional advice,*[3] that the problem of deprivation was one affecting small pockets of population in discrete run-down areas, and one that could be tackled by topping-up the existing forms of social provision with perhaps some attempt at innovation. To quote from one of the officials closely involved in designing the Programme:

'We found that each department had its own little geographical areas. It was accepted by all of us right away that there could be areas of multiple deprivation. "Housing" produced a list of housing stress areas, "Education" produced maps of education priority areas, and "Health" produced a list of areas of high pre-natal mortality. This formed a very crude criterion because we were told to produce our report within a fortnight.'

(Senior Home Office official)

Much of the early discussion centred around the means by which additional resources would be channelled to deprived areas and more specifically at what rate grants should be made. The first

---

[3] But it should be noted that since they had to complete their task in a matter of some two and a half months this was not possible.

point, it would seem, was easily and quickly resolved at official level. The alternatives considered were a specific grant to local authorities or a readjustment of the Rate Support Grant to give additional weightings for deprived areas. There was some deliberation within the Working Party about possible local authority reaction to a new specific grant and about the likely success of either method in achieving the immediate aim of the Programme, to get additional resources into small deprived areas, but it was not an issue upon which the local authorities, through the Local Authority Associations, were consulted, and therefore not one on which they had any influence. The relative merits of each system were considered and a decision reached in the following terms:

'The decision to provide for a specific grant was taken after rejecting the possibility of reweighting the factors on which the distribution of the rate support grant is based under the Local Government Act 1966. It was felt that such a reweighting would give no incentive to local authorities to spend on the preferred type of project, and that as the rate support grant was in aid of all the revenues of the authority and not of any specific item of expenditure, there was no guarantee that any additional grant diverted to authorities whose areas contain districts of special need, would in fact be spent on projects of benefit to such areas'.

(Draft paper on the Urban Programme 1968)

The framework within which such administrative discretion was exercised is illustrated by the comments of one member of the Working Party on Immigration and Community Relations — a body, as already mentioned, composed of officials:

'We fairly quickly came to the idea of a specific grant system so that we had a sanction over individual projects. The alternatives would have been to put money into the general Rate Support Grant. I felt strongly that this would not have been the way because of our concept of geographical areas, that is, areas of geographical concentration of need. I would not myself have thought of a general grant which the local authority could spend at its own discretion, not so much due to distrust of local authorities as because this is not what we had been told to do. We had been told to get a central government programme going.'

(Senior Home Office official)

Within the unspecific framework laid down by ministers, therefore, officials were exercising a fairly wide degree of discretion — to be sure, along lines with which they felt their minister to be sympathetic, but discretion nonetheless.

Having decided upon a specific grant as the most appropriate instrument, attention was turned to the rate at which grant should be paid to local authorities on approved projects, and it is within this discussion that a broader range of influences were brought to bear. Home Office officials argued for a rate of grant at 75 per cent (i.e. central government would meet 75 per cent of the cost of approved projects, local authorities finding the other 25 per cent) — somewhat higher than the level of the Rate Support Grant, then at just over 50 per cent, and the rate for other specific grants, pegged at 50 per cent. The then Home Secretary concurred in this.

The arguments for such a high grant adduced by the Home Office administrators hint at the somewhat ambivalent attitude to the role of local authorities that was to develop during the next six or so years. The primary reason for wanting to pay grants at a rate of 75 per cent was to secure local authority co-operation in the Programme, and this argument was reinforced by the possible desire of central departments to influence priorities in the types of project funded, and by local authorities' reluctance to spend more of their own money at a time when great economies were being urged. A rate of grant of 50 per cent might have been insufficient to secure the co-operation of some authorities.

On the one hand, it was felt to be essential to be able to impose a central government pattern on the Programme, but, on the other hand, it was necessary to anticipate and perhaps to accommodate potential local authority reaction. This was clearly an issue on which it was felt that local authority views could not be overlooked. In a sense therefore it can be argued that the local authorities exercised a passive influence (at this stage) on the deliberations by virtue of their anticipated reaction.

There was some strong and potentially-influential opposition to a 75 per cent rate of grant on the grounds that in 1966 it was decided, in principle, in the discussions preceding the introduction of the then Rate Support Grant, that specific grants should be abolished as far as possible, but that there should be a uniform rate of 50 per cent for such specific grants as it was necessary to retain. This was considered to be neither more nor less than was needed, on the one hand to iron out any unevenness in expenditure between authorities and, on the other, to secure adequate departmental control.

While Home Office and some other departmental officials — no doubt in anticipation of a forthcoming meeting with representatives of the various Local Authority Associations at which the Urban Programme would have to be 'sold' to them — were arguing strongly for a 75 per cent grant, and with equally-strong arguments based on precedent for a rate of grant of only 50 per cent, it became an issue for resolution at ministerial level. When the resolution came, it was in favour of the higher rate of grant. (Quite how and why such a decision was reached at ministerial level, it is of course not possible to detail here.)

By the time of the meeting with the Local Authority Associations on 28 November 1968, therefore, officials were able to offer the local authorities a grant at the rate of 75 per cent. However, at the meeting it was also stated that, though for the first two years of the Programme monies would not be drawn from the Rate Support Grant fund, this would be the case from April 1971 and this fact would be taken into account in the Rate Support Grant calculations. For local authorities this meant that after April 1971 the UP would not consist of additional funds but would simply represent a reallocation of a small part of the total RSG fund. The minutes of the meeting (11.1968) recorded the reactions of the local authority representatives: ' ... the Government would be paying 75% to some authorities but about 57% of this [the then rate of RSG] would have been paid even if the Programme had been financed by RSG from the beginning, while the other 18% could only come out of the pockets of the local authorities as a whole'. In consequence, the Associations argued that grant should be paid at 100 per cent. It is not possible to say whether this was seen as a realistic demand or whether it was rather in the nature of a gesture. As far as the officials present were concerned, it was certainly a non-starter. The minutes record: 'The Chairman would represent to Ministers the LAA's views regarding the RSG, although he could not hold out any hope of a change of policy.'

Whereas the local authorities had been successful as passive influencers of policy over the 75 per cent rate of grant, their attempt at direct influence to achieve 100 per cent was unsuccessful. The level of grant was fixed at 75 per cent.

Within these deliberations, therefore, can be seen an interweaving of influences spread out largely among Home Office and other department administrators, Treasury officials, and local authorities, but with the final decision, because of a stalemate at official level, being made by ministers. And not only were these actors playing the roles traditionally ascribed to them, but all were no doubt influenced to some degree by their perceptions of what constituted the phenomenon called 'urban deprivation' and of the role that the Urban Programme could play in alleviating it. Early participants have spoken of the enthusiasm within the Working Party in the early days and of the strong feeling that with the UP an opportunity had been provided to do something effective about the concentration of multiple deprivation in small geographical 'blackspots' (see pp.50-1). On the other hand, an alternative view taken by one government department was that either the problem was a residual one that could be cleared up relatively quickly with a modest programme or, if it were not residual, it was a significant one and resulted from the failure of existing programmes and policies which should therefore themselves be reviewed and made more effective (government official).

Between February 1971 and October 1973 there was a continual, though sporadic, debate about the necessity of voting more funds to the Urban Programme, which eventually resulted in an increase of £2 million for each of two years. The debate is examined here as an example of the kinds of discussion that have taken place between officials in different departments and between them and their ministers, and of the various influences at work on changing the scale of the Programme.

On 1 February 1971 a meeting of the Working Party on Immigration and Community Relations was held to review the Urban Programme to date, at which the Chairman pointed out that, of the £60 million allotted to the UP for the period up to 1976, between £45 and £50 million had already been committed in approvals and associated running costs, and this meant:

'that the scope left for the feeding of new approvals was extremely limited. It was doubtful whether Ministers were aware of the true position. The Government [Conservative Government elected in 1970] came to power with a commitment to give more assistance to the Urban Programme ... whereas in fact the maximum level of approvals for projects in future years could be no more than £2.5 million [per annum — compared with an average of £6 million in previous years] with the present resources available.'   (Working Party on Immigration and Community Relations Minutes 1.2.1971)

Thus, although there had been a political commitment to expanding the UP, and though the life of the Programme had been extended for four years (in May 1970) as a partial fulfilment of this commitment, it was not until the Home Office Finance Division did some sums that it became clear that, far from increasing, the annual volume of new approvals would have to be reduced. This fact may have been conveyed to ministers informally but it was not until June 1971 that the Under Secretary with responsibility for the Programme minuted the Finance Division of the Home Office to stress that in briefing the Home Secretary for ministerial discussions about the 1971 Public Expenditure Survey Committee report (on PESC see Garrett 1972: 104-7) they should point out that to stay within the existing limits of the UP would mean that ' ... the input of new schemes approved under the Programme will have to be reduced fairly sharply from now onwards, reaching zero in 1976' (Minute to Home Office Finance Division 17.6.1971).

Despite this initiative by officials, it seems that nothing was done at political level to review the situation: the same Under Secretary in a lengthy paper (1972: internal Home Office document) reviewing the Urban Programme, written in late 1971 and early 1972 on leaving the public service (later to become Director, Centre for Studies in Social Policy), again emphasized the need for early action to increase the scale of the Programme to prevent a 'run-down' in new approvals as a result of high commitments in the early years. This paper was unusual in a number of respects: it was, by Civil Service standards, a very long document, and it was designedly written both to stimulate discussion between departments about the UP in general and to elicit some firm policy decisions from ministers (which, for a year since the run-down problem had first been mooted, had not emerged). The author was of the opinion, however, that interdepartmental discussions at *official* level should not take place before ministers had given some hint as to where, broadly, any such discussions should lead, since any expressed differences of opinion could be exploited by parties not sympathetic to the Programme. That this expectation of strong departmental reaction was fulfilled is evidenced in the written departmental responses to the paper, which almost uniformly suggested full official discussion before the paper (or a revised version of it) be presented to ministers.

Most departments were by and large sympathetic to the need for some policy decision about the future of the Programme but all agreed with the Treasury that there should be full official discussion before submission to ministers.[4] Thus very strong departmental influences were brought to bear at official level to keep the issue of a review of the Programme out of the political arena until all departmental interests had been aired at official level.

From this point on, events moved more rapidly. A new Under Secretary took over the Programme and revised and drastically shortened his predecessor's paper, giving more emphasis to the anticipated hostile reaction of local authorities, voluntary agencies, and the public to a reduction in the Programme, but seeking a more modest increase than that proposed in the original paper. His revised paper was also met with critical reaction from one department which argued that it still did not provide an adequate basis for discussion, but by now the issue had entered the political arena and the Home Secretary expressed the wish to announce a modest increase in the Programme. Notwithstanding this, however, discussions continued at official level between the Home Office and other departments in an attempt to forestall any potentially-effective opposition to an increase. It was not long before the debate was extended to ministerial level, with the Home Secretary arguing strongly for an enlarged Programme. It is interesting to note his case, based upon five points: first, that it concentrated help in areas of particularly acute social need in a way that the Rate Support Grant could not; second, that such areas often had a high proportion of immigrants, vandalism, and social tension;[5] third, that local authorities welcomed the Programme and, through the Association of Municipal Corporations, had first asked for its size to be increased; fourth, that a rising proportion of the schemes

---

[4] The following recipients responded in writing to the paper: Department of Education and Science, Scottish Education Department, the Central Policy Review Staff, the Department of Health and Social Security, the Welsh Office, and the Home Office Finance Department; of these, the CPRS gave the most favourable response.

[5] Within the context of community relations this is a curious juxtaposition of items.

were carried out by voluntary organizations (which are well-qualified to ensure that money is spent to the best advantage); and, fifth, that the special help given in such areas produced benefits out of all proportion to the actual public expenditure incurred. At the time there was in fact no evidence to support the second and fifth assertions. However, this representation appears to have had some effect: in August 1972 a modest increase was agreed to with the proviso that expenditure be kept within the Public Expenditure Survey Committee limits for 1972. However, before the debate could go further, another complication arose, and one that illustrates well the complex and interconnected aspects of social policy at the level of financial management.

Until 1972, a large proportion of UP funds had been spent on establishing nursery classes and schools, but in September of that year the decision was made within the Department of Education and Science to establish a separate national programme of nursery education (DES 1972). As a result of this, the provision of nursery education was to fall outside the Urban Programme. It was argued by one department that the Urban Programme budget should be cut commensurately, since the retention of nursery education funds *and* the requested increase would represent an unjustifiable expansion of expenditure. (This argument is interesting in that no part of Programme funds had ever been 'earmarked' for nursery education or for any other particular area of provision apart from specific departmental inputs.)

There was some debate within the Home Office about the continued justification for an increase after nursery education had been taken out of the Programme, and eventually it was agreed, in February 1973, that the Minister should seek a somewhat smaller increase than had been anticipated twelve months previously. A final decision about whether this smaller increase would be granted was, however, delayed until the autumn and it was not until October 1973 that the issue resurfaced. When it did, it was in a more hopeful context: the Home Secretary had been appointed co-ordinator of government programmes on deprivation, and a new Urban Deprivation Unit had been established within the Home Office. The Home Secretary immediately pointed out that, since deprivation programmes had again become a matter of some priority, it was essential to vote additional funds to back up the new initiative, and the long-discussed addition to the Urban Programme should be granted without delay. This was finally effected the same month.

The shifting scale of aid to deprived areas can be seen from the above examination to have been the subject of lengthy and complex discussions and bargaining between officials in different departments and between ministers, and to have been influenced not a little by the varying perceptions current within central government both of the nature and extent of urban deprivation, and of the aims, functions, and efficacy of the Urban Programme itself.

We have devoted a considerable amount of space to an examination of the formulation of policy and the ways in which matters of the scale of the UP were decided. Other aspects of the structure of the Programme will be examined below in the same way, but it is here that the complex influences and interactions between departments, officials, and ministers are most clearly demonstrated.

The relative importance of central and local government as the instruments for implementing the Programme

The relationship between central and local government and the responsibilities of each in the implementation of policy is often fairly clearly defined, as in the many areas where statutory responsibilities are laid upon local authorities by central departments. In some instances, however — and the Urban Programme is a case in point — the relationships are less well defined and the sensitive issue of local authorities' autonomy can easily come to the fore. We have shown, with detailed summaries of evidence from local authority members and officials, that the implementation of the Urban Programme caused this issue to be debated to a considerable extent within local government.

The influences on the shape of a programme ultimately determine those who benefit from it, and an examination of the relative responsibilities and powers of local authorities, as opposed to central government departments, in deciding what kinds of project are to be funded must be of relevance to our present discussion of these influences.

There has been, over the life of the Urban Programme, a definite — though, to the casual observer, not immediately obvious — shift from central dominance to local autonomy. It has been explained how, in the discussions over the rate of grant to be paid,

Home Office officials argued for a high rate on the grounds that this would be an effective way of gaining the co-operation of local authorities. In those discussions the local authorities and their associations exercised a passive influence through official actions designed to accommodate their anticipated reactions. Notwithstanding this, however, in the early years the Programme was clearly conceived as a central government programme using local authorities as the channel through which to effect centrally-determined priorities. In a paper prepared between the different departments in 1968, it was argued that a 75 per cent grant would give a greater amount of government control and that, in a programme largely centralized in conception, this would be useful. The Programme was intended to benefit the areas concerned, but the improvement would be carried out broadly according to a national pattern. Local authorities' willingness to bid and to participate was important, but so also was the ability of the Government, in practice, firmly to convey its policy ideas to the participants.

In the second circular (Home Office 1969) issued in February 1969 the request was first made that local authorities indicate some priority order for the projects submitted, but this was as much for administrative convenience as anything else, and officials maintained the view that in essence the Programme was largely centrally determined. And so it remained for some time. Gradually, however, local authorities came to the view that since they were repeatedly requested in circulars to place their submissions in some order of priority they might expect that these priority listings would be respected by central departments in making allocations. It became an issue on which strong feelings were expressed (see Chapter 7 pp.206-7) and one of three topics raised in June 1973 by a delegation from the Association of Municipal Corporations (AMC) in discussions at the Home Office concerning the UP. The effective result of this meeting — which was chaired by an official who had taken over responsibility for the Programme during the previous year — was a significant shift in the locus of power to influence the direction of the Programme, from central to local government. In short, the AMC requested that, since local authorities were asked to place their submissions in an order of priority, these priorities should in future be respected by central departments. The request was granted and they were assured that in future every effort would be made to ensure that authorities' first priority projects were approved, subject to financial limitations (*Municipal Review* 1973). It can be argued that this was not a request that had necessarily to be granted and that had some other official with different views about the parameters of local autonomy been involved, it might not have been. The implication of this decision was that the power of central government to direct the shape of the Programme and impose a 'national pattern' — and hence determine who should benefit — was severely eroded. With an undertaking that their first priority projects would be approved (except in exceptional circumstances), local authorities were placed firmly in the position of being able to determine the future direction of the Programme. Central departments could (and did) still recommend project types in the circulars, but these were only recommendations.

In practice, the situation turned out to be rather more flexible than might have been expected. It was not always possible to approve every top priority project: in Phase 9 the total cost of all of the first priority capital projects exceeded the total capital funds available because the average cost of projects listed by authorities as their first priority was considerably higher than that of lower priority projects (UP Interdepartmental Meeting Minutes 17.7.1973); in Phase 9 and subsequent phases a number of local authorities did not rank their projects and a larger number sent in separate priority lists for each local authority department, or for capital and non-capital projects, or for local authority and voluntary organization projects, making selection of *the* top priority project a difficult and confusing task. Nonetheless it has consistently been the intention, since 1973, to give considerable weight in the allocation procedures to the priority listings of local authorities, as is evidenced in the minutes of interdepartmental meetings held to discuss allocation procedures at central level (UP Interdepartmental Meeting Minutes 12.9.1973; 4.12.1973).

The situation became even more flexible, however, reflecting the constantly shifting structure of the Programme. The strong move towards local autonomy was somewhat diluted by two factors: first, a shift in the emphasis given to the issue of local autonomy within the Home Office, and an increasingly greater weight accorded to voluntary organizations' involvement in the Programme; second, after the change of government in 1974, the increasing interest in the Programme taken by two new junior ministers at the

Home Office,[6] who began to exert a degree of ministerial influence that it had not felt for some time. On occasions they wished to give emphasis to a particular type of project, particular sector of the population, or particular type of sponsor (e.g. voluntary agencies), and such an emphasis would sometimes clash with the general rule of giving greatest weight to locally-expressed priorities.

At the Urban Programme interdepartmental meeting (UP IDM) to discuss allocation procedures for Phase 11, the Chairman (a Home Office official) gave guidelines to other departmental officials for the selection of projects for approval. These were, in order of importance:

a local authority priorities: 'It was important to take these into account and to appear to have done so' (UP IDM Minutes 20.8.1974);

b immigrant schemes: 'A high rate of demand could be expected this year and Home Office Ministers were known to be specially sympathetic towards this category' (UP IDM Minutes 20.8.1974);

c voluntary/statutory balance: ' ... it would be right to strive for a balance of allocation at least as favourable to voluntary organisations as last year' (UP IDM Minutes 20.8.1974);

d concentration of funds (on particular areas);

e preferred types of project: 'There was new [ministerial] pressure to recognise the claims of sport and recreation' (UP IDM Minutes 20.8.1974);

f alternative sources of finance.

Such a list helps to illustrate the extremely complex and difficult procedures involved not only in juggling the different selection criteria but also in giving appropriate weight to each. For example, should a known ministerial preference for immigrant and voluntary projects outweigh an undertaking given to local authorities to approve top priority projects?

It has been shown that the influences bearing upon this aspect of the Urban Programme (as upon others) were constantly shifting,

---

[6] Lord Harris had responsibility (amongst other things) for Home Office initiatives concerned with urban deprivation (including the UP), and part of Mr Alex Lyon's responsibility was for race relations; but since both these fields of activity were seen to be closely linked, both ministers took an interest in the UP.

and an analysis of who, at any one time, appeared to be exerting the strongest influence becomes extremely difficult. Later events in the life of the Programme (and relevant to the local/central balance) serve to emphasize this and are briefly recounted to conclude this section. Mr Anthony Steen, M.P. tabled sixteen questions about the UP for Priority Written Answer on 4 July 1974. The questions mainly concerned the role of the voluntary sector in the Programme but several were worded in such a way as to ask the Minister if local authorities would be 'required' to undertake certain things (Hansard 4.7.1974: cols.243-47). Draft replies were prepared for each question by officials. Their replies were all fairly negative, and many relied, in making their point, on the view that local authorities were, in the matter of the UP, autonomous, and that central departments could not 'require' them to do anything. Under a strict interpretation of the act (*Local Government Grants (Social Need) Act 1969*) this was true, but it can be argued that it would have been open to officials to have drafted responses suggesting that much stronger *requests* would be made of authorities. As it was, on such issues as payment of grant to voluntary agencies by local authorities after approval, officials suggested in drafting responses that, 'How the local authority arranges payments to particular voluntary bodies is a matter for it to decide, the Home Office has no place to interfere' (Home Office Memorandum June 1974); and on the issue of requiring consultation between local authorities and voluntary agencies: 'Home Office circulars encourage consultation ... to go further would surely seem like interference in local discretion' (Home Office Memorandum June 1974).

The draft responses were approved by the Minister, but his views on the respective roles of voluntary agencies and local authorities led him to ask his officials to consider the possibilities of:

a grants being paid direct to voluntary agencies; and
b local authorities funding their own schemes from the Rate Support Grant.

Officials duly examined the issues involved, and the arguments for and against the two proposals put by the Minister, and their replies were discussed at a meeting with the Minister in September 1974. Neither the substance nor the relative weight of the arguments of the officials and their Minister can be detailed here but what

Gordon has to say in general terms on this issue (quoting Johnson 1965: 284) is of relevance:

'The Minister can make his decision only on the basis of the choices offered him and it defies belief to say that structuring the choices is not something with a powerful and perhaps decisive influence on the outcomes. "When we look at policy-making as fact-finding, analysis and recommendations ... then it is officials who dominate it and will continue to do so".'

(Gordon 1971 : 45)

The outcome of this meeting was that possible changes in the Urban Programme should be left for consideration until government policies for the future development of race relations and programmes for deprived areas had been firmly elaborated. It should be noted, however, that an expressed departmental view is not necessarily monolithic, nor one to which all concerned give complete accord — indeed, it would be extraordinary if this were the case. Two Home Office officials involved in the debate mentioned above argued in discussions with the authors for *more central* direction to the Programme. Thus:

'There is plenty of evidence that some local authorities do find prioritization difficult ... All this reflects an admission, in a way, in local government that they would like central government to play a stronger role. So long as local authorities find the priority listing of projects difficult, or embarrassing, or controversial, and so long as they are under pressures that they cannot rationally meet, then I think there is a stronger case for central government to have its own perspectives generally, and perhaps within a local area, too'. (Senior Home Office Official)

The involvement of voluntary agencies

Over the life of the Programme, the proportion of funds allocated to voluntary organizations has, with some minor fluctuations, been increasing, from 5 per cent in Phase 2 to 28 per cent in Phase 9, 25 per cent in Phase 11, and 37 per cent in Phase 12. In consequence it can be argued that those types of project that the voluntary sector is more likely to promote have fared relatively better as the period has progressed. Little of this shift in resources, however, can be attributed to the influence of the voluntary sector itself: its representations have been received politely by officials, but do not appear to have altered very much the course of events. The improving fortunes of the voluntary sector must be attributed, by and large, to ministers, M.P.s, and individual officials within central departments.

The involvement of voluntary organizations in the Programme was put forward as a theoretical possibility as early as July 1968. By October of that year it appears to have been accepted by officials that local authorities might wish to pay grants to voluntary agencies to undertake work relevant to the Programme, and, in the deliberations about the drafting of the Bill to give effect to the Programme, some consideration was given as to whether special powers should be written into the Bill to enable statutory authorities to do this. The initiative in the involvement of voluntary agencies was taken in the first place by ministers, as is made clear from an internal Home Office memorandum outlining alternative means of effecting it:

' ... it was decided that there were two ways of meeting Ministers' desire that it should be possible for local authorities to give money to voluntary bodies ...

1   to rely on existing local provisions if these should prove to be wide enough;

2   to make provision in the Bill which would probably involve giving powers to local authorities to help voluntary bodies to do any work in an area of special social need which the local authority could itself have done'.

(Internal Home Office Memorandum 5.11.1968)

When the Home Office consulted other departments, the consensus of opinion was that sufficient powers already existed, largely in section 136 of the *Local Government Act 1948*; in consequence, no special powers were written into the UP Bill.

There were numerous representations to the Home Office from various voluntary organizations, including the National Council for Social Service (NCSS) in August 1969 and the Pre-School Play-groups Association, and it is possible that the latter had some effect in impressing upon the already-sympathetic official involved the value of voluntarily-promoted pre-school provision: certainly, as early as Phase 2, grants were being paid through local authorities to playgroup organizations.

However, despite the fact that the proportion of funds granted for use in the voluntary sector continued to increase, voluntary organizations did not emerge as a significant arm of the Programme until early 1972. Then the immediate cause was an initiative by the Prime Minister, Mr Edward Heath, who in a speech to the Annual Conference of the NCSS in December 1971 gave an undertaking of extra government assistance to the voluntary sector. Part of this additional assistance turned out to be the injection of an extra £1.1 million into the UP for projects promoted by voluntary organizations. Since that time it is probably true to say that the continued and increasing emphasis given to the voluntary sector within the Programme has been the result almost entirely of the initiatives of successive ministers (of both parties). The Lords Windlesham and Colville, both junior Home Office ministers with responsibility for the voluntary sector in the Heath administration of 1970-74, were keen on expanding voluntary involvement (and of course made this known to officials) as were Mr Lyon and Lord Harris in the Wilson administration. It is no exaggeration to say that it is largely because of their interest that the voluntary sector has increasingly benefited from the Programme.

There is one aspect of the involvement of voluntary agencies, however, where ministerial influence has been less effective, and it is not unconnected with the issues of local authority autonomy discussed above: should the Urban Programme be enabled to pay grants directly to voluntary organizations instead of through local authorities? This question was first raised seriously in July 1972 following a visit made by Lord Colville to Liverpool, during which he met a wide range of voluntary organizations' representatives. At a meeting with officials held on 4 July 1972, Lord Colville, on the basis of his experiences in Liverpool, asked whether there was a case for the Urban Programme paying grants directly to local 'associations of voluntary bodies' for distribution to individual local voluntary organizations. As in the debate over local autonomy discussed above, officials aired some of the difficulties involved in such a plan, namely that, if local authorities knew that grant was being paid directly to voluntary organizations, they would be likely to cut down their own subsidies, that difficulties of co-ordination between statutory and voluntary bodies would arise, and that ' ... if some separate body was set up at the centre to distribute the money, control by the Treasury would be easier than in a more piecemeal system'.

The last point is of particular interest in that officials were using the threat of a Treasury predisposition to control the UP more closely as an argument for maintaining the existing less easily-controlled arrangements. Again, the weight of experience and knowledge was on the side of the officials, and the issue was 'deferred', only to surface again under a different minister — and different officials — in mid-1974. The immediate impetus was again provided by a ministerial visit — this time to Brixton — and again was the result of contact with the representatives of voluntary organizations — on this occasion, a substantial contingent from the West Indian community. Again as a result of the visit, the Minister[7] discussed the issue of direct funding with officials: his recent discussions with representatives of immigrant organizations had convinced him that the Urban Programme was not giving as much support as it should to the more imaginative schemes proposed by such organizations. He argued further that many such projects were rejected out of hand by local authorities, and those that were submitted to the Home Office were often given low priority on the local authorities' lists. This position would not improve until some means were found of channelling grants directly to voluntary organizations rather than through local authorities. In the ensuing discussion, the alternative arguments reviewed by officials were:

(a) that no change could be made in the administration of the UP without amendment of the *Local Government Grant* (*Social Need*) *Act 1969*;

(b) that the Act was needed to implement the new Home Office initiative on the deprivation front — the Comprehensive Community Programmes;

(c) that the severe limitation of funds made it difficult to use the UP more imaginatively;

(d) that it was not in the interest of the Home Office to raise the future of the UP '...lest in doing so, opposition to it be marshalled';

(e) that local authorities would still have to be consulted about the worthiness of voluntary schemes submitted;

(f) that voluntary bodies had access to funds outside the UP anyway — including funds from local authorities themselves.

[7] Mr Lyon, whose responsibilities included race relations but not the UP; Lord Harris, whose responsibility the UP was, also attended the meeting.

The upshot of the meeting was that no decision would be taken and that the matter would again be 'deferred'. This and the fact that direct funding to voluntary agencies has not been, and within the present framework of the Urban Programme is unlikely to be, implemented is a reflection of the strong influence that officials can bring to bear over their political master by virtue of their monopoly of knowledge and expertise in any one particular complex field. The point has been made by Gordon;

> '...though politicians may dislike the advice given to them, though they may ignore it, procrastinate, argue against it, "the one thing they are rarely able to do without expert assistance, is to question the analysis on which advice to them is based". Where in the existing executive system is such assistance to originate, except with the civil service which monopolises it and which, moreover, vigilantly chokes the flow of information to outsiders? ...what can one minister do to ensure that the officials possess not just the proper expertise, but the indispensable zeal as well?' (Gordon 1971 : 42)

In discussion, Home Office officials expressed views about the role of voluntary organizations (see Chapter 7 pp.208-9) that were broadly in line with the stance adopted by them in the above discussions, even though the then director of the Home Office Voluntary Services Unit thought that voluntary bodies had a very important role to play. In his view the Programme itself was: '...so small that it cannot possibly deal with structural deprivation' (Director, Voluntary Services Unit). He went on: 'So we are really talking about patching and mending, and voluntary organizations are particularly good at this; and so I think they have a very important role to play in the UP.' The director also felt, however, that many voluntary organizations did not appreciate the structure of the Programme. Referring to a delegation to the Home Office of a group called the 'Moving Spirits' (a dining club of directors of national voluntary organizations) to discuss the Home Office response to Mr Anthony Steen's sixteen tabled questions on the Programme (see above pp.128-29), he said that the fact that they (the Moving Spirits) had found the meeting unsatisfactory and the Home Office response inadequate reflected in part a 'fundamental misunderstanding' of how the UP worked. He continued: 'They seem not to have understood the changed relationship between local government and central government. They still seem to think that central government can issue circulars demanding certain things of local authorities and the local authorities will immediately jump to it and see that it is done' (Director, Voluntary Services Unit).

Shifts in the main types of project promoted

More directly related to the question of who benefits from the Programme is the issue of what types of project have been promoted by Programme circulars and what variations these have shown, and why. It has already been described how the initial list of project types was largely the result of a round-the-table discussion of the Working Party on Immigration and Community Relations in May 1968. That list, devised by departmental officials, has remained the backbone of the Programme ever since. The emphasis on educational projects, and especially on projects for the under-fives, can be traced back to various sources: the influence on officials (especially within the DES and the DHSS) of reports such as those of Plowden and Seebohm; the officials' own predelictions; the fact that the Prime Minister's speech had specified education; ministers' apparent interest in this type of provision; and, as one of those very closely involved in designing the Programme said in discussion with the authors, the fact that, in the earliest stages, the DES '...was one of the most responsive takers'. This responsiveness of the DES, and the general move towards pre-school and other educational provision, was well delineated by an Under Secretary who worked on the Programme within the DES for some three years. Of the role of the DES in the formulation of the Programme, he said:

'At that time, Mr Short was our Secretary of State and he brought with him a strong belief in nursery education. Public expenditure had taken a hammering, and there were no resources for new policies, and Short saw the UP as a means of making a small start on the expansion of nursery education. On the administrative side this suited the Department very well. We already had a building programme relationship with local authorities so that the development of nursery schools and classes was a familiar area for us. There were no organizational difficulties. Nobody in the DES disagreed that this was how to use the Department's share of the funds. Thus there was a political thrust and an administrative fit'. (Senior DES official)

More generally, and across departments, it was felt that ' ... you can't go far wrong in doing things for young children', that the money had to be spent quickly and so proposals for day nursery and nursery provision had an advantage in that local authorities were already familiar with the requirements and no new machinery had to be set up, and, importantly, that the provision of pre-school facilities in immigrant areas was an uncontroversial way of giving effect to the immigrant bias of the Programme without appearing too strongly to favour immigrants.

It was, therefore, a concatenation of influences that gave the Programme the strong educational bias that has remained, though to a lessening degree, throughout its life. These might be summarized by saying that academic reports (Plowden and Seebohm) had an influence on both ministers and officials, that ministers pressed most firmly for pre-school provision, that this fitted well with existing administrative machinery and practice, and that it fulfilled other requirements such as speed and the introduction of an immigrant bias.

Though the pattern of projects promoted through successive phases of the Programme has remained fairly constant, new and different types of project have on occasion been advocated or at least discussed. It is worth looking at some of these and the impetus behind their promotion.

The architects of the Programme intended that housing should be an important aspect of it, and the building of new houses is referred to in the early circulars as a possibility under the Programme in the future. Housing provision was seen amongst officials as an important component in the alleviation of deprivation, but it proved in the end to be impossible to include it, notwithstanding an undertaking given to representatives of the Local Authority Associations in November 1968. The reasons why house construction has never featured are largely financial (though other projects related to housing have, of course, been included in the Programme). The Programme is very small and house construction is exceedingly costly; its inclusion in the Programme would have taken too great a proportion of the total funds. Second, the use of a

75 per cent specific grant for house construction would have conflicted with the existing subsidy arrangements for house construction and led to anomalous situations.

Another possibility that never got off the ground was that of social security provision under the Programme. The DHSS had raised this as being a relevant component of the attack on deprivation, but it was short-lived, and official discussion within the Working Party indicated that to attempt to pay preferential rates of benefit to people in UP-approved areas (as was the suggestion) would prove inordinately complicated and impractical.

Probably the most significant development in project types (in terms of number of projects approved, though not financially) was the introduction of 'holiday projects', a generic name to cover a range of activities for children during the school holidays, with a special emphasis on semi-educational activities for immigrant children. Such projects were first founded under Phase 2 (1969), more heavily emphasized under Phase 4 (1971), and from Phase 6 onwards were promoted by a separate circular each year. The introduction of holiday projects was largely the result of the fruitful relationship that existed between the Community Relations Commission (CRC) and the Home Office department responsible for the Programme. It is to CRC efforts that an official involved in the early negotiations has attributed the development of holiday schemes as an integral part of the UP. It is perhaps the only type of project that has been introduced as a result of non-statutory (or semi-statutory) efforts.

Central departments have, on occasion, used the UP as a means of trying out certain types of project or provision to which they did not wish to commit themselves on a wide or universal basis. Selective approvals under the Programme therefore provided a useful opportunity for 'testing the water'. Sometimes such selective testing was accompanied by the injection of additional funds into the Programme from the relevant department. One such addition (of £1.3 million) was injected by the DHSS in late 1970 to assist in the promotion of family planning services. The money was earmarked for this area of provision but, if (as is assumed) it was a 'testing-the-water' operation, there appears to have been remarkably little monitoring of the exercise or feedback from it. Another such injection of funds (£1 million) by the DHSS was made in 1972 for the further promotion of day-care facilities for the under-fives.

These are two instances of the departmental promotion of projects shifting (albeit in a minor way) the overall pattern of promoted projects. A similar attempt by the DOE in 1972/73 to inject funds for the promotion of projects in aid of homeless single people ran into difficulties with the Treasury, which opposed it on the grounds that the Urban Programme was not intended to provide housing (UP Interdepartmental Meeting Minutes 12.12.1972).

There was, in 1972, another instance of interdepartmental influence on the range of projects promoted by the Programme. In the Phase 7 circular of that year, among the list of suggested projects, a lengthy reference to legal aid and advice centres was included. Their inclusion, as types of project that might be funded under the Programme, was in line with the increasing interest in legal aid for the deprived and the rapid development at that time of neighbourhood law centres. However, the reference in the circular attracted the attention of the Lord Chancellor's Legal Aid Advisory Committee, which took exception to the apparent promotion by one government department of a scheme that was still the subject of deliberations in another. In particular they expressed concern that such centres might provide legal representation before tribunals, which at that time was contrary to government policy, that their proliferation might mean that business would be taken away from lawyers (a matter about which the Law Society was concerned), and that if and when they were established there should be some arrangement for means-testing applicants. After much discussion (including a meeting of the Legal Aid Advisory Committee attended by the minister responsible for the UP) the Home Office agreed to curtail its proposals, and however many submissions were received to fund only four at the most, and then only after consultation with the Committee and on the basis that the schemes were experimental, and were presented as such.

A later development was the exercising of considerable ministerial pressure for funds to be diverted towards more immigrant projects and, in particular, immigrant self-help groups. In June 1974 Mr Alex Lyon visited such a group — the Harambee Project — in Islington and, clearly impressed with their work and no doubt mindful of the Community Relations Commission (CRC) report on the employment and housing problems of young West Indians (Community Relations Commission 1974), he expressed to his Civil Servants a strong desire to see more such projects funded under the

UP. This coincided with a collective decision taken by ministers on the basis of officials' proposals, made partly in the context of Phase 12 of the Programme, to provide more aid for black self-help groups. Within a very short time a letter was sent out to local authorities drawing their attention to the CRC report and urging them to see whether there was any scope for easing the problems it detailed. The letter drew attention to the then current phase of the UP (Phase 12, the special 'immigrant' phase — which was only two months from submission deadline) as one useful channel by which such help could be implemented. This was, therefore, an instance of a strongly expressed ministerial wish, coinciding with the fruits of a longer-term ministerial initiative, being translated into administrative action in a very short space of time.

Ethnic minorities as special recipients of Urban Programme aid

The degree to which the UP is an 'immigrant programme' or a programme about deprivation with special emphasis on immigrant areas has from the very beginning been a sensitive and contentious matter. Ministers and officials alike have been well aware of the controversy surrounding this point and have in consequence taken great care in the manner in which it has been handled, mindful always of anticipated public and local authority reaction.

Chapter 3 has described how the Programme arose from the debate about Commonwealth immigration and race relations in general, and, however much it is disguised, it is impossible to hide the fact that the Programme was devised as an attempt to defuse a potentially explosive situation. The extent to which special emphasis has been given to immigrants and areas of immigrant concentration throughout the life of the Programme has, however, fluctuated, and the influences bearing upon these fluctuations are worth examining.

Initial sensitivity over the immigrant bias of the Programme revolved around two related but distinguishable issues. The first was the political sensitivity of discriminating in favour of immigrant areas, or, as a Parliamentary Committee brief expressed it: ' ... the general recognition of the political difficulties of setting up the idea of positive discrimination in favour of immigrant areas however these might be dressed up as urban areas of general social need' (Brief for Parliamentary Committee 5.1968). The second was the need to avoid the confusion in 'the public mind' of 'general deprivation' and the problems of immigrant areas: 'It was agreed that the social effect of Commonwealth immigration was an element of social need for the purposes of the Programme but it was important to make it clear that it was a different kind of social need from multiple deprivation' (Working Party on Immigration and Community Relations Minutes 7.6.1968).

It must be said that great care was taken in the drafting of any public statement to avoid the association between immigrants and deprivation, but the fact remains that the immigrant aspect of the Programme could never be fully disguised and that by its very existence it served to label immigrants as a 'problem' demanding special government attention. The same can be said — though even more strongly — of immigration legislation. It is a dilemma of social policy in general and positive discrimination in particular that the very identification of particular identifiable groups for the receipt of special aid marks them out *ipso facto* as problem groups requiring special attention.

Such was the concern in ministers' minds that the Programme should not become too closely linked with immigrants that, when an approach was made to the Home Office in September 1968 by the Community Relations Commission requesting that it be made known that government would be consulting with the CRC over allocations of grant under the Programme, the request was turned down by the Minister on the grounds that this: ' ... would relate the UP in the public mind solely to social problems arising from immigration. This is something I am anxious to avoid' (ministerial letter).

Though the Programme got off the ground and developed without any serious controversy over the immigration issue, the question of anticipated local authority reactions again arose in July 1970. Lord Windlesham had asked officials to consider the scope for increasing aid to areas with a high level of immigrant settlement. The matter was referred to the Working Party on Immigration and Community Relations (WPICR), which argued that since aid could not be increased within the existing scope of the Programme (for example, by giving 100 per cent grants for immigrant projects), and since it would not be possible ' ... to switch the Programme towards immigrant areas for fear of antagonizing local authorities with low immigrant numbers' (WPICR Paper. 7.1970), the best compromise would be to ' ... use any increase [in funds] to tilt the balance of the Programme towards immigrant projects. The existing flexibility of the Programme would lend itself admirably to this' (WPICR Paper 7.1970). In this instance, therefore, it was the officials who, mindful of the sensitivity of the implications of the Minister's request, proposed a solution that would, without arousing controversy, go some way towards meeting it.

By 1974, however — and for no very clear reason — some of the officials' reticence seems to have been lessened. When the Minister decided late in 1973 to divert £6 million worth of foreign aid originally intended for Uganda to domestic usage, he stipulated that the money should be used for distribution through UP machinery to areas of immigrant concentration (Hansard 6.12.1973: col. 1484). Contrary to earlier practice this money was not 'hidden' within normal allocations; rather, a special phase was instigated to concentrate solely on immigrant projects, and there was less reluctance to divulge the fact that the CRC had on this occasion been fully consulted. Later in 1974, following two ministerial visits, one to the Harambee Project in Islington (an immigrant self-help group) and the other to Brixton (see pp.132 and 137) to meet representatives of immigrant organizations, the Minister urged officials that more aid be given in the future to immigrant projects (and especially West Indian self-help groups). As has been described above in the context of the role of voluntary organizations, steps were taken immediately to give effect to the minister's request.

In the foregoing analysis we have attempted to identify some of the influences that have helped to shape the UP during its life and, in consequence, have helped to determine its beneficiaries. Enough has been said to indicate that the interplay of influences has been both complex and constantly shifting, but what is perhaps especially worthy of note is the extent of the officials' role. There are two related reasons for this. First, as the chapter on the aims and development of the Programme has shown, and as Chapter 7 confirms, the Programme has never had a clearly defined strategy, function, or set of aims and goals. In both structures and purpose the UP has remained without firm direction, and, whilst the flexibility this has afforded has on occasion been useful, it has also detracted from the potential achievements. As one official put it: ' ... it has always suffered from planning blight'. It is in precisely this sort of environment, of ill-defined policy direction, lack of ideology, and lack of purpose, that scope is provided for greater administrative discretion. As Peter Self has pointed out:

'Administrative discretion utilises precedent where convenient but is also sensitive to changes in the political climate and fills in limitations of established rules and policies with pragmatic ideas about fair treatment and commonsense. Senior administrators sometimes make stronger policy contributions — this is most likely when party policies are vague and specialised opinion inadequate. Administrators are the residuary legatees of decisions which nobody else is able to make, though they are prone to take a cautious view of policy innovations.'

(Self 1972 : 176)

The second reason is really a partial explanation of the continuing lack of direction, and hence the maintenance of that flexibility that allows for administrative discretion. The speed with which the Programme was initially constructed precluded the possibility of much consultation or research; but neither has the more leisurely pace of events since proved conducive to such a development. There has never been any systematic review of the direction of the Programme, nor any investigation of the problems it aims to tackle, with a view to giving it more purpose and direction.[8] This has in part been a result of the almost inevitable process of 'fossilization' of administrative structures such that the time was never right for a review of the direction of the Programme; but it has also arisen from the curious relationship that exists in central government between administration and research. The latter is never seen to be an important and continuing concomitant of the former. Indeed, as John Garrett has pointed out (1969:50), research is usually confined to a purely advisory or service role, divorced from the mainstream of policy-making; and, since administrators have no involvement in the research process, they have little familiarity with the contribution that research can make to policy formulation. This situation might have been improved by the further implementation of the Fulton Report recommendations on greater specialization in the Civil Service (Committee on the

---

[8] The authors of this report, though working in the Home Office division responsible for the programme, were not seen to be employed in such a capacity, and were never allowed to make any significant contribution along these lines.

Civil Service 1968), but this is not the place to reiterate the many arguments for and against such proposals.

In the absence of strong ministerial direction, therefore, and with an ill-defined programme strategy, the perceptions of the nature of urban deprivation which officials of all departments brought to their task strongly influenced the scope of the Programme and the areas of provision it was deemed capable of covering. On a more technical level, it was again largely the officials who determined that payment should be by specific grant rather than a readjustment of the Rate Support Grant. The shift from central direction to local autonomy occurred under officials' guidance, and it was officials who maintained this new balance through the debates with ministers over the direct funding of voluntary agencies and the restructuring of the financial arrangements.

Successive ministers, on the other hand, appear to have carried greater weight in the attempts to increase the size of the Programme, in the increasing role played by the voluntary sector, and, in recent years, in the shift towards greater provision for ethnic minorities. Only on rare occasions have circumstances combined to enable the influence of local authorities — largely through their Associations — to determine the course of events, and the power to influence events available to the other main participant in the Programme — the voluntary sector — appears to have been negligible.

In a cross-departmental programme like the UP, it is inevitable that the priorities and special interests of participating central departments should be important factors in determining changes in the shape of the Programme. Sadly — probably because the number of interdepartmental initiatives in the field of social policy is very small — very little has been written about the interplay of departmental influences in shaping policy direction. That such influences have played an important part in determining the structure and financial scale of the UP and the range of projects promoted by it has been made clear above, as has the fact that the Treasury has exerted a strong influence throughout the life of the Programme. Indeed, much of the history of the changing scale of the UP has been of continual debate, conflict, bargaining, and compromise with a department that is determined, for reasons entirely consistent with its traditional role, to 'keep a tight rein and limit the damage that might be done to good financial accounting'.

This chapter has attempted to pinpoint some of the factors,

tangible and less tangible, that influenced both the shape and direction of the Programme between 1968 and 1975 and determined the allocation of Programme funds, to which areas and which types of project and hence, ultimately, which beneficiaries. This examination of selected factors, combined with the preceding chapter's analysis of how the detail of the Programme's administration carried its own less conscious determinants, has shown, in this one small area of social policy, the complex interplay of those influences (including economic circumstance, political pressure, official discretion and intransigence, departmental sovereignty both at local and central government levels, the relationship between the voluntary and statutory sectors of provision, and the shifting ground between local autonomy and central direction) that determine the *practical* outcome of policies.

6 The projects

Between the end of 1968 and the middle of 1975 some 3,750 projects with a total approval value of £34,264,540 were sanctioned under the Urban Programme. These represented the 'on the ground' result of the application and approval processes of thirteen programme phases. Previous chapters have described these processes in some detail, as well as the influences upon them and upon the structure of the Programme which helped to determine the beneficiaries. The present chapter directs attention to the end results of these processes — the projects themselves — and through an analysis of project types, costs, sponsors, and other factors presents a picture of the Programme in its more concrete guise.

Much of what follows is a descriptive account based on an analysis of all projects approved up to and including Phase 9 of the Programme. Given the complexity and time-consuming nature of this task, involving as it did the setting up of a punch-card system to record details of every project, it has not been possible to extend the coverage of the analysis beyond the 2,929 projects approved up to the end of Phase 9 (1973). It is reasonable to assume, however (with one notable exception), as by Phase 9 a fairly stable pattern of applications and approvals had emerged, that after Phase 9 the situation did not alter in any significant way from that which prevailed during the first nine phases. The exception is that Phase 12 represented something of a departure from what had become fairly standard procedure. The phase itself was an addition to the normal run, resulting from the injection of an additional £6 million originally destined to be aid for Uganda but subsequently switched for use in the United Kingdom (see Chapter 5). Approvals under this phase were confined to projects designed to benefit ethnic minority groups and as such were not representative of the wider array of projects normally approved under main programme phases.

In the punch-card system all projects were classified by the following variables:

    (a) type of project;
    (b) type of budget;
    (c) phase of approval;
    (d) sponsor (local authority, voluntary agency, joint);
    (e) approving central government department;
    (f) cost of approval;
    (g) type of local authority submitting the project.

The full range of possible classifications within each of these variables is listed in *Appendix III*. A word should be inserted here, however, about the first of these classifications, the type of project. Given the vast range of different types of project approved under the Programme there is no single self-presenting classification that stands out from the many possibles. Any such classification, therefore, must be somewhat arbitrary, and the one adopted here attempts to combine the categories in common usage among central government departments involved in the Programme with those which, as parsimoniously as possible, include all the other less-obvious types of project[1] Even so, the full list of project types is somewhat long for analytical purposes (there being twenty-five types of project including a 'miscellaneous' category) and a second 'condensed' list of seven types has on occasion been introduced in the following tables.

Applications and approvals

Table 1 shows the distribution of all projects approved up to the

---

[1] It may be thought that 'client groups' would provide a ready-made and effective means of project classification, but since the client group is in many cases unclear (as for example with community centres, community workers, or citizens' advice bureaux) such a method proved impracticable.

end of Phase 9 across the range of project types and *Table 2* gives the same information for the shorter list of project types. (For details of the composition of the categories in *Table 2*, see *Appendix III*. Throughout this chapter, figures in the tables do not necessarily sum to 100 per cent due to rounding.)

Table 1   *Distribution of project types: Phases 1-9*

Type of project	Number	%	Type of project	Number	%
Pre-school			Housing Advice		
playgroups	278	9.5	Centres	92	3.1
Childrens homes	51	1.7	Other advice		
Day nurseries,			centres	28	1.0
day care	162	5.5	Community centres	81	2.8
Nursery education	574	19.6	Community		
Adventure			workers	48	1.6
playgrounds	117	4.0	General community		
Other play			projects	95	3.2
facilities	362	12.4	Volunteer Bureaux	34	1.2
Youth activities	82	2.8	Accommodation		
Care of the elderly	114	3.9	for homeless	88	3.0
Family planning	128	4.4	Language projects	165	5.6
Family Advice			Compensatory		
Centres	61	2.1	education	106	3.6
Neighbourhood			General social		
Advice Centres	27	0.9	work	94	3.2
Citizens Advice			General health	30	1.0
Bureaux	24	0.8	Miscellaneous	80	2.7
Legal Advice					
Centres	8	0.3	*Total*	2,929	100.0

Even though nursery provision was not eligible for funding after Phase 7, it still represents the single most frequently approved type of project (20 per cent of all approvals), followed by 'other play schemes', pre-school playgroups, language classes, and day nursery provision. Four out of these five most frequent types of project represent some form of provision for children (language classes having been included in the 'special education' category in *Table 2*, though they may well also cater mostly for children) and this predominance is reflected in *Table 2*, which shows that more than half of all projects approved have been designed specifically as some form of provision (e.g. play or education) for children. This ignores the other types of project which, though not classified in

Table 2 *Distribution of project types (condensed)*

Type of project	Number	%	Type of project	Number	%
Provision for children	1,544	52.7	Social work/ welfare/health	340	11.6
Other age groups	196	6.7	Special education	271	9.2
Advice/information (general)	240	8.2	Miscellaneous	80	2.7
Community projects	258	8.8	*Total*	2,929	100.0

Table 2 as specifically child-oriented, will nevertheless also provide some form of aid for children. After 'provision for children' the next largest category of project is that consisting of some form of social, welfare, or health provision (11.6 per cent of all approvals, *Table 2*) and a significant part of this is accounted for by family planning provision (4.4 per cent of all approvals — see *Table 1*). The remaining projects are spread fairly evenly over the other major categories in *Table 2,* with provision for youth and the elderly at 6.7 per cent of all approvals being the smallest.

It has been described in previous chapters how, in the absence of a clear conception (both at central and local government level) of the nature of urban deprivation and its constituent problems and their causes, and in the absence of any well-defined strategy or policy based on such a conception, institutional factors and influences have filled the gaps thereby opened up and have strongly affected the direction of the Programme. Thus, from the start, it was the DES rather than the then Ministry of Housing and Local Government or the Department of Employment and Productivity that was the biggest 'taker' (see pp.58 and 134-35) in the early negotiations: from the start, as a result of this, emphasis was given in circulars to provision for children and at local authority level it was the education departments which could respond quickly with concrete proposals for meeting a recognized need (for nursery provision). The very heavy concentration throughout the life of the Programme, therefore, on provision for children has resulted less from design and strategy than from institutional factors which, in default of a clear strategy, have filled the vacuum.

While it remains true that local authorities have responded to circulars in such a way as to give emphasis to child-oriented projects, the question remains as to what extent the total pattern of approvals over all types of project reflects the overall pattern of the applications. It has not proved possible, in view of the very large number of applications (some 12,000) to classify all of them by project type, and so a direct comparison of the total number of applications with all of the approvals cannot be carried out. To overcome this difficulty a sample of applications has been drawn from seven applicant local authorities for three major phases (3, 7, and 9). The authorities selected were Birmingham C.B., Liverpool C.B., Leeds C.B., Haringey L.B., Brent L.B., Lancashire C.C., and Yorkshire West Riding C.C.,[2] and between them they submitted 769 projects over the three phases mentioned. This sample enables us to make a direct comparison between applications and approvals given for these particular authorities in the three phases. While it cannot be claimed that these seven local authorities were strictly representative in terms of the applications and approvals of all authorities using the Programme, there is little reason to believe that as a sample they differed in any systematic way from all the others.

The relevant information for a comparison of applications and approvals for *all* types of project is recorded in *Table A, Appendix IV*, and *Table 3* below presents the same information for the condensed list of project types. Comparison of columns B and C in *Table A, Appendix IV* shows how far the pattern of approvals by project type for the sample authorities and phases differed from that of all projects approved over Phases 1-9 for all authorities. The main differences lie in the proportions of 'other play' schemes and neighbourhood advice centres approved. For the sample authorities only 1.0 per cent of all projects approved were 'other play' as against 12.4 per cent for all projects, and the figures for neighbourhood advice centres were 4.2 per cent and 0.9 per cent respectively. Attention is also drawn to one other major difference, though not concerning project types: whereas only 32.7 per cent of the total number (all authorities, all phases) of projects approved were voluntary agency projects, the corresponding figure for the sample authorities was 49.8 per cent. Thus, for the sample authorities, a much higher proportion of approved projects had

---

[2] Since, at the time of writing, the great majority of Urban Programme projects were approved prior to local authority reorganization, all analyses in this chapter relating to local authorities maintain the pre-reorganization classification of local authority types.

Table 3 *Applications and approvals by type of project for seven local authorities for Phases 3, 7 and 9 and total approvals by project type (all local authorities, all phases)*

	Applications (sample)[1]		Approvals (sample)[2]		Approvals (total)[3]		Applications approved (sample)[4]
	Number	%	Number	%	Number	%	%
Provision for children	348	45.3	122	42.2	1,544	52.7	35.1
Other age-groups	79	10.2	28	9.7	196	6.7	35.4
Advice/information (general)	65	8.6	39	13.6	240	8.2	60.0
Community projects	83	10.8	36	12.5	258	8.8	43.4
Social work/ welfare/health	104	13.6	40	13.8	340	11.6	38.5
Special education	58	7.6	19	6.6	271	9.2	32.8
Miscellaneous	32	4.2	5	1.7	80	2.7	15.6
All projects	769	100.0	289	100.0	2,929	100.0	37.6
Local authority projects	498	64.8	145	50.2	1,972	67.3	29.0
Voluntary agency projects	271	35.2	144	49.8	957	32.7[5]	53.0
Capital projects	393	51.1	115	39.8	1,211	41.4	29.0
Non-capital/'once-only' projects	376	48.9	174	60.2	1,718	58.6	46.0

Notes:
[1] All applications, seven local authorities, three phases: percentage of applications falling within each type of project.
[2] All approvals, seven local authorities, three phases: percentage of approvals falling within each type of project.
[3] Total approvals, *all* local authorities, Phases 1-9: percentage of approvals falling within each type of project.
[4] Percentage of applications approved within each type of project, seven local authorities, three phases.
[5] Includes joint local authority/voluntary organization projects (0.6 per cent of total).

been submitted by voluntary organizations than was the case for all submissions from all authorities. In *Table 3* a comparison of the patterns of application and approval according to the condensed list of project types for the sample authorities shows that, by and large, the distribution of approvals by the type of project fairly closely reflects the pattern of applications, the major differences being in the proportions of advice and information centres applied for and approved (8.6 per cent of applications being for this project type, but 13.6 per cent of approvals), and in the relative proportions of miscellaneous category projects (4.2 per cent of all applications but 1.7 per cent of approvals). A similar comparison for the full range of project types (columns A and B, *Table A, Appendix IV*) serves to reinforce this finding, there being only minor discrepancies between the distributions over project types of applications and approvals with the exceptions of pre-school play groups (8.2 per cent of all applications, 11.1 per cent of approvals) and 'other play' projects (5.2 per cent of applications and 1.0 per cent of approvals).

The final columns of *Table 3* above and *Table A, Appendix IV* present the same information in a different form, giving the percentages of all applications that were approved *within* each project type. Thus, looking at *Table 3* above, it can be seen that whereas 37.6 per cent of *all sample* projects applied for have been approved,[3] the approval rate for different (condensed) types of project ranges (excluding the miscellaneous category) from 32.8 per cent for special education projects to 60.0 per cent for advice and information projects; this latter figure reflects the above finding that advice and information centres are more heavily represented among the approved projects than among the applications. However, apart from the higher approval rates for advice and information projects and, to a lesser extent, community projects, approval rates for other types of project diverge by not very much from the overall rate.

Because of the breakdown into more detailed categories in *Table A, Appendix IV*, the information in the final column of *Table 3* on the percentage of applications approved within each type of project is based on relatively small numbers of projects and is therefore inherently unreliable. It does indicate, however, that the apparent degree of relative stability in the approval rates for the condensed list of project types masks the greater diversity in rates apparent in the more detailed classification of types. Thus the approval rate ranges from zero for children's homes to 80 per cent for neighbourhood advice centres (but, it should be noted, both these are

---

[3] This figure can be compared with that of 34.7 per cent of projects approved out of all projects submitted under Phases 3, 7, and 9 by *all* London boroughs and county boroughs in England, 31.7 per cent for all London boroughs and 36.1 per cent for all county boroughs.

based on small numbers of applications). Among the project types for which applications were sufficiently numerous to provide some degree of credibility to the approval rate, the following high rates of approval may be noted (bearing in mind that the rate for *all* sample projects was 37.6 per cent): pre-school play groups (51 per cent), youth activities (42 per cent), community centres (42 per cent), and accommodation for the homeless (46 per cent). Notable low rates of approval were obtained for 'other play' schemes (8 per cent), care of the elderly (29 per cent), compensatory education (24 per cent), and general social work (28 per cent).

Thus while, with the exception of advice and information centres and community projects, there is a fair degree of correspondence in general terms between the patterns of application and approval, examination by the more detailed breakdown of projects reveals some significant discrepancies, and from this it may be deduced that, whereas at a fairly crude level of analysis the distribution of types of project actually in operation as a result of the Urban Programme's funding largely reflects the pattern of project types initially formulated at local authority and voluntary agency levels, more detailed analysis gives a greater indication of the influence of central department intervention.

The distribution of programme funds compared with the distribution of 'deprivation'

Since the Urban Programme is a programme of positive discrimination, a partial aim of which is to direct additional funds on a selective basis into areas of greater social need or greater 'deprivation', another test of its efficacy is to examine the extent to which this has been achieved by comparing the geographical distribution of funds with some measure of the geographical distribution of 'deprivation'. Such a comparison has been carried out and is fully reported in the series of Working Papers on the Urban Programme which supplement this book (Edwards 1974). In that report, comparison is made between the rankings of London boroughs and county boroughs, separately and combined, on a 'deprivation index' based on local authorities' scores on four census indicators of deprivation and their rankings in the receipt of Urban Programme funds over Phases 1-9 both in absolute sums and in terms of 'funds per head deprived'. (For details of these computations see Edwards 1975.)

Clearly, such a comparison gives only a crude measure of the discriminatory effects of the Programme since the targets for much of the funding were particular areas of social need much smaller than local authorities, and a precise comparison would require measurements at ward or, preferably, enumeration district level for both the deprivation index and the distribution of funds. However, even at this aggregated level of analysis, some indication has been provided of the effectiveness of the Urban Programme in directing funds into deprived areas. It is not intended to reproduce the findings of this exercise here (reference for these should be made to the appropriate working paper) save to say that there were some considerable discrepancies between the rankings of local authorities on the deprivation index and their orders of rank in both receipt of funds in absolute amounts and receipt of funds 'per head of population deprived', and that particular authorities were identified as having been relatively over- or under-funded from the Urban Programme during its first nine phases.[4] The most significantly under-funded authorities (that is, those whose ranking on the deprivation index indicated that they received significantly less from the UP than would have been expected were (in order of the degree of under-funding):

London boroughs	*County boroughs*
Lambeth	Grimsby
Southwark	Hull
Wandsworth	Salford
Westminster	Gateshead
Hammersmith	Bradford
	Manchester
	St Helens
	Dewsbury
	Oldham
	Warrington
	Barnsley
	Oxford

Those most significantly 'over-funded' (with a greater share of

---

[4] Relative over- or under-funding was ascribed to those authorities for which there were large discrepancies in order of rank between the deprivation index and receipt of programme funds (Edwards 1975).

Urban Programme funds than would be expected from the rank position on the deprivation index) were:

London boroughs	County boroughs
Brent	Barrow-in-Furness
Haringey	Dudley
Havering	Leeds
	Portsmouth
	Wakefield
	Wolverhampton
	Walsall

There are, of course, a number of possible reasons for relative over- or under-funding, some the results of action or inaction at local government and voluntary agency level and, some, of decisions taken at central department level. Thus, it could be argued that, because in the process of selecting bids for approval at central department level use is not made of any 'index of deprivation', or of any conception of the relative degree of social need as between authorities, decisions have been taken and allocations made that have inappropriately 'rewarded' some authorities *vis-à-vis* others. This assumes of course that under-funded authorities had in fact submitted sufficient numbers of projects to have enabled central departments to make more 'appropriate' allocations if the relevant criteria had been to hand and had been used. An alternative reason postulated for relative under-funding might be, therefore, that it simply reflects a paucity of applications from the under-funded authorities, such that central departments have not been able to allocate more funds to them. A third alternative is that 'under-funded' authorities, while submitting as many projects as others, have tended to opt for smaller and cheaper projects so that, while, relatively, they have had as many projects approved as other equally deprived areas, the total funds involved have been smaller. Conversely, it could be that relatively over-funded authorities have opted to submit comparatively more expensive projects.

The data in *Table 4* enables further examination of some of these points. The first column indicates the average number of applications made over Phases 3, 7, and 9 for the seventeen 'under-funded' and ten 'over-funded' authorities listed above, and for *all* London and county boroughs combined. The second column shows the average numbers of approvals made per authority over the same phases for the same groups of authorities, and the third shows the approval rate for these same authorities.

Table 4   *Application and approvals: 'over-' and 'under-' funded authorities*

	Average number of applications per authority Phases 3, 7, 9	Average number of approvals per authority Phases 3, 7, 9	Approval rate Phases 3, 7, 9[1]
All 'under-funded' authorities	43	15	33.7
All 'over-funded' authorities	63	23	36.0
All London boroughs and county boroughs combined	36	13	34.7

NOTES:

[1] Approval rate based on *total* number of applications and approvals for Phases 3, 7, 9, not on the average applications and approvals per authority

Far from the 'under-funded' authorities having submitted fewer projects over Phases 3, 7, and 9, they did in fact submit *more* on average per authority than was the case for all London and county boroughs combined (43 to 36) and also had more *approved* per authority than all the authorities combined (15 to 13). Neither is there any indication that 'under-funded' authorities suffered from a lower rate of approval than others, the difference of 1 per cent (33.7 per cent compared with 34.7 per cent for all authorities) being insignificant. The explanation for the relative under-funding of these authorities therefore appears to be neither that they submitted fewer projects than other authorities, nor that central departments unwittingly discriminated against them in any way by approving less of their projects; the explanation appears to lie rather in the relative costs of projects applied for and approved.

As for the ten 'over-funded' authorities, *Table 4* suggests that their advantaged position may in fact have been due to a combination of higher average numbers of applications (63 to 36 for all authorities), a slightly higher approval rate (36.0 per cent compared with 34.7 per cent for all authorities), and hence simply more projects approved per authority (23) than the average for authorities (13). What this serves to highlight is that, with a relatively stable rate of approval hovering at around one-third of applications, the more projects an authority submits, the more it is likely to have approved, and this notwithstanding its position relative to other authorities on any index of social need or deprivation.

Types of project

The beginning of this chapter compared the distribution of projects applied for and those approved, across the various project types. This section takes further the analysis of the projects that are actually operational by comparing their distribution by types with other variables such as cost, kind of local authority, and sponsor. Most of the cross-tabulations discussed make use of the shorter, condensed list of project types, but, where appropriate, reference is made to the fuller breakdown by types.

(a) *Types of project and costs*:   The fact that some types of project cost more on average than others is obviously not a guide to cost-effectiveness, since the purposes, functions, and benefits of different kinds of project are themselves necessarily different, the 'problems' they are designed to tackle are different, and the social needs they aim to meet are of different kinds. No comparison of their effectiveness as instruments for alleviating a nebulous and undefined condition called 'deprivation' can be meaningful because there does not in reality exist any *common* benchmark against which the effectiveness of a wide variety of different types of project can be assessed. What can be provided by a comparison of costs by types is an indication of which types of project are more likely to consume relatively greater shares of a necessarily finite and limited financial resource.

Table 5 details the numbers and percentages (on both axes) of projects as they are distributed by type and cost. Taking the lower end of the cost-band range, it can be seen that more than a third of all approved projects over Phases 1-9 cost less than £2,000, and many more than three-fifths cost less than £6,000. There were, however, considerable differences as between different types of project, with, for instance, a much smaller proportion (24.4 per cent) of community-type projects falling into the lowest cost band and a much higher proportion (41.3 per cent) of special education projects. If 'cheap' projects are taken to be those costing less than £6,000, then advice and information centres and special education projects are seen to be more heavily represented in this category than others, with 63.2 per cent of all projects being 'cheap', but 70.1 per cent and 76.4 per cent respectively of these two project types. On the other hand, projects providing for children are less well represented among 'cheap' projects (58.4 per cent). It should also be noted that whereas community projects are relatively less well represented in the lowest cost band, as noted above, their representation across the three lowest bands (up to £6,000) is about par for all projects.

At the opposite end of the range (projects costing £20,000 or more), while 13.3 per cent of all projects fall in this category, both community-type projects and those making provision for youth and the elderly are more heavily represented (both at 17.4 per cent), and advice and information centres and special education projects are less well represented (6.2 per cent and 7.1 per cent respectively). Thus, taking only the extremes of the cost range, it is clear that while advice centres and special education projects are relatively more common amongst the 'cheaper' projects (largely no doubt because they do not on the whole involve expensive capital outlay but demand rather relatively less expensive rents and salaries), both community-style projects and those involving provision for youth and old people are more likely to consume a greater proportion of programme funds than their overall representation would suggest. Examination of the distribution of projects by the fuller list of project types shows that the over-representation of such projects among the higher cost bands is due to the number of expensive community centres and the provision for accommodation for the elderly, both of which involve considerable capital outlay.

(b) *Types of project and local authority*:   It is not surprising, in view of the different responsibilities of different (pre-reorganization) types of authority, that considerable variation is to be found in the kinds of project approved in them. It is to be expected that education-oriented projects will be less well-represented among the London boroughs, for example, than the county boroughs (the inner and middle London boroughs not being education authorities), and that, given the more limited statutory responsibilities of urban and rural districts and municipal boroughs, the types of project for which they receive approvals will differ markedly from those in London and county boroughs and county councils. Apart from the variation that can be explained by such structural factors,

Table 5   Project types (condensed) by cost band (condensed)

Type of project		Cost band											Total
		£0-1,999	£2-3,999	£4-5,999	£6-7,999	£8-9,999	£10-11,999	£12-13,999	£14-19,999	£20-29,999	£30-49,999	£50,000+	
Provision for children	% (col)	57.3	35.9	41.9	46.2	56.0	62.9	75.7	70.4	58.9	54.4	59.3	52.7
	Number	589	195	116	85	70	83	87	95	86	74	64	1,544
	%	38.2	12.6	7.5	5.5	4.5	5.4	5.6	6.2	5.6	4.8	4.2	100.0
Other age-groups	% (col)	5.5	9.0	5.8	5.4	6.4	3.8	6.1	7.4	8.2	11.0	6.5	6.7
	Number	57	49	16	10	8	5	7	10	12	15	7	196
	%	29.1	25.0	8.2	5.1	4.1	2.6	3.6	5.1	6.1	7.7	3.6	100.0
Advice/information (general)	% (col)	6.9	10.7	14.1	12.0	8.8	10.6	3.5	4.4	4.8	4.4	1.8	8.2
	Number	71	58	39	22	11	14	4	6	7	6	2	240
	%	29.6	24.2	16.3	9.2	4.6	5.8	1.7	2.5	2.9	2.5	0.8	100.0
Community projects	% (col)	6.1	14.4	9.4	8.7	6.4	3.8	5.2	8.1	11.6	10.3	13.0	8.8
	Number	63	78	26	16	8	5	6	11	17	14	14	258
	%	24.4	30.2	10.1	6.2	3.1	1.9	2.3	4.3	6.6	5.4	5.4	100.0
Social work/welfare/health	% (col)	10.6	15.7	12.6	17.4	11.2	10.6	6.1	0.7	8.9	11.8	13.0	11.6
	Number	109	85	35	32	14	14	7	1	13	16	14	340
	%	32.1	25.0	10.3	9.4	4.1	4.1	2.1	0.3	3.8	4.7	4.1	100.0
Special education	% (col)	10.9	10.3	14.1	8.7	6.4	6.1	3.5	6.7	6.2	3.7	4.6	9.3
	Number	112	56	39	16	8	8	4	9	9	5	5	271
	%	41.3	20.7	14.4	5.9	3.0	3.0	1.5	3.3	3.3	1.9	1.8	100.0
Miscellaneous	% (col)	2.6	4.1	2.2	1.6	4.8	2.3	0.0	2.2	1.4	4.4	1.8	2.7
	Number	27	22	6	3	6	3	0	3	2	6	2	80
	%	33.8	27.5	7.5	3.8	7.5	3.8	0.0	3.8	2.5	7.5	2.5	100.0
Total	% (col)	100.0	100.0	100.0	100.0	100.0	100.0	100.0	100.0	100.0	100.0	100.0	100.0
	Number	1028	543	277	184	125	132	115	135	146	136	108	2,929
	%	35.1	18.6	9.5	6.3	4.3	4.5	3.9	4.6	5.0	4.6	3.7	100.0

Table 6   Project types (condensed)

Type of project		Type of local authority													
		London boroughs		ILEA		GLC		County boroughs		County councils		Municipal boroughs, urban and rural districts		Total	
		Number	%	Number	%	Number	%	Number	%	Number	%	Number	%	Number	%
Provision for children	Number	396	51.9	84	73.7	3	42.9	808	49.7	212	66.9	41	41.4	1,544	52.7
	%	25.7		5.4		0.2		52.3		13.7		2.7		100.0	
Other age-groups	Number	28	3.7	2	1.8	0	0.0	141	8.7	17	5.4	8	8.1	196	6.7
	%	14.3		1.0		0.0		71.9		8.7		4.1		100.0	
Advice/information (general)	Number	66	8.6	0	0.0	2	28.6	147	9.0	10	3.2	15	15.2	240	8.2
	%	27.5		0.0		0.8		61.3		4.2		6.3		100.0	
Community projects	Number	73	9.4	2	1.8	2	28.6	143	8.8	17	5.4	21	21.1	258	8.8
	%	28.2		0.8		0.8		55.4		6.6		8.2		100.0	
Social work/welfare/health	Number	130	17.0	0	0.0	0	0.0	181	11.1	26	8.2	3	3.0	340	11.6
	%	38.2		0.0		0.0		53.2		7.7		0.9		100.0	
Special education	Number	57	7.5	24	21.1	0	0.0	155	9.5	29	9.2	6	6.1	271	9.2
	%	21.0		8.9		0.0		57.2		10.7		2.2		100.0	
Miscellaneous	Number	15	2.0	2	1.8	0	0.0	52	3.2	6	1.9	5	5.1	80	2.7
	%	18.8		2.5		0.0		65.0		7.5		6.3		100.0	
Total	Number	765	100.0	114	100.0	7	100.0	1,627	100.0	317	100.0	99	100.0	2,929	100.0
	%	26.1		3.9		0.2		55.6		10.8		3.4		100.0	

however, there are others shown up in *Table 6* that are less easily explained and the more interesting for that.

Leaving aside for the moment the rather special cases of the Inner London Education Authority, the Greater London Council, and the urban and rural districts and municipal boroughs, the following significant features can be isolated from *Table 6*. Notwithstanding the fact that the distribution of projects across the various types for county boroughs does not differ markedly from the distribution of all projects (since they represent more than a half of the total), it can be seen that both 'other age-group' projects and advice and information centres, but especially the former, were relatively more common among county borough approvals than among those for London boroughs, and, also, relatively more common than their representation among all projects would lead one to expect. Thus, while 55.6 per cent of all projects approved were in county boroughs, the latters' share of 'other age-group' projects was 71.9 per cent and, of advice centres, 61.3 per cent. London boroughs, on the other hand, are notable for their low proportion of 'other age-group' projects (14.3 per cent as against 26.1 per cent of all projects) and the high proportion of social work/health projects (38.2 per cent). An alternative way of expressing these signal features for London boroughs can be seen by examining the vertical axis of the table. Thus, whereas 'other age-group' projects account for 6.7 per cent of all projects, they account for only 3.7 per cent of London borough projects, and for social work/health projects the respective figures are 11.6 per cent and 17.0 per cent. For county councils, discrepancies lie in the relatively low proportions of advice and community projects and the relatively high proportion of child-oriented projects.

Such variations as these can only partially be explained by structural factors, for instance, differences in statutory responsibilities, and a full explanation must take into account not only the perceptions of officers and members in the various types of authority as to what constituted an appropriate response, in project terms, to their own perceived needs, but also the differing degrees of involvement of the voluntary agencies as between the types of local authority (see p.163 below); for, as is indicated in the next table, there were significant contrasts in the kinds of project that emanated from the voluntary and statutory sectors. For example, the low representation of advice and community projects in county councils, and the high representation of child-oriented projects can partially be explained by the very low relative involvement of the voluntary sector (which generates a high proportion of the two former types and a low proportion of the latter) in the counties.

Table 7   *Project types (condensed)*[1] *by sponsor*

Type of project		Local authority		Voluntary agency[2]		Total	
		Num-ber	%	Num-ber	%	Num-ber	%
Provision for children	*Number*	1,141	57.9	403	42.1	1,544	52.7
	%	73.9		26.1		100.0	
Other age-groups	*Number*	123	6.2	73	7.6	196	6.7
	%	62.8		37.2		100.0	
Advice/informa-tion (general)	*Number*	135	6.9	105	11.0	240	8.2
	%	56.3		43.8		100.0	
Community projects	*Number*	110	5.6	148	15.5	258	8.8
	%	42.6		57.4		100.0	
Social work/ welfare/health	*Number*	213	10.8	127	13.3	340	11.6
	%	62.7		37.4		100.0	
Special education	*Number*	200	10.1	71	7.4	271	9.2
	%	73.8		26.2		100.0	
Miscellaneous	*Number*	50	2.5	30	3.1	80	2.7
	%	62.5		37.6		100.0	
Total	*Number*	1,972	100.0	957	100.0	2,929	100.0
	%	67.3		32.7		100.0	

Notes:

[1] See *Appendix III.*
[2] Includes joint local authority/voluntary organization projects.

(c) *Project types and sponsors*:   *Table 7*, as would be expected, shows that the voluntary sector was particularly strong on those types of project that fell out with the bounds of what is normally considered to be statutory provision. Thus, whereas about one third of all projects over Phases 1-9 were voluntary agency projects, more than half of all community-style projects were initiated by the non-statutory sector (comprising 15.5 per cent of all voluntary projects, only 5.6 per cent of all local authority projects, and 8.8 per cent of all projects) and 43.8 per cent of all advice and information centres (comprising 11.0 per cent of all voluntary projects, 6.9 per cent of local authority projects, and 8.2 per cent of all projects). Conversely, the voluntary sector was responsible for a smaller proportion of child-oriented and special education projects than would have been expected from the division of all projects between the statutory and non-statutory sectors.

These patterns are again reflected in the more detailed breakdown of project types (details not reproduced). Thus, all legal advice centres were sponsored by voluntary agencies, 95.8 per cent of the citizens advice bureaux, 67.9 per cent of the 'other advice centres', and 69.5 per cent of the community centres.

Sponsoring bodies or agencies

The involvement of the voluntary sector in the Urban Programme is of significant interest in the present context, both for the influence it has had on the pattern of projects approved (there would not have been so many advice and community projects were it not for the initiative of this sector, as is shown above) and for the opportunity this involvement has provided to examine some of the factors that influence and shape the role of voluntary agencies in a multi-department, central and local government programme such as the Urban Programme.

Although one-third of all projects approved over Phases 1-9 as a whole were voluntary organization projects (see *Table 7*), this figure conceals the increasing part played by the voluntary sector over the life of the Programme, as is shown in *Table 8*. Whereas in Phase 3 the voluntary sector accounted for only 22 per cent of all project *applications* in the sample authorities, this had increased, by Phase 7, to 40.8 per cent and, by Phase 9, to 47.1 per cent — almost half of all applications; and in terms of actual approvals, the rise of the voluntary sector was even more marked, constituting 27.2 per cent of all approvals in Phase 3, 60 per cent in Phase 7, and almost 68 per cent in Phase 9 (but see note to *Table 8*). Again, the approval rate for voluntary organizations' projects was consistently higher over these phases than that for local authorities, indicating somewhat favourable treatment from central departments.

The influence of the voluntary sector on the types of project approved under the Programme has been examined above; now we

Table 8   Applications and approvals: local authorities and voluntary agencies: Phases 3, 7, 9 for seven local authorities[1]

	Phase 3			Phase 7			Phase 9			Total: three phases		
	% Applications	% Approvals	% Approval rate	% Applications	% Approvals	% Approval rate	% Applications	% Approvals	% Approval rate	% Applications	% Approvals	% Approval rate
Local authority projects	78.1	72.8	33.0	59.2	40.2	29.0	52.9	32.2	19.0	64.8	50.2	29.0
Voluntary agency projects	21.9	27.2	44.0	40.8	59.8	63.0	47.1	67.8	45.0	35.2	49.8	53.0

Note:
[1] A sample of seven local authorities was used for comparisons of applications and approvals (see p. 148). Comparison of the distribution of approvals between sponsors for the sample authorities and phases indicates that voluntary organizations fared much better in these sample authorities than they did overall.

shall consider how far the involvement of voluntary organizations is affected both by the type of local authority in which they are situated and by the approval policies and procedures of different government departments.

(a) *Sponsor and type of local authority*: The summary of evidence in Chapter 7 deals, in some detail, with the involvement of the voluntary sector in the Urban Programme (see pp.190-96; 208-9), and with the differences in the extent of this involvement as between different types of local authority. Assuming that central departments do not (wittingly or unwittingly) greatly vary the relative approval rates for local authority and voluntary agency projects between the different types of local authority (and there is no evidence to suggest that they do), the differences in the extent of voluntary agency participation in the Programme (as measured here by numbers of projects approved) between the different types of local authority must be considered due to the effectiveness of their involvement at the local level. Chapter 5 has discussed some of the factors that determined the extent to which voluntary agencies took part in the Programme (see pp.129-34), and these might be borne in mind in the interpretation of the data in *Table 9*. These factors included, for instance, the actual numbers of voluntary agencies in an area (which, on the evidence gained in the course of the research, seemed likely to vary more by geographical region than type of authority), the extent to which the circular or information about it was distributed by authorities to voluntary organizations, the effectiveness of other means of communicating information about the Programme, the ability and willingness of voluntary organizations to take part in the Programme, the effectiveness of local authority machinery to involve them, and the prevailing attitudes about voluntary agencies in general and their role in the Urban Programme in particular.

It is clear from *Table 9* that the degree of voluntary involvement in the Urban Programme was greatest in the London boroughs (a third of all projects over Phases 1-9 were voluntary agency projects, but 44 per cent of London boroughs' projects were in this category), and was lowest (discounting the rather special cases of the ILEA and the GLC) in county councils, where only 15.8 per cent of projects were run by the non-statutory sector. County boroughs, of course, because of their large share of all projects, shaped the overall pattern, and, for them, the division between

Table 9   Project sponsor by type of local authority

Type of local authority		London boroughs		ILEA		GLC		County boroughs		County councils		Municipal boroughs, urban and rural districts		Total	
		Number	%	Number	%	Number	%	Number	%	Number	%	Number	%	Number	%
Local authority	Number	428	55.9	99	86.8	4	57.1	1,114	68.5	267	84.2	60	60.0	1,972	67.3
	%	21.7		5.0		0.2		56.5		13.5		3.0		100.0	
Voluntary organisation¹	Number	337	44.1	15	13.2	3	42.9	513	31.5	50	15.8	39	40.0	957	32.7
	%	35.2		1.6		0.3		53.6		5.2		4.1		100.0	
Total	Number	765	100.0	114	100.0	7	100.0	1,627	100.0	317	100.0	99	100.0	2,929	100.0
	%	26.1		3.9		0.2		55.6		10.8		3.4		100.0	

Notes:

[1] Includes a small number of joint local authority/voluntary organization projects.

statutorily and non-statutorily administered projects was close to the average for all projects combined. Interestingly, in the smaller authorities (municipal boroughs and urban and rural districts) voluntary involvement was somewhat higher than the average for all projects though not as high as for London boroughs. The explanation for this may well be that the limited responsibilities and powers of these smaller authorities provided less scope for their own involvement in the Programme, but did not affect the potential role of non-statutory agencies, and that locally-based voluntary agencies were more likely to approach second-tier than first-tier authorities. The greater involvement of the voluntary sector in the London boroughs, on the other hand, is no doubt due in part to the existence of larger numbers of voluntary organizations in London and to the generally more highly-developed pattern of co-operation between statutory and non-statutory agencies. As for county councils, evidence presented by officials in those county councils in which our discussions were held (see pp.190-92) suggested that a dearth of lively voluntary organizations in some regions combined with the inadequate machinery for voluntary agency involvement, often over very large geographical areas, to explain the very low proportion of county council projects that are run by non-statutory bodies.

(b) *Sponsors and central departments*: The varying proportions of voluntary and statutory sector projects approved by the divers central government departments reflect particular structural features, such as the more limited scope in some areas of provision (notably education) for voluntary involvement, the tendency in many authorities (see pp.192-96) to assume that voluntary projects are more relevant to social services departments than education, and hence to channel them through local social services departments in which they are more likely to be considered at central level by the DHSS, and the links and traditions of co-operation with the non-statutory sector which are stronger in some central departments than in others.

The differences that existed in the division of approvals between local authorities and voluntary organizations for the various central departments are shown in *Table 10*. The voluntary sector achieved the largest proportion of approvals from within the Home Office's sphere of activity (46.8 per cent), followed quite closely by the DHSS (44.7 per cent), as compared with the overall figure of

32.7 per cent of approvals given to the voluntary sector. As might be expected from what was said above, approvals to voluntary agencies in the sphere of education were far fewer, accounting for only 9.3 per cent of DES approvals and 9.3 per cent of voluntary organization approvals (compared with 32.5 per cent of all approvals falling overall in the education sector). The DOE also approved relatively fewer voluntary projects (comprising only 1.8 per cent of all voluntary approvals and 14.9 per cent of all departmental approvals). Finally, joint-department approvals again tended to favour the voluntary sector — no doubt reflecting the fact that fewer voluntary organization projects tended to fall neatly within the established realm of responsibility of any one department. The high rate of voluntary approvals in the Home Office field, on the other hand, was probably due to the high proportion of community and advice-style projects (for which the Home Office has responsibility) emanating from the voluntary sector (see pp.160-1), and to the special responsibilities of the non-statutory sector and hence the closer awareness on the part of Home Office officials of the needs of this sector.

Costs

That there are significant (and very large) variations in project costs as between the various types of project is shown above. There are two further factors (amongst others) by which costs will vary, and which are examined here. These are variations in cost by sponsor and by type of local authority.

(a) *Costs and sponsors*: *Table 11* shows that, as might be expected, voluntary organization projects tended to be much less expensive than the local authority projects. A higher proportion of all local authority projects falls into every cost band above £3,999 than is the case with voluntary agencies, three-quarters of whose projects cost less than £4,000 each (as compared with only 43 per cent of local authority projects). At the opposite end of the cost range 17.7 per cent of statutory-based projects cost £20,000 or more as against only 4.3 per cent of voluntary schemes. Again, taking that proportion of each cost band that contains projects run by voluntary agencies, there is a steady decline from the lowest band (51.8 per cent of all projects costing less than £2,000) to

Table 10 Sponsors by central department

Sponsor		Central government department										Total	
		Home Office		DHSS		DES		DOE		Joint[1]			
		Num-ber	%	Num-ber	%	Num-ber	%	Num-ber	%	Num-ber	%	Num-ber	%
Local authority	Number	505	53.2	452	55.3	863	90.7	97	85.1	55	57.3	1,972	67.3
	%	25.6		22.9		43.8		4.9		2.9		100.0	
Voluntary organization[2]	Number	444	46.8	366	44.7	89	9.3	17	14.9	41	42.7	957	32.7
	%	46.4		38.2		9.3		1.8		4.3		100.0	
Total	Number	949	100.0	818	100.0	952	100.0	114	100.0	96	100.0	2,929	100.0
	%	32.4		27.9		32.5		3.9		3.3		100.0	

Notes:
[1] All approvals made jointly by more than one department.
[2] Includes a small number of joint local authority/voluntary organization projects.

the most expensive (6.5 per cent of all projects costing £50,000 or more).

These variations stem from two unrelated factors: first, that voluntary agencies are far less likely to submit costly projects; and, second, that central departments are less willing to approve high-cost voluntary sector projects, this being allied to the fact that most high-cost projects involve extensive capital works which, until recently, central departments have not been willing to fund in the voluntary sector (only 8.6 per cent of capital schemes having fallen into the non-statutory sector compared with 49 per cent of all non-capital and once-only schemes).

(b) *Costs and types of local authority*:   Variations in project costs by types of local authority must be explained largely in terms of the differences in the distribution of project types as between the diverse kinds of local authority, and by variations in the division of projects between the voluntary and statutory sectors (see *Tables 6* and *9* respectively). The more expensive types of project (see *Table 6*) are community-style projects and those catering for 'other age-groups', while less expensive projects tend to deal with advice and information centres and special education. On this basis, it might be expected that county boroughs, in which there were high numbers of 'other age-group' projects, might have administered more high-cost schemes, and London boroughs, with a low representation of this type of project, might claim a smaller proportion of high-cost projects. County councils, on the other hand, ran relatively few advice-style projects and might therefore be expected, on the whole, to have had more in the high-cost band. Reinforcing these hypothesized distinctions for London boroughs and county councils is the fact that voluntary projects (which tended to be cheaper — see *Table 11*) were highly represented in London boroughs but poorly represented among county councils.

Perusal of *Table B, Appendix IV* does in fact indicate that, by and large, the distribution of projects by cost band is oriented towards the higher cost bands to a greater extent in county councils than in London boroughs, with the one exception that a slightly smaller proportion of county projects falls into the highest cost band (£50,000 or more) than is the case for London boroughs, though the difference is small (4.7 per cent and 5.9 per cent respectively). At the low-cost end of the scale, the differences are

Table 11   *Project costs (condensed) by sponsor*

Cost band		Local authority		Voluntary organization		Total	
		Number	%	Number	%	Number	%
£0-1,999	*Number*	496	25.2	532	55.6	1,028	35.1
	%	48.3		51.8		100.0	
£2-3,999	*Number*	350	17.8	193	20.2	543	18.5
	%	64.5		35.5		100.0	
£4-5,999	*Number*	198	10.0	79	8.3	277	9.5
	%	71.5		28.5		100.0	
£6-7,999	*Number*	143	7.3	41	4.3	184	6.3
	%	77.7		22.3		100.0	
£8-9,999	*Number*	105	5.3	20	2.1	125	4.3
	%	84.0		16.0		100.0	
£10-11,999	*Number*	110	5.6	22	2.3	132	4.5
	%	83.3		16.7		100.0	
£12-13,999	*Number*	101	5.1	14	1.5	115	3.9
	%	87.8		12.2		100.0	
£14-19,999	*Number*	120	6.1	15	1.6	135	4.6
	%	88.9		11.1		100.0	
£20-29,999	*Number*	128	6.5	18	1.9	146	5.0
	%	87.7		12.3		100.0	
£30-49,999	*Number*	120	6.1	16	1.7	136	4.7
	%	88.2		11.8		100.0	
£50,000+	*Number*	101	5.1	7	0.7	108	3.7
	%	93.5		6.5		100.0	
Total	*Number*	1,972	100.0	957	100.0	2,929	100.0
	%	67.3		32.7		100.0	

more marked, with 40.3 per cent of London borough schemes falling in the lowest band (£0-1,999) but only 31.2 per cent of county council projects. Though county boroughs might be expected to have more projects in the higher cost bands than London boroughs, there is little evidence from the table to support this notion apart from the fact that a somewhat smaller proportion of county borough projects falls into the lowest band (34.6 per cent) than is the case for London (40.3 per cent).

Types of local authority

Most of the major variations in Urban Programme characteristics by type of local authority have already been covered in previous tables and commentaries. There is, however, one other factor of the variation by local authority type that is considered here, since it reveals some interesting differences. This is the variation in the extent to which approved projects fall within the realms of different government departments as between the different types of authority. Some of this variation can be accounted for by differences in the kind of project submitted by and approved for different types of authority (see *Table 6* and commentary), but, as *Table 12* shows, these variations are highlighted even more by a comparison of the approving central departments. Thus, in taking the proportion of projects from each type of local authority that were approved by the Home Office, wide variation can be seen, from 19.7 per cent for county councils to 69.7 per cent for smaller authorities. For London boroughs the proportion approved by the Home Office is 41.7 per cent and, for county boroughs, only 29.9 per cent. The fact that municipal boroughs and urban and rural districts had fewer statutory responsibilities that fell within the aegis of the major social departments, such as the DES, the DHSS, or the DOE, explains why such a high proportion of projects from these authorities fell to the Home Office, with its less well-defined, but wide-ranging, responsibilities. Again, the fact that many London boroughs have no education responsibilities explains why only 16.3 per cent of London boroughs projects fell to this department (compared, for example, with more than a third of county borough projects), and probably also accounts, by a process of displacement, for the high proportion of projects relevant to the Home Office among London boroughs. Less easy to explain is why county councils had so few Home Office projects but such a high proportion of projects relating to education (51.4 per cent of all county council schemes having fallen into this category compared with only 34.4 per cent of county boroughs' and 32.5 per cent overall). A likely explanation of this phenomenon must be the reaction seen to be appropriate by county officials and members to the Urban Programme, and the types of provision felt by them to be relevant to their dominant problems.

These, then, are some of the features of the more tangible

Table 12 *Types of local authority by central government department*

Type of local authority		Central government department											
		Home Office		DHSS		DES		DOE		Joint[1]		Total	
		Number	%	Number	%	Number	%	Number	%	Number	%	Number	%
London borough	Number	319	33.6	256	31.3	125	13.1	30	26.3	35	36.5	765	26.1
	%	41.7		33.5		16.3		3.9		4.6		100.0	
ILEA	Number	8	0.8	1	0.1	102	10.7	0	0.0	3	3.1	114	3.9
	%	7.0		0.9		89.5		0.0		2.6		100.0	
GLC	Number	5	0.5	0	0.0	0	0.0	2	1.8	0	0.0	7	0.2
	%	71.5		0.0		0.0		28.6		0.0		100.0	
County borough	Number	486	51.2	470	57.5	560	58.8	70	61.4	41	42.7	1,627	55.6
	%	29.9		28.9		34.4		4.3		2.5		100.0	
County council	Number	62	6.5	77	9.4	163	17.1	0	0.0	15	15.6	317	10.8
	%	19.7		24.3		51.4		0.0		4.7		100.0	
Municipal borough, urban and rural districts	Number	69	7.3	14	1.7	2	0.2	12	10.5	2	2.1	99	3.4
	%	69.7		14.1		2.0		12.1		2.0		100.0	
Total	Number	949	100.0	818	100.0	952	100.0	114	100.0	96	100.0	2,929	100.0
	%	32.4		27.9		32.5		3.9		3.3		100.0	

Note:
[1] All jointly-approved projects.

aspects of the Urban Programme. The data given above have shown the outcome of the Programme as manifested in the projects that have been made operational over its first nine phases. Some attempt has been made to indicate where the money has gone, what groups have benefited, what types of project have predominated in which areas and how, in practice, the respective roles of statutory and non-statutory agencies and the various influencing factors — structural and perceptual, outlined in Chapters 4 and 5 — are manifested in the Programme's end product: the projects 'on the ground'.

7 Perceptions and evaluations

If there is one recurring theme elicited by a detailed evaluation of the Urban Programme, it is that the Programme is in large measure a product of the interplay between its structure and process, on the one hand, and its administrators' and its executors' beliefs, on the other. The theme has been approached from a number of angles in preceding chapters but, in essence, the reasoning behind it is that the Programme was designed so quickly and along such general lines that its detailed shape and form were to become manifest only during the course of its implementation, and that, in default of specific guidelines from ministers at one level and central government officials at another, the perceptions of its executors, both about the aims and functions of the Programme itself and about the problems it was designed to tackle, were to play a signal part in determining that shape and form. This line of argument can be extended to suggest that, in its turn, the nature of the practical results of the Programme have in large measure been determined by the form of its implementation in practice.

In order therefore to understand fully the nature of the Urban Programme and its achievements (and failures) it becomes necessary to explore those views and perceptions, on the part of its executors at central and local government and voluntary agency levels, that have had so important a determining influence.

It is also to those responsible for implementing the Programme — at all levels — that we must turn for an assessment of its achievements and failures, its benefits and disbenefits, as they have become manifest during its construction and implementation.

These then — perceptions and evaluations — are the issues to which the present chapter addresses itself. The source of our material was the lengthy discussions held with 147 respondents, all concerned in one way or another with the administration of the Programme. A complete list of all respondents is given in *Appendix VI*. Below is a breakdown of the number of respondents at each level of administration:

central government officials	17
local authority officers	78
local authority councillors	10
local voluntary agency respondents	29
voluntary agency headquarters respondents	12
local authority association respondents	1
other	1.

Within central government, discussions were held with officials in each of the departments involved in the Programme: the Home Office, the Department of Health and Social Security, the Department of Education and Science, and the Department of the Environment. At local government level, twelve (pre-reorganization) local authorities were selected as case studies, and officers and members selected within these. (For details of the selection of the twelve authorities, see *Appendix V*.) All voluntary agencies within these twelve authorities that had any interest in the Urban Programme were also approached and discussions held with their representatives. Finally, contact was made and discussions held with all major voluntary agencies that had expressed interest in the Programme.

Neither in the selection of authorities nor of individual respondents was an attempt made to gain numerical or typological representativeness, and the source material does not, as a result, lend itself to quantification. No numbers are, therefore, quoted in the text, but some indication is given of where the weight of particular opinions or perceptions lay.

The exploration first of perceptions and then of evaluations is arranged under the following headings:

— Perceptions of the goals of the Urban Programme

— Perceptions of the nature of 'urban deprivation'
— Perceptions of the scale and importance of the Programme
— Perceptions of the achievements, results, and benefits
— Evaluation: the administration of the Programme at local government level
— Evaluation: the administration of the Programme at central government level
— Evaluation: local and central government priorities
— Evaluation: the Programme and voluntary agencies
— Evaluation: improvements in and the future of the Programme.

We should say a word about including the fourth of these under perceptions. Although, in some ways an assessment of the achievements of the Programme ought properly to be placed under evaluations, they do in many respects reflect perceptions of the nature of the Programme, and have been influential in shaping its form and usage both at central and local government levels. For this reason they are included under 'perceptions'.

Perceptions of the goals of the Programme

It has been shown in Chapter 3 that there has never been a clear, precise, and definitive statement of the aims of the Urban Programme, and that an analysis of such statements of aims as there have been (by politicians and administrators) indicates not only a lack of clarity but an embarrassing number of different aims, not all of them compatible. For this reason (and because it was felt that it might be a relevant factor in the shaping of the Programme) it is important to see what the various respondents in local and central government and in voluntary organizations thought were the aims of the Programme.

A common response among the local authority respondents was that the aims were quite unclear, or confused, or simply not known to them. To these respondents (and no doubt to others too) the Urban Programme was simply a channel for extra funds that could be used in the provision of additional services for people who needed them, mainly in the fields of education and social services. Nor was this uncertainty over aims (or, rather, conviction that there were no clear aims) confined to local authority respondents. Several Civil Servants (including two in the Home Office) also felt that the aims of the Urban Programme were either confused or unclear. It is worth quoting from the replies of two of these central government administrators, since it is from them that one might expect — if such existed — a definitive statement of aims:

> 'I personally have been surprised at the apparent total wilderness in which the Urban Programme has operated. No-one really seems to have got to grips with this problem of urban deprivation. So in this context the Urban Programme had a difficult task to set itself goals or even to achieve functions for want of goals. Certainly the initial goals were very general, though also very tentative, and there was much uncertainty about where the thrust or the impetus within the Programme would come from, whether it would be from voluntary effort, from local authorities, or from central government. So I think the initial goals were very much off the cuff.'
>
> (Senior Home Office official)

And again: 'The short answer is that I do not see the Programme in terms of having consistent goals which enable one to see whether it is or is not achieving these goals. It is fundamentally a statutory provision which is virtually endlessly adaptable' (Home Office official).

Other respondents, on the other hand, felt able to hazard an opinion as to what the Programme might be about. As might be expected, a fairly wide range of objectives was proposed, some more specific than others, and these have been grouped where possible into those of like kind. Thus, the most frequently-mentioned group of aims revolved round the notion that the Urban Programme was concerned with providing additional help for deprived areas, with meeting special social need, and with providing additional help to areas within authorities that lack resources. This is an unremarkable (and incontestable) group of aims, reflecting as it does the broad indications of the purpose of the Programme given in the government circulars.

Not unrelated to the above was the aim cited by some local authority officers, that the Urban Programme was a supplement to the Rate Support Grant, or provided additional resources for local authorities in need of funds. Again, the Urban Programme did serve such functions (though it would be truer to say that the Urban Programme redistributed a minute portion of the Rate Support

Grant fund than that it was an addition to it, since Urban Programme monies came out of this fund in the first place); but it could be argued that these functions do not constitute statements of aims.

Somewhat different was the view that the Programme was primarily concerned with experimentation and innovation — with finding and implementing new ways of meeting established needs where normal programmes seemed to have failed. Other ideas expressed by local authority officers or members were that the Programme was an exercise in positive discrimination, that it was concerned mainly with alleviating the burden of or reducing the extent of unemployment, and that it was primarily concerned with helping immigrant communities. There was one further aim attributed to the Programme, though only by voluntary organizations, which interpreted it very much in terms of non-statutory activity: namely, that the purpose of the Programme was to provide seed money for voluntary activity which, when it has proved successful, can more justifiably seek (and more hopefully gain) longer-term funding from local authorities or other funding agencies. It was not a view of the Programme's purpose shared by many local authorities.

Perceptions of the nature of 'urban deprivation'

Views about the aims of the Programme become a model of clarity when compared with the delineation of those problems that it is assumed to set out to tackle. Again, the purpose here is not to discuss the matter of 'urban deprivation' — this is done elsewhere in the book — but more simply to attempt to reflect the views of respondents on what deprivation was, on the assumption that it was urban deprivation that the Programme aimed to deal with.

It is necessary, first, to touch on one of the broader issues concerned with the nature of urban deprivation, and the reactions of some of our respondents to it. In a much-simplified (and perhaps over-simplified) form, it can be argued that there is a continuum of thought about the nature of 'urban deprivation' with two very different conceptions at the poles (see Chapter 8). One view sees deprivation in terms of pathology, whereby the deprived are those who, for a complex of reasons, but mainly because of social, personal, emotional, mental, or physical inadequacy, are less able to bear the stresses and strains of urban life and, for this reason, need additional aid of one kind or another from statutory and non-statutory agencies. At the opposite end of the spectrum is an analysis that sees deprivation as the result of competition on a free market for scarce but fundamental resources such as housing, education, and employment. The structure of this competition is such that there will always be 'losers': those who will not benefit from the competitive processes and will be inadequately served with society's basic resources (Holman 1973; Edwards 1975).

The implications for social policy of these two polar conceptions are of course radically different and, in reality, the Urban Programme could serve no purpose in the context of the latter formulation. Nonetheless, it was felt to be important to discover towards which end of the continuum central government respondents tended in their conception of urban deprivation, and what place they felt the Urban Programme had in the continuum. It should be added that, in discussion, the dichotomy was not necessarily articulated as it has been here. It was clear that, in the two main 'service' departments concerned with the Urban Programme (the DES and the DHSS), the problem was seen in terms of meeting needs, and that urban deprivation represented a concentration of people with additional and often multiple social need. Two officials in the Home Office, however, said they inclined towards the structural view of deprivation, but both felt that the scale and scope of the Urban Programme disqualified it from any claim of being able to have any impact on that form of deprivation.

Turning to some of the observations made by respondents about the nature of 'urban deprivation', these can be divided into two kinds: those that are more general and discursive, and those which cite particular problems or situations that might represent deprivation or some aspects of it. Of the first, quotations from some of the responses obtained cannot be bettered.

'Firstly, my personal view. I cannot see much difference between urban deprivation and general deprivation. I do not recognise anything special, either in quality or quantity, in the urban situation that makes deprivation so much worse than it is in rural areas. Secondly, there is a range of things which affect or influence the happiness or contentment of people, and these might range from genetic factors, to family upbringing, to personality, etc., and other things which the government is powerless to do anything about. And so one comes back to the third point which is that of social justice. It seems to me that there is an underlying obligation to make some sort of adjustment between those to whom the goods of society flow to those to whom they do not flow.' (Senior Home Office official)

'...it would be hard to mount an across-the-board research effort on urban deprivation. I see such an exercise rather as like "hunting the Snark". I find it curious that great concern is expressed about a thing to which the name urban deprivation is attached and then it is necessary to expend great effort and time to try and say what this thing really is.' (Home Office official)

'I think the definition of urban deprivation is one which requires a great deal more sophisticated analysis than it has yet received — if you are saying the concept of urban deprivation is a vague and "political" slogan, I would agree with you.'
(Chairman of the Community Relations Commission)

Specific observations about the nature of urban deprivation were many and varied and are best presented in list form, as below. These were mentioned by various respondents as being features of urban deprivation, and some were mentioned more frequently than others; they are presented in the list in order of frequency:

— immigrant concentrations/immigrant language difficulties
— poverty or low income
— the problems of the handicapped (mental and physical)
— lack of community facilities/the quality of life
— unemployment/poor industrial base/poor job opportunities
— single parent families
— overcrowding
— urban renewal problems
— declining industry, declining rate of income, decaying infrastructure
— large families
— poor health
— level of crime
— bad housing
— non-involvement in local affairs and local politics.

Either by implication, or explicitly, all of these 'problems' were seen to occur at their worst or in greatest concentration in the inner-city 'stress areas'. A number of respondents, however, also made explicit reference to the 'problems' of outlying housing estates (new or inter-war) and were concerned that they should not be excluded from consideration as deprived areas — and hence from being considered worthy of attention from the Urban Programme. The range of concerns in such estates was hardly any less catholic than that in the inner city, as is evidenced in the list below — all relating to suburban or more outlying estates:

— the lack of facilities
— loneliness
— the lack of a community
— problems of expensive housing
— problems of expensive transport
— wrong educational attitudes
— problems of isolated housewives
— large families
— 'problem' families.

Perceptions of the scale and importance of the Programme

Expressed in terms of a proportion of all expenditure on social services, the scale of the Urban Programme was miniscule. Notwithstanding this demonstrable fact, it is interesting to note the reactions of respondents to the scale and significance of the Programme. Was it universally condemned as miniscule in scale — or did some see the sums involved as not insignificant? Did it have a significance beyond and belying the small financial investment in it? What significance did it have in the context of major programme provision in the fields of social services and education?

In response to the last question, very few were prepared to dismiss the Programme out of hand as totally insignificant, and most could see some virtue, some measure of significance, in it. Several respondents, whilst acknowledging some of the benefits accruing under the Programme, laid greater emphasis on its smallness. Against this, a rather larger number gave greater weight to the significance of the Programme notwithstanding its scale. The gist of these comments was that the significance and importance of the Programme was out of all proportion to its financial scale, among them being that it enabled work to be carried out that could not be otherwise, that it allowed of innovation and experiment, that its underlying philosophy was of great importance, treating as it did of a grave social problem, that it heightened awareness of social need, and that it was of great importance to voluntary organizations, especially in the context of the contraction of other sources of finance. Other central government officials felt that the Urban Programme had an importance that went beyond its slim financial base. An assistant secretary in the DHSS commented: ' ... if you compare it with the size of our main programme on the capital side, the Urban Programme constitutes about one fiftieth — so from that point of view it is not very significant. But this is not the most important aspect. I think it is a very important programme in terms of the educational effect it has.' And an assistant secretary in the DOE, while acknowledging the small size, thought that it could bring 'shafts of illumination to the problem'. He added, however, that the Programme could not constitute a major attack on deprivation, but could only stand in a pioneering role as long as it was oriented towards projects: 'you will get back bids for projects if that is what you ask for. You won't get a sustained analysis of the problem followed by the development of non-project programmes.' Obvious as this point may seem, it sums up in a few words one of the fundamental weaknesses of the Programme: that at the end of the day it would not have added to the corporate body of knowledge about the nature of and solutions to deprivation.

In addition, it should be added that when asked directly about the scale of the Urban Programme, all respondents who replied were unanimous in saying that it was far too small, some dismissively, an equal number adding that this was true 'in relation to the size of the problem it is tackling'.

Another aspect of the importance or significance of the Programme, not directly related to its scale, was the conceptual significance attached to it in the eyes of those who administered it. Was it seen primarily as an innovative programme, both in itself and in terms of the work it funds, or as an extra envelope of money on top of the main programme budgets — a mechanism for the delivery of small additional resources? It is not hard to see the significance of the form of the Programme and of the use made of it by any particular authority; indeed, the way it was administered at central government level may well have been influenced, if not determined, by which of these two conceptions predominated.

Opinion was naturally divided on this issue, but approximately twice as many respondents saw the Programme primarily as a small extra resource as those who saw it in terms of an innovatory programme or an experiment in social policy.

Perceptions of the achievements, outcomes, and benefits of the Programme

Assessment of the achievements of any programme or policy must, at least in part, be made in relation to set goals. The absence of clear goals for the Urban Programme makes assessment difficult not only for the evaluator but also for administrators and implementors. Nonetheless, most respondents voiced some opinions on this matter, and opinion was weighted to the view that, on the whole, the Programme was not achieving such aims as could be identified for it. More than half, however, felt that the Programme was not without some achievements or at least some spin-off benefits, and in this respect local authority respondents were far more optimistic than those from voluntary agencies.

The most frequently-mentioned point, however, cannot be construed so much as an achievement than as a benefit arising from the Programme's more generous grant level and its character as a special and specific-grant exercise. These features were seen to be of considerable help in easing innovative or experimental schemes through otherwise doubtful service committees.

A second, more positive spin-off that was cited was that the Programme had stimulated much new thought on the nature of social need and new or alternative ways of meeting it, had produced a number of new ideas for the alleviation of deprivation, and had encouraged experimentation in this field.[1] Whether or not the stimulus to fresh thought provided by the Programme will have a lasting benefit, and whether the experience gained is still being drawn upon in the planning of more general and regular programmes, it is impossible to say, but this would be a more pertinent measure of the real benefits accruing from the stimulus provided.

[1] In an earlier study of a sample of Urban Programme Projects it was found that more than half the projects were felt to have produced similar sorts of benefit or spin-off apart from any direct help they may have brought to recipients. It can be argued, therefore, that both at project formulation and project operation stages these less tangible benefits were produced by the programme (Edwards and Batley 1974).

A number of other spin-offs were mentioned (though less frequently) by respondents. Amongst these were suggestions that the
Programme had acted as a basis of new provision (that projects
once tried and tested under the Urban Programme had been
replicated by local authorities using regular funds); that the Urban
Programme had led to more interdepartmental co-operation and
discussion within authorities; that the Programme enabled an
immediate and unprogrammed response to local need; and that it
had been an educative experience for officers and members.

Within central government, feelings about the achievements of
the Programme were somewhat less sanguine. One DHSS official
speculated that the DES experience of nursery education provision,
gained under the Urban Programme, in all probability was not
uninfluential in the establishment of the Nursery Education
Programme of provision when Margaret Thatcher was Secretary of
State for Education in 1973. (Since 1960 local authorities had been
explicitly forbidden to provide more nursery education except for
the children of schoolteachers, and between 1969 and 1973 the
Urban Programme had been the only means by which local
authorities could provide nursery education for deprived children.)
However, another official in the DES doubted that 'the experience
of nursery education under the Urban Programme in any way
contributed to or was used to justify DES's current programme'.
What could have been affirmed as a major and significant achievement for the Urban Programme must therefore be left in doubt.

Within the Home Office itself response was measured. One
official, while admitting that, at one level, the projects on the
ground and, at another, the stimulus to new thought and innovation
could be claimed as achievements, felt that 'the "fame" of the Urban
Programme seems greater than its substance', and another, in similar vein, said, 'I suppose the main achievement has been the publicity
the Urban Programme has got. The brand name "Urban Programme" is fairly well known and I would say perhaps not deserved.'

Evaluation: the administration of the Programme at local government level

Within the general topic of the local administration of the
Programme, the following were the issues most frequently raised
by respondents:

1 difficulties arising from inadequacies of the local administration:
    (a) a lack of organization or interdepartmental co-ordination;
    (b) insufficient anticipation of the Urban Programme circular and a lack of planning to enable the machinery of administration to come into play rapidly on receipt of the circular;
    (c) inadequate budgeting arrangements in some departments;
    (d) doubts in the minds of some officers about the effectiveness of councillor involvement in the Urban Programme;
2 difficulties arising from external constraints imposed by the Home Office and other government departments in the regulations governing the administration of the Programme;
3 problems involved in mounting capital projects once approved due to escalating costs (especially in the building industry), an inadequate compensatory inflation factor in Urban Programme grants, and the difficulty in some areas (particularly the North East and London) in getting builders to tender at all for some capital works;
4 difficulties arising from the reorganization of local government in addition to the reorganization of personal social services, and the necessity for new machinery and channels of communication to be developed;
5 the degree of administrative structure and policy developed for the administration and use of the Urban Programme;
6 the internal effects of the Urban Programme on the local authority by means of increased interdepartmental discussion and co-ordination and heightened debate about improved assessment of need and new ways of meeting it;
7 the involvement of voluntary organizations at local level;
8 local authority administration and voluntary organization involvement as seen by voluntary organizations;
9 the cost effectiveness of the Urban Programme for local authorities and voluntary organizations and whether the effort involved in making submissions was worth the benefits direct and indirect that would accrue.

That the body of this evidence on local administration consists in large measure of comments about difficulties and problems involved does not *necessarily* imply that such problems were, in the minds of respondents, the most significant features of the Urban Programme, but rather that, in any wide-ranging discussion of such a piece of machinery, problems and criticisms tend to provide more scope for complaint than smooth-running does for praise. A number of these issues can pass without further comment since they have no long-term implications; others require some elaboration.

Difficulties arising from the inadequacies of the local administration

Within the structure provided by central government, the efficacy and success of the Urban Programme was, in large measure, determined by the local authorities' inventiveness of attitude, determination, and the particular procedures brought to bear on it at the levels of local government and voluntary organizations. Indeed, the point was often made within central government departments that the Urban Programme was in essence a *local authority* programme, with central departments acting largely in the role of enablers. It is of interest, therefore, to examine what seem to local authority officers and members to be the problems and difficulties they faced in putting the Programme into operation. In this context it is noteworthy that, while much of what has been written about the Urban Programme has concentrated on the constraints imposed by central government (*The Times* 14.4.1971; 6.4.1972; *Community Action* 1972; Holman 1971; *Spectator* 21.10.1972), comments from respondents in local government were, more frequently, on the problems caused by the inadequacies of local organization or administration in one form or another — statutory or voluntary — than on the difficulties imposed by central government constraints.

Foremost among the local difficulties affecting the use of the Programme adduced by local government respondents were those arising from the inadequacies of organization and interdepartmental co-ordination.

In general, it was thought that there was insufficient co-operation and co-ordination between social services and education departments (the main users of the Urban Programme) to make the fullest use of the Programme and exploit its potential for interdepartmental initiatives. Second, that as a result of this very few interdepartmental projects were emerging. (The fact that a departmentalized response to the Programme is now seen by a number of respondents as a failure — or at least a disappointment — reflects the fact that the Programme is viewed in many quarters as a potential instigator of cross-departmental effort.) Third, the overall running and management of the Programme was seen to be inadequate by a number of officers as a result of the lack of appropriate machinery, and, fourth, local authorities were seen on occasions to fail to respond quickly enough to government circulars, so leaving themselves insufficient time to prepare bids adequately.

There is considerable evidence, therefore, from within local authorities themselves, that the administration of the Programme at local level is often not as smooth and efficient as it might be (and this excludes the important issue of the involvement of voluntary agencies by local government which is considered later). The sorts of factors mentioned above must, at least to some degree, detract from the successful utilization of the Programme on the ground and lend some support to Teresa and George Smith's remark that '...developments at the centre are sometimes not helped by the creaking machinery at local level' (1971).

Difficulties arising from external constraints

It is probably not surprising that, when criticism has been levelled at the Urban Programme, it has most frequently been directed at central government. The role of central government is not only the clearer, it makes an easier target. (The exception to this has been the criticism levelled at local authorities over their involvement of voluntary agencies — a topic dealt with later.) Little of this criticism has, however, tried to take into account, from the local authority's point of view, the difficulties imposed on local administration by centrally-imposed rules and regulations. As noted above, there was a greater volume of scepticism among respondents themselves about the efficacy of local administration than about central constraints.

The most frequent complaint about external constraints concerned the difficulties of being able to budget adequately for the 25 per cent local authority contribution for Urban Programme projects. Such difficulties were seen to arise most frequently from the timing of Urban Programme circulars and the fact that the commitment to meet the 25 per cent local authority contribution (on an *unknown* total sum, since the total actually involved would not be known until the final approvals were issued) had to be made at a time when it was not possible to make compensating savings and a consequent continual call on contingency funds. Another complaint was that the sheer novelty of some Urban Programme projects made costing a difficult business.

Another difficulty raised on a number of occasions was that, by its very nature, the Urban Programme was incompatible with any attempt by the local authority at long-term planning. This complaint is rooted in a broader issue (indeed, one of the major bones of contention in the Urban Programme) which is dealt with when considering central government policies (see Chapter 5): it is the requirement that projects submitted for urban aid should not be ones that the local authority has already considered, drawn up, or included in its main programmes. The general point has been made before: '...the Government's insistence that local authorities should not use the grants to subsidise regular work which is already timetabled has often led to a desperate scraping around to initiate projects for which to claim, a process which is the absolute antithesis of good planning' (Smith 1972 : 645). Local authority reactions to this requirement in general are examined later in this chapter, and concern here is with the views of our respondents as to how this requirement affected the local administration of the Programme. On the whole, the impression was given that most authorities did not undertake to meet this requirement in any absolute or literal sense, but some considered it to be sufficiently serious to cause problems for long-term planning. In general, however, it was thought that the Urban Programme was accommodated in existing plans fairly easily by most authorities either because they ignored this particular requirement or because the Urban Programme commitment was so small as to make no inroads in existing plans and budgets.

A third external constraint which sometimes made the local administration less smooth running than it might have been was the time restriction imposed by the Home Office deadline for submissions. During the early phases of the Programme, the time allowed for local authorities and voluntary agencies to devise and submit projects was very short but, in response to general pressure

from local authority associations and some voluntary organizations, this time period was extended to some six months in 1973. It
remains true, however, that the timetable of phases made no
allowance for the more extensive procedures needed in counties and
other large authorities and this may have acted to their disadvantage.

*The degree of administrative structure and policy developed for the
administration and use of the Programme*

The majority of authorities had not established any special
structures to administer the Programme, but the majority of
respondents in these authorities felt that the Programme would
have been more effectively used and exploited had such structures
existed.

Again, on the matter of whether specific policies had been established to exploit and govern the use of the Programme, all but one
department in one authority had either failed to do so or thought it
unnecessary. The exception was an education officer at divisional
level in a county council, who said that although the county had
developed no strategy, they had, within his division, adopted a
policy of innovation whenever possible. Of course, it is largely a
matter of definition as to what constitutes a policy (and it is
unlikely that a decision to innovate wherever possible would
constitute a policy in many informed people's minds) but at the
very least it might constitute the development of some purpose for
the use of the Urban Programme rather more specific than that of
'meeting social need' or 'alleviating deprivation'. In concrete
terms, therefore, a distinction could be drawn between an authority
that responded to each circular as it came along and drew up an ad
hoc and unco-ordinated packet of projects, and one where for
example Urban Programme projects were seen as an integral part
of a strategy of action for a particular area. In the latter (hypotheti-
cal) case it is possible to envisage an overall policy being developed
for an area where part of the policy (in the form of a number of
projects) would be seen to consist of Urban Programme funded
schemes. These schemes would be drawn up along with the rest of
the strategy in readiness for the arrival of the next Urban
Programme circular.

This more purposive use of the Programme does not contravene the 'rule' that Programme funds should not be used for projects already included in major local programmes since, in such an instance, they would not have been budgeted for in main programmes. However, there is one major drawback to such a constructive approach to the Programme, one that has been mentioned before and one to which a number of respondents alluded when discussing local policies for the Programme: it is that the 'lucky dip' aspect of the Urban Programme is antithetical to any attempt at long-term planning. It is one thing to devise projects for submission to the Urban Programme as an integral part of a broader strategy; it is quite another to get them all approved, or even some approved. Failure to do so (of which there is an 83 per cent chance)[2] leaves an important hole in the overall strategy. A number of respondents commented along these lines, pointing out that it was impossible to devise policies for the use of the Programme in the absence of any central government strategy, taking into account the temporariness of the Programme and the high chances of not gaining grant approval. For the rest, response to the Programme was either ad hoc or in order simply to use it in the context of existing departmental policies and to further those policies.

Such evidence adds much weight to the view that the Urban Programme has failed to generate anything other than an ad hoc and unco-ordinated response to the problems it set out to tackle and that, in the absence of a more clearly defined central government policy, no local strategies can be developed, and the Programme must perforce remain little more than a financial channel for the minor redistribution of resources to deprived areas.

The internal effects of the Programme on local authority administration

Notwithstanding the rather dismal picture painted above, it has been shown (Edwards and Batley 1974) that the Urban Programme can give rise to benefits other than through the direct provision of projects on the ground, by way of stimulating new thought about ways of meeting need, of widening the debate about policies for 'deprivation', and of extending and improving the degree of

[2] Up to and including Phase 9 an average of one out of every six projects submitted was approved.

interdepartmental co-ordination of debate and action at local authority level. The general topic of the unintended benefits of the Programme is discussed at more length in a later section of this chapter but an aspect of it, relating to local administration, is taken up here, i.e. the extent to which (if at all) the Programme has inspired further interdepartmental discussion and action.

It can be argued that, since the Programme operates across a number of departmental fronts and involves activities within the realm of a number of departments at both central and local government level, it could and should act as a stimulus to activity that is *not* departmentalized, but rather recognizes that both the problems that the Programme is aimed at and the actions necessary to solve or alleviate those problems involves an intermeshing of the responsibilities and activities of a number of discrete departmental fields. This is a topic upon which a number of respondents expressed views, and the great majority were of the opinion that the Programme had in fact led to an increase in interdepartmental co-ordination.

The involvement of voluntary agencies

If there is one aspect of the local administration of the Programme that has caused more criticism and comment in literature than any other inside or outside local authorities, it is the involvement by local authorities of voluntary agencies.

A great deal of evidence was provided on this general topic both by respondents in local authorities and by the voluntary agencies themselves. The discussion of their comments has been divided into two main sections, the first dealing with local authority evidence and the second with that from non-statutory agencies.

The involvement of voluntary agencies: local authority evaluation

Evaluations of voluntary agency involvement can be classified into four general types, each of which can be subdivided:

(a) criticism of local authority involvement of voluntary agencies
   — inadequate local machinery for voluntary organization involvement
   — only established agencies 'in the know' are involved

— general criticism of local authority involvement of voluntary agencies and suggestions for improvement;
(b) expressions of general satisfaction with voluntary agency involvement
— general expressions of satisfaction
— specific examples of successful involvement;
(c) constraints upon effective involvement
— institutional constraints
— time as a constraint;
(d) criticisms of and lack of sympathy with voluntary agencies
— criticisms of voluntary agencies or the quality of their submissions
— wariness of voluntary agencies on the part of local authorities.

In the specific criticisms of the authorities' involvement of voluntary agencies, the two most common features were the lack of adequate local government machinery to achieve this end, and the view that only well-established and non-radical agencies were involved by the local authorities, the more radical organizations either not being kept adequately informed or being positively discouraged (Holman 1969; *Community Action* 1972; Bourne 1972; Smith 1972; Adeney 1972; Holman 1971).

In the context of criticisms of local authority involvement of the voluntary agencies, the most frequently-made suggestions revolved around the need for authorities to do more by way of encouraging agency involvement and specific suggestions as to why and how this could be done. Comments ranged from the fact that an authority had been 'off-hand in its public relations with voluntary organizations', and the view that voluntary organizations ought to be more closely linked with the authority and a joint package of submissions made, to the view that the Home Office should make it mandatory to involve voluntary agencies, and (a frequent comment) that authorities had simply made little attempt to involve agencies.

On the more positive side, there was a not insubstantial volume of comment to the effect that the involvement of voluntary agencies was being achieved with some degree of satisfaction. Successful arrangements specifically cited included the use of the local Council of Voluntary Service as a channel of communication or the establishment of a voluntary organization liaison committee or similar piece of machinery. Overall, however, there were more comments from local authority offices critical of local procedures *vis-à-vis* voluntary agencies than there were expressing satisfaction with these arrangements.

On more neutral ground, some respondents emphasized the difficulties involved in effectively communicating and working with voluntary agencies. Such difficulties were of three kinds, resulting either from the wide geographical areas to be covered or from the great variety of agencies that might want to be involved, or from the lack of time. This last was the most frequently-mentioned difficulty — that even with the six months now allowed for submission it was often difficult in the time to contact voluntary organizations and encourage them to submit bids in time for them to be considered by officers, vetted by committee, and submitted to the Home Office.

There has been much criticism of local authorities over the way they involved voluntary agencies in the Programme, both from such agencies themselves and from other commentators (*The Times* 1971; Hudson 1974; Harrison 1975; Smith 1971). Local authorities have understandably been less willing to air in public such criticisms as they have of voluntary agencies but it would be unusual if there were not some misgivings about voluntary agency involvement on the part of some local authority officers and members.

There were two general areas of concern over voluntary involvement expressed first in terms of criticisms of certain voluntary agencies themselves and the quality of the submissions they made, and, second, in terms of a general wariness of voluntary agency involvement in areas that have traditionally been the province of the statutory services. Interestingly, this latter feeling was given far more expression in Labour-controlled authorities (even among officers) than in those that were Conservative-controlled. Unfortunately, it is not possible on the evidence available to state with any certainty whether or not such expressions of adverse sentiment reflected feelings that were positively detrimental to voluntary agency involvement in practice.

The involvement of voluntary agencies: voluntary organization evaluation

Almost all voluntary agency respondents both at local and

headquarters level commented on the involvement of voluntary organizations by local authorities, though the specific areas that concerned them differed to some extent from those given expression by local authority respondents. In summary these areas were touched upon by comments concerning:

— the distribution of the circulars to voluntary bodies
— the general level of communication between local authorities and voluntary agencies
— the general relationships between local authorities and voluntary agencies
— the procedure of prioritizing bids before submission to the Home Office
— the effects of local authority departmentalism
— the local role of the Council of Voluntary Service.

Some of these issues can pass without further consideration; others require more comment.

The process of the distribution of circulars to voluntary agencies was one that came in for considerable criticism. The majority of local authorities in the sample were criticized for the unsystematic and dilatory fashion in which Programme circulars were distributed to voluntary agencies. Many agencies either received the circular too late to take effective action before the deadline, did not receive it at all, or heard about it only on 'the grapevine'. Most local Councils of Voluntary Service received copies from the NCSS (and most Community Relations Offices from the CRC).

If this is a reflection of the situation generally up and down the country, it seems a highly unsatisfactory means of communicating information, essential for voluntary agency involvement, to the agencies themselves. It can amount, as one of our respondents commented and as was suggested in Chapter 4, to a rationing of funds by ignorance.

There are, in theory, two means by which this situation could be improved, though one is fairly impractical — but, given the political will, not impossible. The first, as a number of respondents suggested, is to make it a requirement on local authorities to distribute the circular to all known voluntary agencies in their area.

The alternative possibility would be for the Home Office itself to take on the responsibility of sending the circular to as many voluntary agencies as possible. This would not be without difficulties — especially if distribution were to be ensured to all the less well-established agencies as well as the well known ones (a function that the NCSS and CRC can perform in any case) but could be effected by means of widespread advertisements in the national and local press inviting requests from voluntary organizations for a copy of the circular.

It has to be added that the Home Office, in all recent circulars, has strongly urged local authorities to pass information on to voluntary agencies but, it would appear, without sufficient success to ensure the fullest involvement of non-statutory agencies seen by most of those involved (not least the government departments) as an important aspect of the Programme.

Closely related to the topic of the distribution of the circular was the more general one concerning the level of communication about the Urban Programme between local authorities and voluntary organizations. Again, with only one exception, the comments from voluntary agencies were generally critical of the way in which authorities kept agencies informed on all aspects of the Urban Programme. Even when voluntary agencies had heard about the latest phase of the Programme (from the local authority or elsewhere), they complained that they were not apprised of the progress of their submissions or of the priority ranking attached to them.[3]

The views of local agencies on this topic were reflected by representatives of some of the major voluntary agencies: Shelter, Age Concern, Pre-School Playgroups Association, Task Force, National Council for Social Service, and Young Volunteer Force. All spoke of the need for more, and more effective, communication about the Urban Programme between local authorities and their voluntary bodies.

The single greatest body of comment from voluntary agency respondents concerned the general quality of relationships between local authorities and either a particular voluntary organization or voluntary organizations in general. Such comment reflected the feeling that the local authority was unsympathetic to the particular agency ('we shall not make a submission under Phase 11 because

---

[3] It should be added that the issue of communication between local authorities and voluntary organizations has also been the subject of an exchange in the House of Commons between Mr Selwyn Gummer, M.P. and the then Home Secretary, Mr Carr (Hansard 14.6.1973: cols.1689-90).

we have no confidence that the authority will back us — it's in the council minutes that they won't help us any more'; 'we had bad relations with the local authority until they discovered we weren't all Marxists'); or to voluntary work in general ('the local authority is unwilling to accept/does not encourage voluntary bids'; 'the Labour council is suspicious of voluntary organizations'; 'Labour wants all the glory for itself — they're not interested in voluntary organizations').

Two further sources of irritation for voluntary organizations are the process of ranking all submissions to the Home Office, both authority and agency bids, into a priority order as requested in the circulars, and the inconvenience (and sometimes difficulties) imposed by the departmentalisation of local authority activity.

A number of voluntary agencies complained that they were not made a party to the ranking process, and one claimed that this had become a source of some friction between voluntary agencies and the authorities. This is no doubt just one aspect of the more general issue of communication and co-operation (or lack of) between voluntary agencies and local authorities, but it can be identified as a specific cause of friction, or at least of mistrust, in so far as, as long as voluntary bodies do not know what priority ranking has been attached to their bids, there is always the suspicion that the authority's own projects have taken precedence in the list. The fact that this suspicion might be unfounded is, of course, irrelevant in the absence of any manifest demonstration of the contrary.

The issue of departmentalism can be divided into two parts. The first is that, though much voluntary activity does not fall neatly within the purview of any one local authority department, the machinery of submission is such that projects must be channelled through one department. The consequences are that the voluntary body must — whatever the real nature of its project — 'present [its] projects in terms of the area of interest of one department', or search out the most sympathetic department (a process requiring not a little skill and knowledge of the authority), or take pot luck with one department in the hope that they will be prepared to carry it to committee. A concomitant of this situation, as one respondent pointed out, is that local authority departmentalism acts as a barrier to innovation, which should know no departmental boundaries.

The second consideration is that different departments may have different views about voluntary bodies, and while education (say) may take a sympathetic view, social services may be quite obdurate. This may not matter if a project has an education content; it certainly will if it is oriented more towards the social services.

The evidence presented above reflects, as accurately — and adequately — as possible, those issues relating to the local authorities' involvement of voluntary agencies that appeared to most concern the voluntary organization respondents. It should be added that these agencies covered a very wide range of concern and of style, from social-work oriented old people's groups, to fairly militant radical community groups. It hardly needs to be said that the radical groups were more critical of local authorities than the others, though, as the evidence shows, the overall weight of opinion from the voluntary agencies was critical of the statutory agencies and unsympathetic towards them. This general criticism can be traced to various sources: the role and area of concern adopted by some of the more radical voluntary agencies will often put them on collision courses with local authorities (though this is a very important and necessary role: much *can* be achieved by challenge and conflict); in part the criticism reflects a seemingly inbuilt distrust about local authorities on the part of some agencies; and it is partly due to the *generally* very poor level and quality of communication between statutory and voluntary agencies at local level, which can only engender mistrust on both sides. These then, represent the views — or particular evaluations — of the local administration of the Programme by those concerned with putting it into effect. Clearly, if one sets out to invite comment and criticism that is precisely what will be received — and, in this instance, in abundance. Similarly, no programme or policy can be administered at any level with such a degree of perfection that no-one will be dissatisfied about some aspect. What is important is that the process of discovering this dissatisfaction provides the opportunity for airing constructive criticism, for showing to what extent concerns felt in the isolated context of one authority or agency are in fact shared by others, and for pointing out those areas where improvement is possible.

Evaluation: the administration of the Programme at central government level

The summary of the evaluations of central government administration is presented under the following heads:

1 views on central government administration generally
   — lack of strategy and policy, the 'lottery effect'
   — central government's project selection procedures
   — timing of the operation
   — inefficiency of central administration
2 views on the provision of information
   — need for fuller and clearer statements and guidelines on policy and central UP strategy
   — need for more explanation of project selection procedures
3 views on the requirement that submissions be new and unplanned
4 possible improvements in administration
   — the possibility of direct voluntary agency submission to central government
   — the possibility of block grants rather than specific grants
   — other improvements.

At the outset it must be said that the great majority of respondents outside central government were largely ignorant of the procedures adopted by central government for the selection of projects to be aided. This is neither surprising nor a reflection on them since central government has never made these procedures publicly explicit, though it should be added that the general framework of selection, that is, the farming out of bids by the Home Office to interested departments, could have been ascertained by a telephone call to the relevant division of the Home Office. It is this latter aspect of the overall selection procedure that came as a surprise to many respondents, who thought that the complete selection procedure was conducted within the Home Office. The sheer complexity of the actual project selection processes within different government departments, the different procedures adopted by those departments, and the absence of any clear definition in these procedures have been outlined in Chapter 4. No doubt if the knowledge of the details of these procedures had been in the possession of our respondents, their comments on the central government administration might have been more incisive and precise. As it is, they leave unscathed many of the details of administration which a deeper awareness might have led them to question.

Views on central government administration in general

The most frequently-voiced comment about central government administration from respondents (and in published material about the UP) was concerned with the apparent lack of any clear strategy or policy statement on or identity of the Programme, and with the consequences of this. Indeed, if there could be said to be one general criticism of the Urban Programme more common than any other, it would be that the Programme has seemed to be all things to all men; it has appeared to lack clarity, purpose, and definition. Whilst the money it provides is welcome and useful, its recipients have frequently asked 'just *what is* the UP trying to do?' (*The Times* 6.4.1972; Holman 1971; *Quest* 1973: 4080-83).

This uncertainty was reflected in many of the comments given by local authority officers and councillors and was clearly recognized by several of the central government officials interviewed. Only among voluntary organizations, both at local and headquarters level, did this seem to be less of an issue, either because they thought they knew what the Programme was about or because it was an irrelevant question as long as the money continued to appear to fund the sorts of activity that they thought important.

The general misgivings about the Programme are not met without some sympathy within the Home Office. It was agreed by two of the officials principally concerned with the administration of the Programme that it lacked clarity and precision of purpose and both of them adduced as the reason for this the continuing uncertainty over the future of the Programme and the lack of any definite political statement about what its life span was likely to be.

'The UP has been in a state of uncertainty for some time. Notwithstanding the fact that it has a statutory basis and that we have made fairly long-term commitments, it is still true that the future of the Programme has never really been certain and this general air of unsureness has stultified the scope for any real initiative and has discouraged any deeper thought and deeper effort in developing the Programme.'   (Senior Home Office official)

The next most frequently-mentioned area of concern was the more specific one of the selection of projects for grant approval by central government departments and the acceptance by central departments of local authority priority ranking of bids. The wider issue of the clash between local and central government priorities within the Urban Programme is considered later in this chapter; it is a matter of concern here in so far as it reflects local authority views about the central administration of the UP. Criticisms ranged from the view that the Home Office appeared to ignore local authority priority ratings, to the demand that, when the selection departed from a strict adherence to local authority priorities, the 'Home Office' should offer an explanation, and to the view — expressed by a number of voluntary agencies — that 'Home Office' selection procedures were unfathomable and apparently irrational. In addition, one Deputy Director of Education wanted to know what these 'National considerations which may override local priorities' were — a reference to the UP circulars that on occasions have cited national purposes or considerations as reasons for not always being able to adhere to local priorities (Home Office 1972:para.6; 1974: Annex C). It is a reasonable question but one to which the answer might have to be so detailed, involving an explanation of the basis upon which projects are actually selected in the different departments, that the Home Office — or any other department — would be unlikely to offer a comprehensive reply (see also Bennington 1971).

The local authority respondents were not the only ones to comment on the central administration of the Programme, and it is of interest to examine what some Civil Servants had to say about their own job.

First, there was the issue of the lack of follow-up on projects, which had aroused the concern of some voluntary agencies (as well as some, though fewer, local authority officers). As a corollary of this, the question was raised as to why there had been no attempt to provide the means by which lessons learned and experience gained in using UP funds could be disseminated or shared by others (for example, by spreading the knowledge and experience gained by the people in local authorities and voluntary agencies in setting up UP projects through some sort of broadsheet, UP newsletter, or annual report). No single reason was given but it is clear that a combination of circumstances — small staff complement, the uncertainty over the future of the Urban Programme, the difficulties imposed by the interdepartmental nature of the Programme, the absence of a *professional* Home Office interest in the areas covered by the UP, and Home Office officials' unwillingness to seem to be taking initiative in areas possibly within the responsibility of other departments — all these played a part. Two quotations from Home Office officials give some indication of these above points:

'If you set up a broadsheet or a newsletter, then you need a commitment to the future, you need a certain sureness about the future, and you need to be sure that it is a virgin field you are moving into, that you do have new things to say that can make an original contribution, that it is proper to enlarge, that you won't be running up against other departments. Maybe, in my time, the UP has been too timid ... But the real frailty of the UP is its complete lack of certainty; its lack of structure means that you are in mortal peril if you go out into the field and make big promises if in fact at the same time you do not know what you can and what you cannot promise, what you must avoid, what you are positively going for.'   (Senior Home Office official)

'Yes, I think it is a matter for regret [that no feed-back mechanism has been set up] though I think it would not have been possible to do this well, with the staff complement we have had. You would also have to be sure that you only reported on things that were worthwhile reporting on and that you are not endlessly pushing out reports and broadsheets just for the sake of it.'   (Home Office official)

On the question of central administration in general, however, the predominant feeling among Home Office officials was that, given the small size of the staff quota, the administrative task had been carried out fairly well. There was one aspect of the process, however, that did inspire comment: it was that of ministerial involvement in the administrative process. For Home Office Civil Servants, ministerial interest and involvement must be important elements of the administrative process.

In the early days of the UP there was considerable and persistent (and fairly detailed) interest in the Programme from the 'top of the office', but, as the political sensitivity wore off, as political danger points were passed, and as the Programme got into its stride, interest waned and officials were left freer to oversee the Programme's general running.

However, there is one point in the process when ministerial involvement must be invited by officials. This is when the final list of project approvals is sent to the Minister for his consideration and approval. Successive Ministers have taken varying degrees of interest in this process, some requiring only minor changes, others rather more extensive ones (sometimes in the course of fulfilling 'promises' made during ministerial visits to towns, or because a Minister might have taken a particular interest in one town or one project, or because for political reasons he wants to ensure that a little extra goes to one town or another). During Phase 9 of the Programme, the Parliamentary Under Secretary of State at the Home Office (Mr David Lane) asked to retain the approval list for a while, and requested that in future phases he be given two weeks to go through the list in detail. Commenting on this particular occurrence, a Home Office official pointed out that ministerial intervention might be more effective and constructive if it took place throughout the process of selection and approval rather than just at the end.

In addition to the administrative process itself, central government officials also commented on two aspects of the structure within which that process took place. The first of these was inter-departmental co-ordination at central level. That there is little real interdepartmental co-ordination on the Programme and virtually no truly joint-departmental activity has been shown in Chapter 4. The majority of Civil Servants agreed that this was the case and, with varying degrees of enthusiasm, welcomed the idea of an increase in interdepartmental activity. Only within the Home Office, however, did there seem to be any real enthusiasm for seeing more co-ordinating activity put into practice.

Allied to the question of interdepartmental co-ordination is that of the role of the Home Office itself in the Urban Programme and the suitability of the Home Office as the co-ordinating department. On the whole, there appeared to be general satisfaction among the Civil Servants, both in the Home Office itself and other departments, with the part played by the Home Office and its appropriateness for the task of co-ordination. The main reason adduced was that, alone among the involved departments, the Home Office had little professional involvement in areas that might be considered relevant to the Programme and could therefore act as mediator between the other departments. Before leaving this topic, it is worth noting the comment of an informed non-Civil Servant on the position of the Programme within the Home Office.

Mr Mark Bonham Carter, Chairman of the Community Relations Commission, when asked in interview about this, said:

> 'The Home Office has never been a department which has seen itself as an initiator. It has always seen itself as a wicket-keeper to catch the ball that goes by. And, therefore, they are being asked to do something which is not altogether in tune with the spirit of the department. Now this may be an excellent way of infusing a new spirit in the department, but it presents certain psychological problems for those who are responsible for running it.'

Views on the provision of information

To return to the evidence of local authority respondents, the second main area of concern about central administration as far as they were concerned — and one that worried a large number of voluntary organizations — was that of the quality and quantity of information flow between central government on the one hand and local authorities and voluntary agencies on the other. Two aspects to this issue were raised (by a number of officers and councillors): the first, closely reflecting the concern about the lack of strategy or policy on the Urban Programme, was the expressed need for more guidelines from central departments about the general direction and purposes of the Programme — a need which, if fulfilled, would enable them (local authorities) to give more direction to their own efforts in relation to the UP (see also Smith and Smith 1971); and, the second, that the Home Office should give more information about its project selection procedures and especially about the criteria used to select projects for approval. This issue has been dealt with above and need not be elaborated upon here. On the reverse side of the coin, however, it should be noted that an almost equal number of local authority respondents expressed satisfaction with the quality and quantity of information provided by central government.

Such was not the case with voluntary organizations, which almost universally condemned the lack of information they received from central government, about both the general UP issues and the details of submission and selection. This in large measure is a reflection of the situation whereby local authorities are considered by central government departments not only as the intermediaries for the channelling of funds to voluntary agencies but also of information.

When this point of information flow was taken up with Home Office officials, it was agreed (by both the Assistant Secretary and the Principal) that there was a need for more consultation with local authorities, both directly and through the local authority associations, but that lack of opportunity had prevented this from happening more fully in the past.

Views on the requirement that submissions be new and unplanned

There is an anomaly for local authorities in one of the UP requirements imposed by central government administration. This is the 'Catch-22' situation whereby, though projects submitted should be important enough to go 'to the roots of deprivation' (and, it might be added, important enough to attract a 75 per cent central government subsidy), they must not be ones that the local authority has already thought up and put into its planned programme. The contradiction is obvious, and a number of local authorities complained about or commented on it. The great majority of both officers and members, however, said either directly or by implication that they ignored this regulation, and very few maintained that their authority tried to abide by the rule by drawing up projects either on receipt of or in anticipation of the programme circular rather than submitting those that were 'already on the books'.

The practice of submitting projects already planned (and possibly already included in local programmes), whilst often seeming to be justified (for otherwise the Urban Programme is simply providing a higher rate of central government subsidy for low priority work), has attracted the criticism that many authorities are simply using the Programme to fund work that they would have carried out themselves in any case and are thus simply saving on the rates by using the higher subsidy attaching to UP grants (Smith and Smith 1971; Holman 1971; *Community Action* 1972).

Possible improvements in administration

One final aspect of central government administration that was discussed was of possible improvements that the respondents would welcome. Discussion of improvements centred on two specific points: first, whether voluntary agencies should be able to submit projects directly to central government without having to go through the local authority (and either receiving 100 per cent central funding or finding 25 per cent themselves: see also Ball 1971; Smith 1972); and, second, whether a block grant system to local authorities was thought to have advantages over the present project-specific grant.

Evidence from local authorities on the first point was equally divided between those in favour of direct funding and those against. The main argument in favour of direct submission was that it would save a great deal of work (or 'bother') for local authorities. A qualification was often added however to the effect that voluntary agencies should still consult with the local authority to prevent duplication of effort. This was also the most frequently advanced reason for keeping the present arrangement. Other reasons given were that local authorities were in a better position to assess voluntary organizations and their bids, that local authority/voluntary agency co-operation was an important feature of the Programme, and that local authorities needed to keep a watchful eye on voluntary activity in their area.

These points are largely in accord with the 'Home Office view' on this point. The prevailing view of officials is best summed up in the following comment from the Assistant Secretary with responsibility for the Programme:

'My main counter-argument when this question has arisen before is "how would central government deal convincingly with all the applications that would come in?". I do not see how central government could dish out grants to voluntary organizations without some consultation with local authorities. If one did have such consultations then the views given by local authorities might be very different, if they did not have a financial stake in the project. Then if one holds the view that the UP should somehow be a relevant response to deprivation in areas of special social need for which local authorities ought to be taking a responsibility, then any decisions by central government ought to have some regard to the local authority's general plan for the area. The only alternative would be to have some central agency dishing out money to voluntary organizations on quite different criteria. That would imply a greater central commitment to community work, community development, and community action and I wouldn't have thought that that yet seems to be the case.'

Again, the then director of the Voluntary Service Unit within the Home Office felt that the present arrangements were not the right way to give money to voluntary agencies and that some entirely different procedure was necessary (outside the Urban Programme), but that: ' ... under the present rules and structure of the UP there is no other way of doing it. The Programme is an agreement between central and local government and I think many voluntary organizations do not understand this.'

That the Programme as it stands is an arrangement between central and local government that simply does not allow of direct voluntary agency involvement is not of course for many voluntary organizations a sufficient reason why in the future it should not do so. Most voluntary agencies, not surprisingly, had something to say on the issue. As with local authorities, opinion was equally divided for and against direct submission, but there was a significant distinction between local and headquarter agencies in their responses. The great majority of local agencies expressed themselves to be in favour of direct submission while the majority of headquarter offices were balanced against it. The reasons for these different divisions of opinion were made clear in the amplifying statements that, at local level, reflected the general frustrations experienced by local groups in having to submit through local authorities and, at head office level, reflected the wider view (that local authority/ voluntary agency co-operation was of fundamental importance) that might be expected of workers not embroiled in the immediate task of trying to establish projects on the ground.

Specific grants like urban aid have the advantage of ensuring that funds are spent in accordance with certain central government dictates and can be used in direct pursuance of certain central government policies.[4] They have the disadvantage of appearing to usurp local government's freedom to set its own priorities within the wider central policies. For this reason such specific grants

4 It must be added, however, that in this respect — as in others — the Urban Programme is peculiar in so far as the advantages accruing to central government by the use of specific grants have to a large extent been sacrificed by an allocation system which gives greatest weight to local authority priorities thus producing the worst (or best) of both worlds.

are, understandably, not entirely welcome among local authorities. A possible alternative system of grant aid, which might conceivably be more attractive to local authorities, is that of the block grant. In UP terms this would simply mean that selected authorities would be given a lump sum for expenditure in deprived areas rather than have to submit and get approvals for and spend the grants on specific projects. The arguments for and against such an alternative were well rehearsed in the evaluations of local authority respondents. Opinion was again fairly evenly balanced, but with a slightly greater weight in favour of block grants. The most frequently-cited arguments in favour of a block grant system were that it enabled local authorities to decide their own priorities (though the present UP allocation system does not rule this out) and that it reduced the level of central government intervention; the most frequent arguments against it were that service departments might lose the money (because it would not be specifically earmarked for their use), that there *should* be imposed certain national priorities, and (this was put forward surprisingly frequently by local government officers) that local authorities could not always be trusted to spend the money wisely and in the best interests of the deprived. (It is noteworthy that such comments came from local government officials and not from Civil Servants.)

The above section, which has evaluated the central administration, points up the major areas of concern at all three levels of involvement and complements the previous section on local administration. Together they provide an overview of the Programme at both levels of government by those involved in it.

Evaluation: local and central government priorities

Notwithstanding that prime importance is attached to local authority priority rating in the selection of projects for approval by central departments, the Urban Programme as a whole presented some local authority officers and councillors with the potential for a clash between the operation of locally-determined priorities and central government intervention. This issue was raised above in relation to the discussion of block grants as opposed to specific grants, but it was also raised by a number of local authority respondents as a significant issue in its own right. The weight of opinion that was concerned about the apparent usurpation of local authority autonomy was twice as great as that which was, by and large, content with the degree of central intervention inherent in the Programme. In the latter instance, three main reasons were given for the acceptance of central intervention. The first was that the direction of funds by central government allowed local committees to channel funds into deprived areas or immigrant areas — action which, if seen by the local electorate as the result of local determination, would incur hostility and opposition among ratepayers. To this extent it allowed local politicians to avoid the consequences of politically unpopular action. The second saw the justification for central intervention in the need to take a nation-wide view of the problem, something that local authorities could not do. And the third saw it as a useful means of promoting schemes that would otherwise have a low priority within the authority.

The concern over central intervention was less specifically articulated and, on the whole, simply reflected the view that the incursion of central departments into the traditional preserve of local autonomy was a thing to be resisted. Secondarily, and less frequently, it was adjudged that different authorities had different problems and should therefore be left free to determine the most appropriate local solutions.

Within the Home Office itself, central intervention was defended. It is worth quoting from one official's response since it sheds rather a different light on the issue:

'So long as local authorities find the priority listing of projects difficult or embarrassing or controversial, and so long as they are under pressures that they cannot rationally meet, then I think there is a stronger case for central government to have its own perspective generally and perhaps within an area too. There is plenty of evidence that some local authorities do find prioritization difficult, some send in separate prioritized committee lists, some do not prioritize the list at all, some send separate local authority and voluntary organization lists, and some dodge the issue by having "joint equals". All this reflects an admission in a way in local government that they would like central government to play a stronger role.'

This in part reflects the view that the Urban Programme enables local politicians to escape the consequences of unpopular decisions and indicates that to an extent some authorities *are* so using it. It also indicates that the abrogation of responsibility to central government for the selection of projects may be used locally as a means of avoiding internal friction between committees and dispute between authorities and voluntary agencies.

Evaluation: the Programme and voluntary agencies

Much has already been said about the administrative involvement of voluntary organizations in the Programme (see pp.190-96) but, beyond this, the more general issues of the role of voluntary agencies in the Programme and its significance for them were also raised (see also Harrison 1975).

The most frequently-made point on this general issue was the importance of the Urban Programme for voluntary agencies and the need, therefore, to concentrate more of its funds on them. For voluntary organizations the Urban Programme is a significant source of funds, increasingly so as money becomes tighter. Over recent years their various alternative financial sources have been rapidly eroded. For some, the funding of voluntary agencies was seen to be the most important function of the Urban Programme.

Set against this, however, was the concern expressed by some local authority officers over the financial and other implications for local authorities of the existing and possibly increasing level of funding for voluntary agencies. Of relevance to this were the possible direct financial implications for local authorities of meeting 25 per cent of the costs of voluntary projects, and possibly 100 per cent of the costs in future years; doubts were expressed about the efficacy of voluntary effort; and complaints were made about the amount of work involved for officers in working up voluntary bids into a 'reasonable' form.

The most extensive comment received on the role of voluntary organizations in the Programme came from the then director of the Voluntary Services Unit in the Home Office — probably the person in central government most directly concerned with the activities of the voluntary sector in general. He felt that, while two years previously voluntary agencies could concentrate on innovatory and experimental projects and the sort of work that local authorities could not or would not do, the change in economic circumstances over the past few years — circumstances that have affected the voluntary sector as much if not more than others — meant that innovation had become a luxury few could afford. There was no longer any guarantee that money would be forthcoming to continue and consolidate innovative efforts and the result might therefore be a great waste of money and effort. The need now, as far as the voluntary sector was concerned, was not innovation but more funds simply to continue with their basic tasks. It had, the director felt, been easier for voluntary organizations to get grant aid for innovatory and unusual work than for the day-to-day running of their operations and this, in the present circumstances, was misconceived because there was a growing danger that some agencies simply would not be able to maintain their operations at all, let alone continue with experimental work.

It seems clear, therefore, that, while the Urban Programme has in the past provided an important source of funds, enabling the voluntary sector to carry out innovative schemes, it has become even more important as a means of sheer survival and this alone might argue for a greater concentration of Urban Programme resources on the voluntary sector. Given the present structure of the Urban Programme, however, the view of local authorities on this issue cannot be ignored and account may have to be taken of some degree of opposition from them if such a shift in the direction of funds was contemplated.

Evaluation: improvements in the Programme and its future

This final section of evaluation looks to the future of the Urban Programme in one fairly specific and three more general matters: first, the likely future of existing UP-funded projects; second, ideas about what sort of project the Programme should focus upon; third, reactions to the idea of increasing the size of the Programme; and, fourth, suggested improvements for the Programme in the future.

Though the suggestions made by respondents for future improvements or amendments to the Programme were subsequently overtaken by the recasting of the Programme in 1977, they are recorded here because they represent the legacy of views about central and local government co-operation in the implementation of an area-based positive discrimination programme resulting from the experience of those involved in administering such a programme.

Programme funding is for a five-year period in the first instance for revenue projects and for the running costs of capital schemes[5] with the possibility of renewal for a further five years if this is desired.[6] However, sooner or later (after five years in some cases and ten years in others) the 75 per cent government grant will terminate and some decision will have to be made by local authorities about the future life of their own and voluntary organizations' projects, for which they at present (1977/78) meet 25 per cent of the costs. The issue of the future of UP-funded projects was raised with local authority respondents. Clearly, in many cases it was too early to say with any degree of certainty what decisions might be made about specific projects and the climate of uncertainty over public expenditure restrictions also made prediction hazardous.

The single most frequent response looked favourably towards the continued funding by the authorities of all projects when Urban Programme grants terminated, though some had reservations about the condition of local authority financing when the actual time for a decision came. In all these cases, however, it was the intention that all projects, both local authorities' and voluntary agencies', should be continued with 100 per cent local authority funding. A further group of respondents felt that, while some projects would be continued with local authority funding, others — often after a review of their success or otherwise — might be terminated. Another group felt that it was unlikely that their authority would be prepared to meet the full running costs of voluntary agency projects for which they currently met 25 per cent of the costs. In these cases it was felt that either the projects would terminate or alternative resources would have to be found by the operating agency.

Moving to the three more general topics, the first of these — ideas about what types of project the Urban Programme should focus upon — can be despatched fairly quickly. Responses usually

---

[5] A grant is generally paid for the life of any loan taken out for capital expenditure.

[6] As the first grant approvals were made in late 1968, this position had already been reached for a number of projects and at the time of writing a number of specific applications for renewal had been received at the Home Office. However, despite promises of guidance to local authorities on renewal procedures for the previous year, none was forthcoming, and policy on renewals remained to be decided. However, blanket extensions on all renewable projects were given until the end of the financial year 1975/76.

reflected the area of concern of the individual, and almost all mentioned the types of project currently financed by the Programme. The most frequent responses were calls for more innovative projects, more community-action style projects, more accommodation for the homeless, and more concentration on immigrant projects. Apart from these, the list consists of individual suggestions such as 'more day nurseries', 'more home-school links', 'more neighbourhood law centres', etc.

Most people who commented on the issue of an enlarged programme were in favour of an increase in the level of funds,[7] but many who thought that the Programme should be enlarged added reservations or qualifications. Others took it as axiomatic that an increase in funds would be beneficial. Among the qualifications or reservations added to responses otherwise generally in favour of an increase were that such an increase should not be at the expense of more central government intervention, that an increase in the level of grant aid from 75 per cent would also be needed, that an increase, while welcome, would require an expansion of staff resources, and that an inherent danger in an expanded Urban Programme would be that there would be less selectivity of projects and therefore a greater chance of 'unworthy' projects being funded.

Response within central government departments was more measured and non-committal. Assistant Secretaries in both the Department of Education and Science and the Department of Environment were in favour of some increase, but only a modest one on the grounds that the Programme was fundamentally about providing seed-money for innovation, or that since solutions to urban problems did not lie in special projects only limited funds should be committed to them.

A smaller number of respondents (all in local authorities) were more critical of an increase in the size of the Urban Programme. The reasons given were that the Urban Programme already pre-empted the freedom of local government to implement its own priorities and an enlarged Urban Programme could not but extend

---

[7] Such comment as there has been about the scale of the Urban Programme in the press and specialist journals has, without exception, drawn attention to its inadequate size and the need for enlargement (*The Times Educational Supplement* 1969; 1975; Bennington 1971; *The Times* 1971; 1972; *Community Action* 1973; *Guardian* 1973; Price 1974; Jenkins 1972: 56).

this (for them) undesirable consequence, that it would impose an undue burden upon local authorities in terms of additional work in involving voluntary agencies and additional resources of manpower and buildings, and that it was doubted whether it would be right for local authorities to expect the Urban Programme to meet more of their responsibilities. Whilst only the second of these reasons would appear to be a *necessary* concomitant of an enlarged Urban Programme, all can be seen to reflect genuine anxieties for local authorities concerning such an enlargement.

The respondents' evaluations of the large number of facets of the Programme and its administration recorded in this chapter suggest in themselves certain areas where alterations in structure, regulations, or administration might prove beneficial. Besides these, however, a number of specific suggestions for improvements were made, some reflecting the criticisms already covered, others supplementing these. The greatest single number of comments concerned the need for more direction and explicitness in the Programme. Taken together they included needs such as firmer policy directives from central government, a more definite framework, clearer and explicit parameters, a narrowing down of the range of and more direction to the phases of the Programme, and an explicit statement of selection criteria on the part of central government departments.

The second most frequently-suggested improvement was the need for evaluation and consolidation of the experience gained from the implementation of Urban Programme projects. There was a much stronger representation of voluntary organization respondents among those alluding to this aspect. Their main concern was that there had been no corporate accumulation of knowledge and experience from the Programme, which, in itself, in tangible terms, is evidenced only by a (large) number of discrete projects. Such a situation, it was felt, could be overcome by the creation of some forum (such as an Urban Programme bulletin) for the collection, exchange, and dissemination of knowledge and experience.

The third most frequently-suggested improvement was an extension in the time allowed either for the submission of projects or for their implementation after approval. Five respondents went further than to suggest improvements in the existing structure of the Urban Programme by formulating — in varying degrees of detail — other means of administering the Programme or alternatives to it.

These schemes are described below because they represent important and constructive comment on possible alternatives for the
future of the Programme.

A two-stage submission procedure

It was suggested by a councillor in a London borough that, in order
to reduce the amount of abortive work involved for local authorities in drawing up project submissions (only a proportion of which
would be approved for grant aid), a two-stage submission procedure might be adopted. A preliminary list of projects would be
drawn up in rough outline only and with only rough estimates of
costs and would be submitted to the Home Office. This department, in consultation with other central departments, would vet the
list and select those projects that, in principle, it would be prepared
to approve and would inform the local authority that it might
proceed with a more detailed submission of those projects but
would be advised not to proceed with the others. The local
authority could then draw up the necessary detailed submissions
for projects approved in principle in the knowledge that a higher
proportion of them (if not all) would be approved for grant aid.
This final short-list would then be submitted to the Home Office in
the normal way. Such a procedure could well have the advantage of
reducing the amount of abortive effort for local authorities and
voluntary agencies. It may indeed have other advantages, but also
some possible shortcomings.

A concentration of funds to be more freely spent

A second alternative procedure was put by members of one education department. It was argued that there should be a concentration
of funds in larger amounts on a limited number of authorities,
possibly selected by central government departments. Funds would
be allocated with the requirement that they be spent on schemes to
aid the deprived in their areas of concentration, but not on the basis
of detailed project submissions. The allocation of such funds
would be treated as an experiment and the results of the expenditure in the various recipient authorities would be monitored,
evaluated, and compared. This is an argument, therefore, in favour
of a block grant system (as opposed to a specific grant) but with

the added dimension that results would be compared and lessons learned for application in future fund allocation.

Two-stage submission with stipulated expenditure ceilings

A more detailed suggestion for a different allocation system was put by members of another education department. It was suggested that for each phase of the Programme (or each year, since it might be difficult to fit more than one phase into a twelve-month period) the total national funds available would be computed and a proportion of these funds would be notionally allocated as a block grant to all local authorities with areas of deprivation (as decided on the basis of social indicators or on a capitation basis: details were not spelled out). Each authority would then be invited to submit, in outline, projects for the alleviation of deprivation to the value of the ceiling of their notional allocation. Discussion would then be initiated between local authorities and relevant central departments and the latter would decide, on the basis of outline submissions and subsequent discussions, whether an authority had made a sufficient case to use the money notionally allocated to it. If it had, it would be free to proceed with the projects with grant aid. If not, the money allocated to that authority would be returned to the national 'kitty' for redistribution in the same or subsequent phases. It was admitted that this could prove to be a time-consuming and cumbersome procedure, but not impossibly so if the approval cycle was a twelve-month one.

An Urban Development Commission for non-statutory bodies

The then director of the Home Office Voluntary Services Unit said he would like any future development of the Urban Programme to be along the lines of the existing Rural Development Commission, and for it to channel funds solely to non-statutory agencies. Such a scheme would be designed to overcome what he saw to be one of the main problems of the existing situation — not only with the Urban Programme, but more generally with central government funding of voluntary agencies — namely that there is no way by which central government can channel funds directly to *local* voluntary agencies. Most activity in alleviating deprivation was, he felt, carried on at the local level, but it was an implicit tenet that central government funds, if used to assist voluntary agencies, should go to the headquarters organization of such agencies, and that funds for local voluntary agencies should come from or through local authorities. There was, possibly, a working arrangement, he thought, sanctioned by the Treasury, that central government money should not go into local voluntary activity; neither was there any structure to ensure that they received funds. Nor even could money easily be channelled to the local level through the headquarters of voluntary agencies, because they were frequently organized on a federal basis, with each local organ financially autonomous.

An 'Urban Development Commission' would therefore be a funding agency for national and local voluntary effort in the field of urban deprivation. In outline some of its features would be that: it would have an independent board; it would have a guaranteed long life (the Rural Development Commission had been in existence for sixty-six years at time of writing); it would have a broad brief — say 'to improve the quality of life in urban areas'; it would itself decide where the main areas of need were at any particular time, but might be fed with information on local conditions by the National Council of Social Service, and would leave the more systematic work in the field of urban deprivation to the new Comprehensive Community Programmes and other initiatives. Such a scheme is clearly an alternative to the existing Urban Programme rather than a refinement of it and leaves open the question of how local statutory activity in the field of deprivation might be funded and carried forward.

Strategic plans to combat urban deprivation

The final one of this set of suggested refinements of or alternatives to the Urban Programme is the idea put forward (as a personal view) by a secretary of the Association of County Councils. He proposed that all local authorities that contained areas of deprivation (selected on the basis of social indicators, other information, and consultation) should draw up plans to combat deprivation over the next five to ten years, the next three years, and the forthcoming year. These plans, which would include some costings, would be submitted to central government and, if approved, would attract a 75 per cent grant, as with the present Urban Programme. In this way the aims of any particular set of plans to alleviate urban deprivation would be specific to an area and designed to meet the needs of that area while at the same time reflecting central government's overall priorities. In drawing up its plans, however, it would be important for a local authority, as a strategic social planning authority, to consult with and involve as far as possible all relevant voluntary agencies. It was felt, however, that a prerequisite to the drawing up of 'strategic deprivation plans' may be the existence within an authority of a corporate planning unit or some form of corporate planning structure since a number of different departments would have an interest and be involved in any subsequent implementation.

Conclusion

To say that the Urban Programme is a product of the beliefs of its administrators is not to suggest that individual assessments are directly influential. We saw that even central government 'policy-makers' may have quite different personal views about the nature of the problem of deprivation that the UP (in terms of its output and public statements: see Chapter 8) is apparently concerned with. One conclusion is that officials perceive and *respect* the constraints of, for example, the Programme's size, timing, administrative capacity, established channels of information and approval, and organizational autonomy, often in spite of their own criticism of the lack of planning, co-ordination, and feedback. The dissonance between personal views and departmental practice is one important measure of the strength of institutional inertia. But, within these constraints, the assumptions and evaluations of the operators of the Programme have helped to determine its course and, accretively, even its structure, 'providing an inventory of legitimate logics and axioms, and a repository of acceptable vocabularies, legitimate motives and laudable ambitions' (Dillon 1976: 58). In these terms, we can see the Programme as an *arena* for the expression and furtherance of a variety of interests rather than as an *instrument* of pure and coherent policy. Given the variety of perceptions we have outlined, such an understanding begins to explain and even to justify the amorphous nature of the Urban Programme.

8 Programmes, policies, and problem definitions

The social and physical characteristics that go to make up the condition known as 'urban deprivation' are not new. It is only the label that is new. It is a phrase that entered the social scientist's vocabulary (and later the politician's) as a form of all-embracing label to describe the range of diverse and sometimes unrelated problems that were manifested predominantly in some of the large cities. More recently it has come to be associated with a number of social policies and programmes of positive discrimination, which have been referred to in Chapters 2 and 3. The phrase itself is not without significance — as is argued below — for the way in which its conception has influenced the development of thought, policy formulation, and programme construction in this area of social policy, and, if only by force of circumstance, the Urban Programme has come to be included, both by commentators (Price 1974; Meacher 1974; Barnes 1974) and politicians (Hansard 29.7.1974: cols. 237-53), amongst the initiatives influenced by it. In this final chapter, therefore, the Urban Programme is examined in the wider context of other government programmes and policies directed variously at inequality, poverty, the 'inner city', and urban deprivation, against the background of the developing debate about and changing conceptions of what constitutes 'urban deprivation', and, more generally, in the context of theoretical ideas about the social construction of social problems. There is a sense in which the Urban Programme has been peripheral to the developing debate about urban deprivation. Although reference has on occasions been made to 'social deprivation' (Hansard 27.7.1968: col. 40), 'deprived areas' (Home Office 1972), 'areas with acute social problems' (Hansard 22.7.1972: col. 253; 11.12.1972: col. 276), and 'areas with acute social needs' (Hansard 14.6.1973: col. 342; 24.1.1974: col. 1877), there has never been any attempt, as previous chapters have shown, to develop, clarify, or define the aims of the Programme or the problems to which it is addressed. While the Programme is generally assumed, as a result, to be a part of the total package of government initiatives directed at urban deprivation, it was born partly of the debate on immigration and race relations and has remained in essentials an exchequer subsidy to be spent on whatever — with central department sanction — local authorities and voluntary organizations feel at any particular time constitutes social need — more especially, social need among immigrants. It would therefore be inappropriate to judge the effectiveness of what is a very modest effort both in scale and intent against the sort of government activity implied and required by more recent conceptions of urban deprivation. There is another sense, however, in which the Urban Programme cannot meaningfully be isolated from other government initiatives and the debate on deprivation. It has already been said that, unavoidably, the Programme is seen as part of a package of programmes and policies; but in a more fundamental sense it has been a significant part of the development of ideas and activities in the area of urban problems over the past decade. Even though it has remained *in essence* a piecemeal subsidy programme, it cannot historically be isolated from what went before nor from what has developed since its inception. While its contribution to developing thought and ideas has been small (compared for example with that made by the Community Development Projects) it cannot be assumed either that its influence has been nil nor that it has remained completely outside the mainstream of developing thought and ideas.

There have been two divergent but complementary strands running through the earlier chapters of this book. On the one hand, the birth and development of the Urban Programme have been examined in the context of organizational, administrative, and structural constraints and opportunities. On the other, emphasis has been placed on the role of significant actors and the influence they have exerted on the Programme through their perceptions of the nature of the Programme itself and of the problems it was designed to alleviate. This latter theme will be developed somewhat further in the present chapter by looking at the variety of meanings that have been attached to the concept of 'urban deprivation' as the social problem that lies at the core of many area-based positive discrimination programmes, and at the policy implications of the way in which this social problem has been conceived or constructed.

The approach to social problems that sees them not only in terms of objective ('real') manifestations but also as in some measure social constructs is by no means a new one, but it is a particularly appropriate one with which to examine the notion of urban deprivation. As Becker (1966: 2) points out, the idea that social problems have both an objective and subjective element was developed as long ago as the early 1940s by Fuller and Myers (1941), but it is Becker himself who has done more than anyone else to explicate and extend the theme, especially in relation to deviance theory. In an often-quoted passage, Becker remarks:

'The central fact about deviance [is that] it is created by society. I do not mean this in the way it is ordinarily understood in which the causes of deviance are located in the social situation of the deviant or in "social factors" which prompt his action. I mean, rather, that social groups create deviance by making the rules whose infraction constitutes deviance, and by applying those rules to particular people and labeling them as outsiders. From this point of view, deviance is not a quality of the act the person commits, but rather the consequence of the application by others of rules and sanctions to an "offender". The deviant is one to whom the label has successfully been applied; the deviant behavior is behavior that people so label.'

(Becker 1963 : 9)

Though in dealing with the concept of urban deprivation we are not on precisely the same ground as Becker (since only a part of the complex of manifestations subsumed under that label is considered deviant), some of the ideas contained within his thesis can profitably be applied here. Thus, before a social manifestation can be called a social problem, it must be recognized and labelled as such by significant groups in the population. Further, before it becomes a social problem about which something must be done — that is, before it can enter the arena of social policy — it must be recognized by significant groups as being of sufficient importance (in terms of common humanity, or of the transgression of valued norms and standards, or as a threat to social order and stability)[1] for the State's apparatus to intervene for its mitigation. The question that such a formulation immediately raises — of who and what we mean by 'significant groups' — is not one that can be pursued in the present context, though, as far as the Urban Programme and its relation to urban deprivation is concerned, earlier chapters have at least shed some light upon it. Of more immediate concern is the point that can be teased from the above formulation: that, before any social policy can be formulated to alleviate, mitigate, or solve a social problem, that problem itself must be defined. The implications of this are not as simplistic and obvious as they might appear: defining the problem is *itself* a social process (a theme developed by Carrier and Kendall 1973) that results from the interaction and conflict between the perceptions and interests of the groups involved (in the present context, the inhabitants of deprived areas, voluntary groups both of the interest and promotional kind, other community activists, politicians, political parties, government departments, academics, the Government, etc.). And not only will the nature of the policy response be influenced by the way in which the problem is defined but, in contrast, the definition of the problem may well be influenced by what administrators and executors see to be possible, practicable, and expedient by way of policy response.[2] Thus, whilst in no way denying the real, objective existence of social problems (in this case, those manifestations labelled urban deprivation), it is argued here that these problems are also social constructs. Just as we construct our social reality, so relevant groups in society construct social problems, and before any social policy response can be formulated, the problem at which it is directed must be articulated and constructed in such a way as to make the response relevant

[1] For example the introduction of rent control in 1915 has often been ascribed to the threat to social stability and the war effort posed by the threatened strike of Glasgow munitions workers.

[2] It has been argued that the gross underestimation of the number of slum dwellings revealed by the 1967 House Condition Survey was at least in part due to previous under-reporting by local authorities wishing their estimates to be more in line with what they saw to be practicable and possible by way of the policy response of slum clearance and redevelopment (Berry 1974).

and meaningful (or at least, appear so).

Clearly, not all social problems are equally well articulated or constructed and the social construction of a particular social problem or group of problems will change over time and will differ from one group or interest to another. (Hence we can speak of poverty as absolute or relative, of the Welfare State as being institutional or residual, of homelessness as being the result of personal inadequacies or the operation of the housing markets.) We can now turn this approach to the examination of the social problems which have been labelled 'urban deprivation'. This has been done to some extent in foregoing chapters but here the conception and construction of urban deprivation is examined more systematically as it is manifested in the rationale behind and explanations for a number of programmes (including the Urban Programme) concerned with its alleviation. What becomes clear from such an exercise is the lack of clarity and precision in the social construction of urban deprivation and, in consequence, the diversity and imprecision of the instruments designed for its alleviation.

Notwithstanding that the Urban Programme has never developed a coherent policy or a clear definition of what is meant by 'social deprivation', 'areas of deprivation', or 'acute social need', it is still possible to see at what particular issues (and client groups) its money has been directed by means of an examination of the suggestions made in successive circulars for projects to submit and, on occasion, the rationale given for such suggestions (see Chapter 3). These circulars can be revealing not only of the intended beneficiaries of the Programme and the reasons for the promotion of certain types of project but also, in consequence of this, of prevailing departmental conceptions of what constitutes 'social deprivation' or 'acute social need' in the context of the Programme.

Thus, in promoting nursery schools and classes and day nurseries in the first phase of the Programme it was argued that:

'In the case of nursery schools and classes there are educational grounds in addition to social, health and welfare considerations which would make the proposed extra provision desirable. Day nurseries can make a significant contribution in areas of acute social need by providing for those pre-school children who have a special health or welfare need for care during the day. These would include the children of unsupported mothers, children who need temporary day care because their mothers are ill, and children whose health and welfare may be affected by home conditions such as gross overcrowding or lack of opportunity to play with others.'   (Home Office 1968: para. 6)

The argument for day nurseries, therefore, was couched not only in terms of useful compensation for the disadvantages that might accrue from a 'poor' home environment (using 'poor' in a wide sense), but also in terms of health and welfare handicaps *per se* — about which there is nothing necessarily urban or area-based, though it could be argued of course that physical, mental, and emotional handicaps impose an additional burden in the struggle to compete in the urban environment. In addition to such social and health reasons, nursery education was promoted on more positive educational grounds — though these were not specified in the circular.[3]

In Phase 7, among the other types of project promoted, but for which, in addition to a simple mention, there was again some reasoning given, were family, neighbourhood, and legal advice centres. Of family advice centres it was said: ' ... these are aimed at detecting families at risk and preventing family breakdown. They are principally designed to cope with the problems of youth and juvenile delinquency' (Home Office 1972: Annex G para. 3). The circular continues, with reference to neighbourhood advice centres:

' ... [they] offer a wide range of advisory and assistance functions to all members of the community, ... and provide a means of communication with the local authority. Their function varies from simply giving information about where to go for advice on specific problems to actually giving advice and assistance.'
(Home Office 1972: Annex G para. 4)

And of legal aid and advice centres the circular said:

'People living in deprived areas often need legal help in matters relating to their daily lives, for example, landlord and tenant disputes. The statutory legal aid and advice scheme covers some

---

[3] It can be assumed, however, that the educational arguments in the Plowden Report (1967) for more nursery provision for 'children in socially deprived neighbourhoods' were influential.

of these matters but, for various reasons, people in deprived areas do not make much use of it. One reason is that few solicitors practice in deprived areas, another, that people are often ignorant of their legal rights, fearful of the expense, and apprehensive of the whole legal process.'   (Home Office 1972:
Annex G para. 7)

Some of the assumptions behind the promotion of advice centres, especially legal advice (and aid), are therefore well-defined and are concerned with compensating for the lack of other provision (in the case of legal aid, the lack of solicitors in some urban areas).[4] In the case of neighbourhood advice centres, there must be an inherent assumption that the inhabitants of 'deprived areas' are less able to communicate any grievances or queries they may have to the local authority (or vice versa) and, in the case of family advice centres, argument is again (as with day nurseries) couched in terms of social pathology (delinquency and 'the problems of youth').

Yet again, in Phase 9 it was suggested that educational visits, 'nurture groups', and 'sanctuaries' might be established to meet the needs of slow learners in secondary schools or children with behaviour difficulties, reflecting once more a social pathology approach to deprivation (there being nothing inherently 'urban' about slow learners or children with behaviour difficulties). The same can be said about the promotion of projects in Phase 11 for alcoholics, the mentally ill, the mentally handicapped, the elderly, and the physically handicapped (Home Office 1974). In the same circular, family day centres, mothers' and toddlers' groups, child minding training schemes, toy libraries, and intermediate treatment schemes were all promoted on the grounds that they were: '… preventive projects directed towards the support of families, in which parents can be encouraged to participate and so to acquire deeper understanding of their own role as parents and of the needs of children' (Home Office 1974: Annex A para. 2). On the education front, the same circular suggested that: '… some authorities may wish to pursue a policy of positive discrimination by providing extra teachers in schools in deprived areas …' (1974: Annex A para. 9); and 'The appointment of staff able to help with the

---

[4] It should also be noted that there was a wider debate on the issues of legal aid and advice current at the time involving both Conservative and Labour lawyers, the Lord Chancellor's Office, and the Law Society.

problems of children in difficulties, e.g. teacher-social workers, counsellors or extra educational welfare officers, may also be considered' (1974: Annex A para. 9). And in the field of adult education, schemes to overcome adult illiteracy and for 'instruction in the domestic arts' were proposed.[5]

What does all this tell us about conceptions of the nature of urban deprivation prevalent during the life of the Urban Programme? The passages cited above from various circulars are not selective. They represent a catalogue of all instances where some reasoning is given for the promotion of particular types of project — as opposed to the many other instances where types of project have simply been mentioned but not justified — and as such they convey some idea of the sorts of problem and the sorts of client group which central departments involved in the Urban Programme have considered to be the appropriate 'targets' of programme funds. (Or, to use the phenomenological terminology alluded to earlier, they make possible some degree of insight into the way the social problem of urban deprivation has been constructed by some of the most significant actors involved: the administrators in relevant government departments.) With the exception of nursery education (for which it was argued that there were educational grounds), neighbourhood advice centres, legal aid and advice centres, and additional teachers for schools in deprived areas, both the client groups mentioned and the reasons given for the need for projects to assist them clearly reflect a concern, *albeit unconscious*, with people who are not necessarily deprived or disadvantaged because they live in 'areas of acute social need' or in areas characterized by 'overcrowding, poverty, high levels of unemployment, old and delapidated housing and rundown and poor environment' (Home Office 1973: para. 2), but rather people who are disadvantaged as a result of physical, emotional, mental, or psychological difficulties. In short, the prevailing conception of deprivation as illustrated in the circulars is one of social pathology and personal inadequacy rather than of any disadvantage, deprivation, or inequality resulting from (or represented by) some of the more important features of the areas to which money was to be directed, as defined in the circulars themselves. At the

---

[5] In the field of child education, of course, such recommendations were in direct line with those of the Plowden and earlier Newsom Reports.

very least, it seems a little strange on the one hand to describe recipient *areas* in terms of poverty, unemployment, and overcrowding and on the other to promote projects directed only peripherally at such problems and rather more directly at 'poor parenting',[6] 'the problems of youth', delinquency, slow learners, adult illiterates, alcoholics, the mentally ill, the physically handicapped, and battered wives.

It has been argued above that it would be inappropriate to judge the effectiveness of the Urban Programme against more structural conceptions of urban deprivation. It has been modest in scale and intent and has in practice proved to be a small social and educational welfare programme. This does not absolve it, however, from charges that it has involved some muddled thinking, that while it talks of poverty and unemployment it spends money on projects that, however worthwhile, are not directly aimed at these issues, and that for want of strong policy direction it has been the continual victim of departmental and sociological fads and fashions.

If the Urban Programme has failed to produce a coherent policy framework, and a clear diagnosis or construction of the nature and boundaries of the problems it is designed to treat, have the other programmes with which it has been associated by commentators and politicians fared any better in this respect? What can be learned about the nature of 'urban deprivation' and the changing constructions of it from these related programmes? Does any more thorough and vigorous analysis emerge from an examination of them? To answer these questions, it is worth looking briefly at the prevailing and changing conceptions of 'urban deprivation' as exemplified in the Community Development Projects, the Cycle of Deprivation (or Transmitted Deprivation) studies, the Inner Area Studies carried out under the auspices of the DOE, the Comprehensive Community Programmes and, most recently, the White Paper on *Policy for the Inner City*.

The aims of the CDPs have been variously stated. Greve notes that they are ambitious: ' ... little less than re-assertions of the fundamental ideals of social policy and of democratic politics'

---

[6] The projects promoted under Phase 11 for families and children (see above) closely reflected the concern in the DHSS with 'poor parenting', being an important link in the 'Cycle of Deprivation' studies promoted by Sir Keith Joseph when Secretary of State and since continued in that department jointly with the Social Science Research Council.

(1973 : 7); and he goes on to summarize the four main components as:

'i To improve the quality of individual, family and community life in areas with high levels of social need through programmes of social action related to local needs, resources and aspirations.

ii To increase the range of social and economic opportunities available to people living in the community.

iii To increase individual and communal capacity to create or take opportunities and to make effective and rewarding use of them.

iv To increase the capacity of the individual and the community to exercise self-determination of their own lives and control over the condition and use of the environment.'

(Greve 1973 : 7)

More succinctly, the CDP described its own initial conception as 'a neighbourhood-based experiment aimed at finding new ways of meeting the needs of people living in areas of high social deprivation' (Community Development Project 1974: 1). Underlying these initial conceptions of the aims of CDP there were, as the *Inter-Project Report* states, a number of basic assumptions about the nature and causes of urban deprivation.

Since the CDP was governmentally conceived, the assumptions must be seen as those prevailing within government departments (and primarily the Home Office) at the time of its inception in 1969, though it should also be recognized that, as recorded in the *Inter-Project Report*, they represent an *interpretation* by the Project's teams of governmental thinking. The underlying assumptions about the problems of urban deprivation which fuelled the CDP initiative as interpreted by the teams were that they ' ... had their origins in the characteristics of the local populations — in individual pathologies — and these could best be resolved by better field co-ordination of the personal social services, combined with the mobilization of self-help and mutual aid in the community (Community Development Project 1974: 1). It is hardly surprising (given the then conventional wisdom on the subject) that this conception of urban deprivation closely resembles that which, though unarticulated, has been shown implicitly to underlie the Urban Programme. Whereas the Urban Programme has proved to be a resource delivery programme, however, enabling the provision of more standard services, which in the main reflect a social pathology conception of deprivation, the CDP was conceived as an action-research exercise, which among other things would seek improved means of delivering services to the deprived. Such improvement (so the *Inter-Project Report* argues) would be brought about — in the tenet of the prevailing government conceptions — by better self-help and more co-ordination of locally-delivered services.

There can be no doubt that, when the first CDPs were established, most members of the action teams would not have demurred at the governmental conception of deprivation. Five years in the field, however, wrought a transformation, and the *Inter-Project Report* firmly rejects a social pathological approach to deprivation:

> 'Analyses of the wider context of CDP areas has led us to recognise what many social scientists have been asserting in recent years; that problems of multi-deprivation have to be re-defined and re-interpreted in terms of structural constraints rather than psychological motivations, external rather than internal factors ... the symptoms of disadvantage cannot be explained adequately by any abnormal preponderence of individuals or families whose behaviour could be defined as "pathological".' (Community Development Project 1974: 8)

It goes on to say, 'They [the project teams] have begun to develop perspectives which better account for the unequal distribution of both private and public goods and services, and provide explanations for the powerlessness of CDP populations to influence these distributions' (Community Development Project 1974: 23). Unfortunately, the authors do not proceed to elaborate what these perspectives are, nor to spell out the social policy consequences for rectifying the unequal distribution of private and public goods and services, nor to discuss the nature, context, and causes of the powerlessness of the populations in project areas. On the last of these issues, and in the context of a discussion of three models of social change, they merely recite that within a structural/conflict model of change, 'The problems are defined mainly in terms of inequalities in the distribution of power ... ' (Community Development Project 1974: 23). Such an entirely superficial analysis is, at its best, unfortunate, not least because this model in all probability provides a more realistic perspective from which to approach the issue of 'urban deprivation'. Simply to speak of 'inequalities in the distribution of power' is of course tautological rhetoric (power is *by definition* unequally distributed), and ignores the more important issues of, on the one hand, whether it is power, authority, influence, or control that is most salient, and, on the other, which of the many power models (e.g. Horowitz 1963; Dahrendorf 1959; Olsen 1970) provides the most useful device for an analysis of the reasons why social structures and processes act to constrain, to the greater degree, the implementation of choices and the taking of opportunities by populations in areas such as those selected for the CDP experiments.

Very different in conception, but no less relevant to the Urban Programme, are the studies in transmitted deprivation initiated by the DHSS and sponsored jointly by that department and the Social Science Research Council. The cycle of deprivation concept (as it was initially called) was first publicly articulated by Sir Keith Joseph when Secretary of State for Health and Social Services and is particularly germane to the UP since many of the ideas developed during its formulation, especially those on 'preparation for parenthood' (drawing on Bowlby 1965), had a strong influence on some of the projects promoted under the Programme (see p.225). Though placed within an all-embracing concept of deprivation, including 'poverty', 'emotional impoverishment', 'personality disorder', 'poor education attainment', and 'depression and despair' (Joseph 29.6.1972), the concept itself is more specific and concerns the transmission, from one generation to another, of family and personal characteristics that may be defined as social problems.

This, however, gives an over-simplified picture of the 'cycle of deprivation' as, during the development of the thesis, it has manifested in abundance the confusions and contortions of thought which, at the beginning of this chapter, it was suggested have been a feature of discussions about 'deprivation' and largely caused by the imprecision of the term. Thus, in the speech quoted from above and in subsequent talks on the issue, Sir Keith Joseph used the terms 'deprivation' and 'maladjustment' almost interchangeably,[7]

---

[7] For example: '...it seems in a proportion of cases, occurring at all levels of society, that problems reproduce themselves within families from one generation to another, and that there are some cyclical processes at work here by which some *deprivation* and *maladjustment* [our italics] is transmitted' (Joseph 27.3.1973).

and appears quite clearly not to have had in mind any form of structural deprivation, but rather emotional, physical, psychological, and health handicaps (leading to 'maladjustment'); however, subsequent research outlines (in the seven-year joint DHSS/SSRC programme) have quite firmly included structural factors such as low income, unemployment, and bad housing on an equal footing with delinquency and heavy and chronic dependence on social service agencies (Social Science Research Council 1974; Rutter and Madge 1976). True, all these features may be found in ecological association in some urban areas but, conceptually and analytically (and diagnostically for social policy purposes), it is less than useful to group them in this way. Even less useful is this gestalt approach in the context of 'transmitted deprivation' where it can lead to the inclusion in the same list of 'intergenerational continuities', of 'income', 'poverty', 'reliance on the social services', 'colour' (*sic*), and 'housing' (SSRC 1974). This is a long way from Sir Keith's concern with the family ('...the basis, sanctified by the main sources of our Western religious traditions for the healthy development of children': 29.6.1972), and with 'preparation for parenthood', and is difficult to reconcile with his assertion that 'transmitted deprivation' occurs at 'all levels of society'. It is certainly true that the children of poor, ill-educated, and insecurely employed parents will also tend to have low incomes, lower than average educational attainment, and poorly-rewarding jobs[8] but, for the purposes of formulating relevant and effective policies, it is both unhelpful and misleading to conceive of these issues as 'transmitted deprivations' as if the processes involved were the same as those in child-rearing practices.[9] The point appears so obvious, but it seems whenever the notion of 'deprivation' is raised it produces a severe atrophy in the corporate capacity to think and conceptualize.

The three 'inner-area studies' (in Birmingham, Liverpool, and Lambeth) were part of the DOE 'total approach' to the improvement of town environments generally and inner-city areas in

[8] They may, on the other hand, improve their housing position by securing better municipal property.

[9] Professor Peter Townsend, in a talk at the National Conference of the British Association of Social Workers, has more articulately criticized this thesis on similar grounds as '...a mixture of popular stereotypes and ill-developed, mostly contentious scientific notions. It had its roots in historical analyses which attributed blame for poverty to the poor rather than society' (4.1974).

particular. The three inner areas (one in each city) were selected because they displayed many of the characteristics associated with 'urban deprivation' or 'urban stress', and each of the three studies was conducted by a different group of consultants under the general auspices of the DOE. As might be expected, therefore, each study tended to concentrate on slightly different issues and conceived the framework of problems with which they were concerned in somewhat different ways. It is constructive in the present context therefore to examine what each study had to say about the complex of issues to which the term deprivation has been attached.

The Lambeth study was the one that made the most explicit use of the term 'deprivation' itself and, again, it is used interchangeably with others and hence imprecisely. Thus, in the introduction to one of their reports, the consultants state: 'There has in recent years been growing recognition, first that *deprivations* or *handicaps* [our italics] are often cumulative or reinforcing and, secondly, that such multiply-deprived families are probably concentrated in the inner city' (Department of the Environment 1975b: 1). And at this point deprivation (or multiple deprivation) is seen to be separate from, or not to include, poverty or low income: thus, 'The original intention was to study multiple deprivation alone. The subject has been broadened out, as indicated in the title, partly because poverty is obviously linked with other kinds of deprivation ... ' (DOE 1975b: 1).

Later on in the report, however, where an attempt is made (in the results of a household survey) to correlate components of deprivation with other characteristics such as household structure, a measure of low income is included *as* one of the components along with overcrowding, lack of housing amenities, contacts with friends or relatives, holidays taken, 'evenings out', leisure activities, disability, unemployment, and rapid job turnover. It was discovered (not surprisingly for an area with a high proportion of municipal housing) that while low income restricted leisure activities and was associated with unemployment, the housing measures were less closely related to other 'deprivation' features. (In an earlier part of the report, low income had been found to be closely related to stage in the life (or household) cycle,[10] but the latter had been more closely related to other components of

[10] Echoing Rowntree's findings in his beginning-of-the-century study in York.

'deprivation' (leisure activities, disability) than had low income itself.) Thus, while the survey is of considerable interest for what it reveals about some of the characteristics and activities of the area population, it again suffers from a confusion of ideas attributable to loose use of the term 'deprivation'.

Though the studies in Birmingham (DOE 1975a) and Liverpool (DOE 1974) cover almost as wide a canvas, they lay far less emphasis on pathology and on personal handicap. The term 'deprivation' is less in evidence (somewhat more so in the Birmingham than the Liverpool study) and, where it is used, the trap of 'Gestalt sociology' is largely avoided and both studies identify the main underlying problem of their respective areas as one of low income and income insecurity. Thus, of Small Heath in Birmingham, it is said, 'The basic problem which people ... share to varying degrees is restricted opportunity or choice, determined by low household spending power' (DOE 1975a: 1), and, of the people in the Liverpool area, that they experienced ' ... a sense of alienation, brought about by poverty, a lack of power to influence events affecting their home lives, and feelings of insecurity about their future' (DOE 1974: 3). These are probably closer approximations to the most important problems of such areas though it is perhaps unfortunate that in the latter case they have been couched in the more fashionable than illuminating terms of 'alienation' (from what?) and 'power' (over what, precisely, and under whom?).

The Urban Deprivation Unit at the Home Office, as part of its review of urban deprivation in general and in the course of preparation of the Comprehensive Community Programmes (announced by the Home Secretary in the House of Commons in July 1974), commissioned from the Institute of Local Government Studies at the University of Birmingham a study of aspects of urban deprivation as perceived by local authority officers and other agencies in Birmingham and Nottingham (Stewart, Spencer, and Webster 1974). The report does not set out to present a clearer definition of deprivation but rather to discover the manifold interpretations of it to be found among a large number of local government and other officers with a very wide range of responsibilities. It argues that most local departments, even if they do not recognize or articulate the fact, are involved in some way in dealing with urban deprivation, and hence justifies throwing the research net so widely as to encompass (for example) fire prevention officers, librarians, directors of passenger transport, and baths managers as well as the more obviously implicated departments' respondents.

In common with the findings from the investigations in twelve local authorities for the present research (see pp.177-80), the work in Birmingham and Nottingham found that there was no consensus of opinion among local authority officials on the meaning of the term 'urban deprivation' and that the views expressed were either conditioned by the field of responsibility of the individual officer or were direct reflections of it. A number of recurrent theories or components of deprivation were, however, identified and the breadth of these clearly reflect the all-embracing (and hence imprecise) nature of the concept. Most frequently mentioned was the state of the physical environment and, in particular, the physical state of and lack of amenities in dwellings, and second in frequency was economic deprivation, chiefly interpreted as the problem of low income (Stewart, Spencer, and Webster 1974: 2-3) and associated with lack of job opportunity and unemployment. The other chief components mentioned tended to revolve around a social pathological view of deprivation so that for a number of officers it was largely to do with 'problem families' and was manifested by such factors as 'low intelligence, low social class, neglected and emotionally deprived children, inability to manage household budgets, illiteracy and family breakdown' (1974: 3). And another group of officers mentioned related but alternative indicators of a social pathological type such as 'anti-social behaviour, vandalism, juvenile delinquency, alcoholism, criminal activity and the number of mentally handicapped ... ' (1974: 3). Yet other groups cited the lack of community spirit or of an atmosphere of mutual self-help and interest, the lack of access to services and facilities, and the 'lack of power' of some individuals or families to influence their own lives (1974: 9). Again, echoing the findings of the present research, it is reported that, while many officers equated one of these dimensions with 'urban deprivation', others felt that deprivation implied a situation in which a number of these dimensions could be found located together in the same area (and hence the concept of multiple deprivation) and this again stresses another dimension of commonly-held views about deprivation — that it is an *area phenomenon*. It is not made clear in the report, however, (and probably not by the original respondents either) whether this is meant to imply *only* that a number of features that are commonly held to characterize deprivation are found together in the same area (as opposed to being widely scattered), but not necessarily affecting the same people, or, more than this, that they are found to affect the same people or *families* within an area. The two are very different, of course (in concept and policy implication), and to ascribe multiple deprivation to families and individuals within an area from the association of a number of area-based statistical measures is a classic example of the ecological fallacy, one unfortunate result of which has been the association of ethnic minorities with social problems simply on the basis that the two can be found in concentration in the same areas.

One further overlap between the findings of this report and those from the present research was the stress given (by respondents) to the fact that areas of urban deprivation were not only to be found within the inner city but were also present in large inter-war and post-war housing estates where lack of 'community spirit' and facilities were common features (see p.180 and Stewart, Spencer, and Webster 1974: 5).

One feature of 'urban deprivation' that has not yet gained a mention in this catalogue but to which the authors of the Birmingham and Nottingham study draw attention is its *subjective* and *relative* nature. A significant number of officers apparently suggested that deprivation was subjective to the extent that it was essentially a question of whether people *felt* 'deprived' or not, and was relative in so far as people compared their own situation with that of others they knew or with whom they had contact. This is not a dimension of the concept to which a great deal of space can be devoted here though it *is* one that should not be ignored. There is a considerable body of social theory that is of direct relevance to the subjective and relative aspects of deprivation (in particular, on reference-group theory: Merton 1957: 225-80; 281-386) and which could profitably be brought more directly to bear on any thorough investigation of the limits and components of the concept. This has already been done to a certain extent (Runciman 1966; Goldthorpe 1974: 55-8) but the field is far from exhausted and is still the subject of contentious argument. It should also be noted, of course, that this *subjective* notion of the relativity of deprivation is quite different from *objective* relativity as often applied to the concept of poverty (e.g. Townsend 1974), though of course 'deprivation' in any sense wider than poverty itself is just as relative in that there are not and cannot be (as with poverty) any *absolute* measures of it.

Apart from this commissioned review of local authority perceptions of 'urban deprivation', the Home Office Urban Deprivation Unit itself examined the concept and the implications of its various interpretations for the Comprehensive Community Programme (CCP). During the course of a three-year review, ideas within the Unit about the important and predominant features of urban deprivation shifted, and this is reflected in the shift of emphasis that has taken place in the design of the CCP's projects themselves.[11] As originally conceived, these were to be based on small (and 'deprived') urban areas selected jointly by the local authorities that had agreed to participate in the exercise and the Urban Deprivation Unit. It was later decided, however, that the programmes should not be area-based, but rather should be exercises in which the test authorities would (with central government help but no financial assistance) review those of their policies and priorities that were relevant to some conception of 'urban deprivation' with a view to identifying how a rearrangement of priorities as between existing programmes over the authorities as a whole might affect and alleviate those conditions held to represent 'deprivation'. There has occurred, therefore, a significant shift from seeing the causes, manifestations, and remedies of deprivation as being contained within finite urban areas to a recognition of its wider manifestations and implications.[12] Subsequent to the shift in thinking within the unit, or concurrent with it, has been the move away from viewing deprivation in pathological terms, to a conception that takes more account of basic inequalities in the distribution

[11] Of the original arrangements with local authorities only two have come to fruition.

[12] Particularly influential in bringing about this shift has been the recent work carried out at the Department of the Environment examining the distribution of census-indicators of deprivation over the country as a whole. Significantly, the ecological distribution of deprivation as measured by a number of indicators was found to be far less concentrated than had been assumed (DOE 1975c). The implication was that, even at the statistical level and even if they were effective, area-based programmes would exclude more of the 'deprived' than they would include. Similar results have been obtained in a study of the distribution of children who fell within the definition of those eligible for help under the Educational Priority Area programme. They also were far less concentrated than had been assumed (Barnes 1974). More substantively, thought has no doubt been influenced by the arguments put forward by the CDP teams (Community Development Project 1974) to the effect that solutions to urban deprivation cannot be found in area-based policies or programmes.

of goods and services. To what extent such a structural view with its more fundamental implications for policy can be effectively articulated in practice within the Comprehensive Community Programme remains to be seen.

In April 1977 the Secretary of State for the Environment announced that the Urban Programme was to be recast as part of a wider review of policies concerned with the inner city, and this review subsequently appeared in June 1977 in the form of a White Paper (DOE 1977b). The underlying aims of the new policy were fourfold:

'a strengthening the economies of the inner areas and the prospects of their residents;
b improving the physical fabric of the inner areas and making their environment more attractive;
c alleviating social problems;
d securing a new balance between the inner areas and the rest of the city region in terms of population and jobs.'

(DOE 1977b : 6)

And these major aims were to be effected through six specific programmes of action, to:

'1 give a new priority to the main policies and programmes of government so that they contribute to a better life in the inner areas;
2 strengthen the economies of inner areas as an immediate priority;
3 secure a more unified approach to urban problems;
4 recast the urban programme to cover economic and environmental projects and to increase its size;
5 review and change policies on population movement;
6 enter into special partnerships with the authorities — both districts and counties — of certain cities.' (DOE 1977b : 10)

This new policy direction was formulated largely on the basis of the series of consultants' reports from the three inner area studies (see pp.229-31) and incorporated the form of initiative that had been attempted with the Comprehensive Community Programmes. It is not surprising, therefore, that the description of the problem at which the proposals outlined in the White Paper were directed bears a close resemblance to the conclusions of the inner-area study reports and of the CCP. There are some departures, however, from preceding conventional wisdom. The components of urban deprivation (a term used with marked parsimony in the White Paper) are, as in previous formulations, numerous and varied, but the emphasis is laid upon economic decline and physical decay as well as on social disadvantage. Thus pathological formulations of urban deprivation appear to have given way, at least in part, to others based on social/structural and physical factors. Recognition is given to the fact that the inner areas vary greatly as between one local authority and another, and indeed even within authorities. They may be characterized nonetheless (says the White Paper) by economic decline, manifested by high proportions of household heads in semi-skilled and unskilled occupations, a loss of jobs in traditional industries and thus high rates of unemployment, and by an insufficiency of investment in new manufacturing. Second, they frequently display physical decay, in the forms of poor housing, old housing, high population densities, lack of amenities, much unused and derelict land, and a general aura of decay. Third, there is social disadvantage: many poor people, due not only to unemployment but also to low wages; concentrations of 'those least able to cope in society', among which the White Paper included the homeless, alcoholics, and drug addicts; too many badly-educated children and too many bad schools, and, finally, what the paper refers to as collective deprivation — a deprivation greater than the sum of its parts. To these three major types of deprivation, the White Paper adds a note on ethnic minorities, but is at pains to point out that, though there are frequently high proportions of ethnic minorities in some inner city areas, 'inner area problems and racial problems are by no means coterminous ... '.

It is also illuminating to compare the description of the nature of inner-city problems as contained in the Secretary of State's announcement in April 1977 with the earlier formulations in the Urban Programme. In 1977, the Secretary of State said:

'Over the past decade, inner cities have suffered a massive and disproportionate loss of jobs and a major exodus of population. Substantial ethnic minorities in some cities have added an extra dimension of difficulty. The old problems of poor-housing — and in some areas, congestion — have still to be overcome, but in many areas they have been joined by the new problems of high unemployment, decay and dereliction, unbalanced population structures with disproportionate numbers of the disadvantaged and the elderly, and an accompanying loss of internal morale and external confidence.'

(Secretary of State for the Environment 6.4.1977)

Almost a decade earlier, the first Urban Programme circular described potential recipient areas as marked by: ' ... notable deficiencies in the physical environment, particularly in housing; overcrowding of houses; family sizes above the average; persistent unemployment; a high proportion of children in trouble or in need of care; ... A substantial degree of immigrant settlement would also be an important factor, though not the only factor ... ' (Home Office 1968: para. 2). And again, five years later in 1973, the ninth circular described such areas as characterized by: ' ... overcrowding, poverty, high levels of unemployment, old and delapidated housing and a rundown and poor environment' (Home Office 1973: para. 2).

The White Paper certainly provides a more thorough and thoughtful analysis of the problems involved than many previous statements, but the quotations above indicate that while there have been some changes in emphasis over the past decade — the addition of population and job exodus and unbalanced population structure, a smaller emphasis on children in need of care, and some changes in terminology ('immigrants' becoming 'ethnic minorities') — the description of perceived problems has not changed a great deal over the past decade. Indeed, that the Secretary of State could describe as 'new problems' in 1977 some of the very same components that were included in the Urban Programme circular of 1968 does raise doubts as to how deep and thorough has been any rethinking about the nature of urban deprivation.

The truth of the matter is no doubt that the most obvious characteristics of inner-city areas have *not* changed greatly over the past decade — except perhaps in degree; but, if the unruly social constructions of these problems that ten years ago spawned inadequate solutions are not much less unruly today, then progress towards more effective policies might not be so advanced as we think. What is important, of course, is whether the problem as it is constructed provides clear guidelines for effective action. Whether this is the case with the 1977 White Paper will be examined shortly.

Attention has been focussed in this review of the conceptions of deprivation not on academic studies of the subject but rather on such notions as are found to be operational in practice and which result from or have significantly influenced specific government programmes or studies, because it is in this interface of thought and practice that the social and policy effects of the confusion engendered by the widely-varying conceptions of urban deprivation are most clearly exhibited. And what this review serves to show is that any policies or programmes that take 'urban deprivation' as their quarry without any clearer articulation of the components that might be open to amelioration are unlikely to be either realistically goal-orientated or even simply, indeed, effective. In actual fact, what appears to have happened, especially in the case of the Urban Programme, is that not only has there been an inadequate and imprecise construction of the social problems of urban deprivation (as pointed out above — see page 224) but that, no doubt in large measure as a result of this, the problem has been continually (and in large measure implicitly) constructed within and in terms of the exigencies imposed by the size, structure, and organization of the programme itself. It is as if the political (and perhaps moral) pressures to do *something* (and to be seen to be doing it) were so great that something *was* done, even in ignorance of what it was hoped would be achieved and how it would be accomplished. What is clear from this discussion is that the nature of the policy responses to urban deprivation have been strongly influenced by the social construction of the problem itself, and that, paradoxically, this construction has been in some measure determined by the exigencies of the programmes of positive discrimination.

Perhaps the most fundamental explanatory variable in assessing the form and function of the Urban Programme and of the other programmes with which it has been associated is, therefore, that of the context of problem-definition and construction, in which they were produced and within which they have had to operate. There are three dimensions to this question, each of which must be given due consideration in any future review of deprivation programmes and policies. They are, first, the primary issue of problem definition and construction itself (determining the inadequacies of the current construction or conception of 'urban deprivation' and how this construction must be amended in order that the policy responses to it can be more effective); second, discovering what are the implications of such a reconstruction for the policy tactics of area-based positive discrimination; and, third, the implications for the issues of corporatism and the co-ordination of policies and programmes. The three dimensions are interrelated, but the latter two stem largely from the first.

Sufficient has been said above to show that the current social construction of the social (and physical) problems to which the label 'urban deprivation' has been attached is too inadequate and imprecise to provide a goal or target for clear and *effective* programmes or policies. In consequence the Urban Programme (and, it can be argued, most of the other area-based positive discrimination programmes) has suffered for the want of goals that can be both stated clearly and achieved. At the same time, it is clear that the manifestations to which the label 'urban deprivation' has been attached are considered by many of the actors or groups involved (though not necessarily by all)[13] to constitute social problems — and, more, social problems of such a degree of 'unacceptability' as to warrant government attention. The very fact that such programmes as the Urban Programme existed bears sufficient witness of this. The key issue, therefore, is that, while the social problem is acknowledged, its social construction has been sloppy and inadequate. It follows, therefore, that as long as these manifestations are held to constitute a social problem about which government action should be taken, what is required is a reconstruction of our conceptions of what that problem constitutes. A careful disaggregation of the many manifestations of 'urban deprivation' is required before any thorough analysis or formulation of relevant and effective policies to attack the whole range of disadvantages and deprivations can be carried out. (Whether this was achieved in the policy review that resulted in the 1977 White Paper will be touched upon later.)

We know too little about the mechanisms by which social problems are thrust into public attention or into the government arena (though this is a growing area of interest among social scientists) and even less about the ways in which social problems are socially constructed, and why one particular construction will predominate

---

[13] No doubt most coloured people (or, in common but largely erroneous parlance, 'immigrants') would resent the imputation which is implied in the Urban Programme that they constitute a social problem.

in any given period. What can be said, however, is that particular constructions and conceptions of the causes of certain social problems will, in large measure, be determined by broader ideas of the nature of social structure and process (for elaboration see George and Wilding 1976). Thus, certain parallels can be drawn between conceptions of welfare as either institutional or residual, of the power structure of society as predominantly elitist or pluralist, of poverty as an inherent part of either the economic infrastructure or the culture of poverty, of the comparative wisdom of universal or selective welfare benefits, and of social problems (including urban deprivation) as being structural or pathological. The parallels may not always be close, but it is fair to say that whether we attribute urban deprivation to personal pathology or to social structure and process will depend, at least in part, on our broader view of the natures of social structure and process themselves.

In previous chapters, two polar explanations of urban deprivation (or the ways in which the concept has been socially constructed) have been used: the social pathology view and the structural view. In some respects such a bi-polarisation is misleading in as much as it overemphasizes two forms of explanation and undervalues others (such as life-cycle variations in income (Donnison 1974) and the culture of poverty), but it does provide a useful starting-point in the disaggregation of the components of 'deprivation' (see further Holman 1973). Unquestionably, in many towns in the country, areas of dilapidation exist, containing, in varying degrees, concentrations of social and physical manifestations that would be described as 'unacceptable' in any relatively affluent society. There is no need to catalogue them here: the reading of earlier chapters should have made them familiar. The fact that they are found in ecological association, however, is not an indication that they have common causes and will therefore be sensitive to the same remedy, be it an Urban Programme, a CDP, a Total Approach, or a CCP. Indeed, the association between them is not an indication, either, that they are each geographically concentrated, as recent census research has shown (see above). As an heuristic device in identifying the policy implications of the different ways in which social problems are constructed, the pathology/structural dichotomy will be retained. On the one hand we have manifestations of 'structural deprivation'. These are no more and no less than manifestations of the inequality of society — inequality in income and wealth, in housing, and in education — and it is in itself socially significant that, while few would disagree that we live in an unequal society, we have socially constructed the problem of deprivation in such a way as to sanitize the manifestations of this inequality by uniting them with other different (but sometimes related) manifestations such as delinquency, vandalism, illiteracy, mental and physical handicap, and even skin colour, and labelling the whole as 'urban deprivation'. We have then set about designing intricate research projects to discover what 'urban deprivation' is ('hunting the Snark' as one respondent put it) and spawning more and more small-scale, low-budget, area-based programmes to deal with the problem.

On the one hand, therefore, there are problems of poverty (financial poverty), problems of inequality in educational provision and motivation (on the part of both parents and children), and problems of inequalities in the housing stock and the distribution of and access to this stock. It hardly needs to be said that low-budget, area-based positive discrimination programmes are largely irrelevant, as effective instruments, in rendering significant changes in these three fields.[14] Each represents a different situation (which, at some stage, becomes defined as a 'problem') and each will be sensitive to and affected by radically *different* policies.

The disaggregation and reconstruction of the elements of deprivation is not therefore a matter simply of semantics but has fundamental policy implications. The fact that poor and poorly-educated people tend to be concentrated in particular areas of sub-standard housing is not a symptom of a common cause between deprivation in education and housing but simply the result of the operations of the housing markets in the three major tenure sectors: more than half of the total stock of dwellings is allocated not on a 'social need' basis but on criteria of financial resources and credit worthiness; the demand/supply ratio in the public sector is seriously out of balance in many large towns; and some local authorities still give emphasis to such moral considerations as social worthiness in allocation: the 'dumping ground' council estates in some areas are extreme manifestations of this (on public housing allocation see Central Housing Advisory Committee 1969).

---

[14] This is not to deny, however, that such programmes can and do bring some help to some people, or that they may have long-term and cumulative incremental effects on the direction of social policy and the choice of priorities within it.

The final conclusion of these processes is that the discriminatory (in the widest sense) practices of estate agents, flat agencies, building societies, and insurance companies serve to exclude those with low income and unstable jobs from all but the worst of the housing stock and possibly from owner-occupation altogether; they may be faced with long delays in municipal housing,[15] or a declining private rent sector (on results of housing allocation procedures see Greve, Page, and Greve 1971; Pahl 1970; Edwards 1973; Burney 1967; Harloe, Issacharoff, and Minns 1974; Murie, Niner, and Watson 1976). Given, therefore, that we have a large inheritance of housing in poor condition with inadequate facilities and within a poor environment, it takes no great skill to see why there is a congruence between the distributions of bad housing and of people with low income and insecure employment. Neither is it difficult to visualize the sorts of policy necessary to improve this situation: a continuing and much-enlarged programme of clearance and rehabilitation of dwellings and their environment, and a radical reappraisal of the means by which we allocate the social asset of housing. (DOE 1977c recognizes some at least of these issues.)

It is not within the scope of this report to examine the nature of the other two major dimensions, poverty and poor education, nor to suggest policies for their alleviation. There is already a sufficiently large body of knowledge about the scale and causes of poverty to make it possible to formulate more effective policies to reduce inequalities: for example, the reports of the Royal Commission on the Distribution of Income and Wealth (1975a; b) have charted the statistical pitfalls in assessing the extent of monetary inequality; Abel-Smith and Townsend (1965), Field (1973), and Syson and Young (1974) have all identified the demographic characteristics and primary sources of the income of poor households; Atkinson (1974) has examined the shifting patterns of income inequality in Britain; Nicholson (1974) and Kincaid (1973) have compared the differential effects of taxation and benefit systems; evidence on the question of the take-up of means-tested benefits has been well reviewed by Ruth Lister (1974); attention

[15] The prospects for many applicants of being granted council housing in an urban centre such as London are worsening rather than improving. A number of boroughs are not able to make any inroads into their ever-increasing waiting lists because other allocations (for slum clearance, other public works such as road building, and social need cases) are exhausting the available supply.

has been drawn to the higher marginal rates of taxation of poor people with children, resulting in the 'poverty trap' (Field and Piachaud 1971; Bull 1972); the arguments for a national minimum wage have been articulated by (among others) Hughes (1972); and Townsend (1975: Chap. 8) has highlighted some of the problems associated with a negative income tax system. The steps necessary in the field of educational policy to reduce inequalities in provision are also well articulated by the experts in that field (Central Advisory Committee for Education 1959; 1963; 1966; Halsey 1972: vol. 1; Gray 1975), though it must be ceded that, in so far as child and parent motivation is recognized as an important aspect of educational achievement, the necessary policy steps are less clear.

Quite apart from these issues of housing, poverty, employment and education there is a host of other and causally-unrelated social issues that have at one time or another been defined as social problems and all of which have on occasion been incorporated with the former under the umbrella of 'urban deprivation'. As explained above, they include issues as diverse as delinquency, vandalism, 'poor parenting', illegitimacy, illiteracy, mental and physical handicap, and children and old people at risk. Wife and baby battering have in recent years been added to the list. These represent the 'pathology' side of the structural/pathology dichotomy referred to above. They are social problems (in the sense that they are issues of concern for politicians, administrators, and professionals) as much as are poverty, housing, and education, but they are of a different order. They are perhaps in some ways linked — and even causally linked — with poverty, housing (Schorr 1964; Chapin 1961), and education, but in terms of practical social policy it is of limited use to assume common causes either between these pathologies or, certainly, between them and the more fundamental issues of inequality.

Though the move towards corporatism and co-ordination within local if not central government was under way before the advent of 'urban deprivation', the two have matured together and it seems likely that they have mutually reinforced one another. It is not hard to see why this might be so. Within the field of urban issues generally, the unanalytical use of the phrase 'urban deprivation' and the form of its social construction as a problem has subsumed under one convenient label a multitude of manifestations, which administratively are the responsibility of a number of different central and local government departments. It has also encouraged the view that all these problems are in some way interrelated (though such linkages as there might be have rarely been investigated thoroughly) and therefore require for their mitigation a concerted interdepartmental strategy. Co-ordination has thus become the by-word and vehicle for action and in the field of urban problems alone, quite apart from education, housing, health, planning, and the social services, a series of recent reports have called for the greater co-operation between departments and co-ordination of their programmes.

In the field of urban management the call for co-ordination has gone out from the three reports emanating from the urban guidelines studies sponsored by the Department of the Environment (1973a: 17-18; b: 42-4; c: Chap. 1). In the field of inner-city problems, the report of the Shelter Neighbourhood Action Project (1972) calls for more co-ordination at local and central level, and this theme has been taken up again in the design of the Urban Programme Neighbourhood Schemes and the Comprehensive Community Programmes. More recently, the need for more interdepartmental effort has been articulated by the Central Policy Review Staff (1975) in their call for a Joint Approach to Social Policy (J.A.S.P.) involving regular (six-monthly) meetings of ministers from the Departments of Education and Science, Health and Social Security, Employment and Environment, and the Home Office, periodic 'forward looks' at possible developments in the social field, improvements in social monitoring, and a series of research studies. It is difficult not to be a little sceptical about the possible benefits and advances that might accrue from more interdepartmental discussion (especially if, as usually happens, each minister turns up with his departmental brief), more research, and more data collection.[16] And, finally, the 1977 White Paper on the inner cities (DOE 1977b) commits the Government to the achievement of greater co-ordination. While there is certainly a need for greater co-ordination between departmental activities where the definition of a problem is such that it does not neatly coincide with

---

[16] In passing, it is worth noting that nowhere in the CPRS review is it acknowledged that social problems may have a subjective as well as an objective reality. Nowhere in their enquiry into social problems and policy responses do they consider the issues of problem definition and construction referred to earlier in this chapter. This can be seen as an unfortunate omission and an opportunity lost.

the division of departmental responsibilities and where the social costs of one department's policies fall to be met by those of another, there is a real danger that the promotion of corporatism and co-ordination will become, at least for a while, another substitute for effective policy formulation. In the field of inner-city initiatives there is a strong case for arguing that more corporatism and co-ordination of departmental policies and programmes should be secondary to a reformulation of the variety of problems that are being dealt with. A reconstruction of the notion of urban depriva-tion should be the first priority.

The third of the major issues to be considered here is that of positive discrimination. It is a generic term applied to a number of strategies, all of which are designed to intervene 'more directly at strategic points in the social structure' (Miller and Rein 1966: 516) and, as Titmuss has argued (1968), positive discrimination can only have any meaning within a universalist framework. Most usually, the strategies are the means by which selective services or other provisions can be directed on a partial basis to groups of the population considered to be most at risk or most in need, and, as such, any group of the population so defined can in theory be the beneficiaries of positive discrimination programmes. There have, however, over recent years (see pp.17-20) been a number of pro-grammes aimed at discriminating positively in favour not of groups of the population but of specific designated areas ('priority areas'). The Urban Programme is one such programme. As with the increasing demand for greater co-ordination, so it can also be argued that the dominance of the Gestalt 'urban deprivation' concept has encouraged the proliferation of priority-area positive discrimination programmes. As is argued above, the concept of 'urban deprivation' has helped to succour the idea that, because the processes of the housing and employment markets serve to concen-trate the poor, the poorly-educated, the unstably employed, and the unemployed, in particular, relatively small areas, and because there is an ecological statistical association of the manifestations of other social problems in these areas, that there is also some common causal link between all these various manifestations and, furthermore, that these common causal factors are to be found also *in the areas* themselves. Hopefully it has been sufficiently argued that this is a misconception of the nature of social process and the causation of socially-defined problems. The thesis is, however, attractive because it is simple, finite, has tangible parameters, and is administratively convenient, and for these reasons it is entirely conducive to the formulation of programmes designed to 'home in on' an urban blackspot, root out the malady, and cleanse it. There are other (and formidable) arguments against area-specific positive discrimination programmes, as articulated, for example, in the work of Davies (1968) who points out that, since there is rarely a concentration of all service needs in one area, the application of *comprehensive* programmes of provision on such a partial basis would represent an inefficient allocation of resources,[17] but it would seem that the misconception upon which many of such programmes are based is the most telling argument in their disfavour, and probably in itself sufficient to throw serious doubt on their efficacy. As with the call for more corporatism, the effective application of area-based positive discrimination programmes should only be subsequent upon a reformulation of the nature of the problems implied by the phrase 'urban deprivation'.

There is, however, one further questionable aspect of the poverty programmes of the 1960s and 1970s; it is a debatable point, but one worthy of consideration. It is that area-based positive discrimination programmes are not only founded on a misconception of the nature of social structures and process but that they also raise expectations that they cannot fulfil. They are based on an assumption that there exist *in vacuo* social problems which by virtue of having been defined *as problems* are then thought capable of being solved. In other words, the social problem of urban deprivation has been constructed in such a way as to give the firm impression that it is solvable and it is not difficult to see some of the mechanisms at work that have produced this impression. It was argued earlier that the relationship between problem definition and policy response is not uni-directional, but that there is interaction. Not only is the policy response in some measure determined by the problem definition, but this definition itself may be strongly influenced by what is conceived to be practicable in terms of policy response. This interaction, therefore, has produced a definition of urban deprivation that is compatible with practical policy expedients, and policy responses that give the impression of being solutions to the problem. Sadly, experience has shown both to be illusory.

[17] In this context he makes an interesting distinction between 'priority area' discrimination and what he terms 'territorial justice' (Davies 1968).

Rather than social problems that are amenable to solution it might be more realistic to conceive of *situations* in a constant state of flux wherein some people are better placed at certain points in time than others, and some improve their situation while that of others worsens. Thus, it can be argued, for example, that we do not have a finite 'housing problem' that one day will be 'solved' but rather a situation in housing which over time gets better for some but deteriorates for others. Perhaps, therefore, we should begin to think less in terms of *programmes to solve problems* and return to conceiving of *policies to alter situations*. While this may be a contentious argument in the face of some (relatively) small-scale pathologies, it is surely the case that major issues of poverty, employment, housing, and education will never be 'solved' by finite programmes (implying as they do fixed budgets and time scales) but will only be sensitive to more robust social policies.

The two years from mid-1975 to mid-1977 saw a more rigorous debate within government and the Civil Service about the nature of urban deprivation and the problems of the inner cities. This debate was stimulated in large measure by the reports from the Inner Areas Studies (DOE 1977a), and perhaps to a lesser extent by the deliberations of the Home Office Urban Deprivation Unit, and culminated in the 1977 White Paper outlining a new policy (or rather, set of strategies) for the inner cities (DOE 1977b).

The construction of the social problem of urban deprivation detailed in the White Paper has been discussed above and, whilst in some respects it marks an advance on earlier and more confused formulations, whether it can lead to the implementation of sets of policies with clearly defined and attainable goals remains to be seen. It certainly goes some way towards the disaggregation of the component parts of urban deprivation which, it is argued in the following pages, might be a necessary starting point for effective policies; whether it goes far enough will depend on the precise strategies adopted. These strategies are in part spelled out in the White Paper (and are briefly listed above: see pp.235-36) but one major component remains — perhaps rightly — undetailed. It is recognized that since the nature of the inner city differs as between different cities and since the characteristics of the major problems also differ, so the policy response must be tailored to fit particular circumstances. To this end, partnership arrangements are proposed between central government and five local authorities[18] in each of which an inner-area programme will be drawn up to meet the particular needs of each area. Such a flexible response is no doubt a sensible one but it shifts the onus of rigorous problem definition, and subsequent derivation of potentially effective and manageable policies, onto the partnership teams involved. It further suggests (though this might not necessarily be the case) that the programmes evolved will be specific to the chosen local authority areas if not to the particular inner cities. It is hard to see how any policy tactics can be determined at national level (or even regional level) to tackle the problems of particular areas within five related local authorities. To the extent that effective action on inner cities may require national policies (be it on housing, education, employment, etc.), these will not be possible within the partnership arrangements which, by their very nature, continue to conceive of inner-city problems as *local* problems.

Since the White Paper represents a recent stage in the development of inner-city policies of which the Urban Programme was an earlier and contributory stage, two further comments upon it, relating to our previous observations, and arising from an assessment of the UP are made here. It was argued above (see pp.246-47) that a tentative case could be made for shifting the burden of ameliorative action in the inner cities away from finite *programmes* with fixed budgets, time scales, and goals (however unclear), and towards the use of more broadly based and flexible policies. It will be recalled that one Treasury official (though not necessarily expressing a 'Treasury view') argued that if inner-city problems were significant and not simply residual then the relevant major existing policies of some government departments should be reviewed and themselves used to effect change in the inner city (see p.120). If the six proposals of the White Paper are implemented then there will be a shift in this direction. The first of the six points was indeed to ' ... give a new priority to the main policies and programmes of government so that they contribute to a better life in the inner areas' (DOE 1977b: para. 41). If nothing else, this may be one way of directing greater resources into the inner cities than would be possible with smaller limited budget programmes.

The second point concerns the use of area-based positive discrimination. While there remains a strong case for using area-based

[18] The White Paper listed five such partnership arrangements. Others were subsequently added.

programmes to alleviate *some* of the component problems of urban deprivation (see below and p.250), there remain cogent reasons and arguments for questioning the over-ambitious use of such tactics. This has been a consistent theme of the present chapter but reference is made in particular to the points above in footnote 12 of this chapter, and pp.245-46. The White Paper recognizes that not all the problems of the inner cities can be solved within the context of inner areas themselves but, at the same time, extends the practice of area selectivity by concentrating the major policy effort in five local authorities. If 'urban deprivation' is not as geographically concentrated as had previously been thought then the wisdom of extending selectivity this far must be questioned. Though the White Paper agreed that careful thought and analysis had been given to selecting five authorities which had the worst inner-city problems, it cannot be by coincidence that three of the authorities selected are those which agreed to participate in the Inner Areas Studies established in 1973.

Disaggregating deprivation

The disaggregation of the notions of urban deprivation requires that we return to first principles and examine precisely what it is that is of social concern (or what, with some degree of unanimity, is thought to constitute a social problem) from within that complex of manifestations. It may well be argued that this would be a pointless exercise since we all 'know' what urban deprivation is. The response must be that, while we do all 'know' what it is, what we know turns out to be different things for different people — as the foregoing evidence has shown. Only when we have catalogued the variety of problems that until now have been subsumed under one name can we begin the task of formulating relevant and potentially-effective policies. Some of the implications of questioning the wisdom of area-based positive discrimination programmes have been mentioned above in relation to housing, education, and employment. The *housing* problems of inner cities can only *partially* be tackled by area-specific policies (improvement and rehabilitation programmes would be among such policies); in large measure effective policies must be directed elsewhere: at the processes of allocation of housing in all tenure sectors, at the systems of housing finance and subsidies, at the 'red-lining' policies of some building societies,[19] and at stock distribution — to name but a few. The same type of argument would hold for education and employment policies: there are some aspects of inner-city education and employment problems (again, particularly environmental aspects) that might be amenable to 'treatment' by area-specific policies; but, by and large, effective action must be directed at broader issues and, to the extent that existing problems are the result of current policies, at these policies themselves. Such an attack on some of the major constituents of the problems of urban deprivation requires a major restructuring of the current conceptions of these problems and their causes; and whether such a reconstruction can be both realistic (in conceptual terms) and compatible with effective ameliorative measures that are politically acceptable (that is, within the bounds of what is currently accepted as legitimate for State intervention) remains a debatable point. Certainly, some of the policy implications of a restructuring of the concept of deprivation and its causes would not be compatible with programmes as ideologically neutral as existing ones such as the Urban Programme.

Housing, education, employment, and poverty are not the only components of urban deprivation, however (though it may be argued that they are the most fundamental). A disaggregation of the concept of urban deprivation such as has been suggested would also throw up the many other manifestations to which reference has been made in this and the previous chapter. Again, the sort of conceptual restructuring that has been suggested would require an examination of each of these in terms of manifestation, distribution, and causation. Ecological association of a number of such problems (for example, high rates of juvenile delinquency, illiteracy, truancy, baby battery, illegitimacy, and petty crime in the same geographical areas) should not be taken as an indication of common origins or even of common association in the same people or families. Where common causality and association can be established then, of course, this must be done; but it would be to repeat the error of many current programmes to assume that either the causes or the remedies of any, some, or all of these problems lie in the areas where they are manifested. The *extent* to which this is the

---

[19] That 'red-lining' policies are followed by some building societies is given official recognition in a housing policy consultative document (DOE 1977c: para.7.32). For more details of red-lining policies see Wier 1976.

case must be established prior to the formulation of any policy initiatives.

Where research indicates that there is sufficient reason to believe that some problems — or groups of problems — might be amenable to alleviation by intervention on an area basis, then there would be a case for retaining or instituting area-based positive discrimination programmes. Where no indications of this kind are given, the application of such programmes might be worthless and wasteful — as is the case to some extent at present. In short, what is required is a much more discriminating approach to the application of area-based positive discrimination than the programmes of the late 1960s and the 1970s — and especially the Urban Programme — have displayed.

What then would be the prescription for the future if the implications of these arguments were to be translated into policy? It would be the development of a more intellectually-discriminating response to urban deprivation wherein the major tactic would be to employ broad-based policies that would be supplemented only where research deemed them expedient by limited area-specific programmes. If this were to be the direction in which policy evolved, then future generations of social policy makers and analysts might acknowledge the Urban Programme — and its sisters — as a necessary stage in the intellectual development of a more discriminating application of positive discrimination; but they might also judge them to have been more the children of enthusiasm than wisdom.

Appendix I: Implications for programme organization

Notwithstanding that the 1977 White Paper *Policy for the Inner Cities* appears to set the course for the Urban Programme for a number of years to come, this evaluation of the Programme has elicited a number of findings, raising more general implications for the involvement of central and local government and voluntary agencies in area-based positive discrimination programmes and for the formulation of potentially more effective programmes, that remain relevant. It is the purpose of this appendix to outline some of these.

Problem definition and programme construction

The most frequently-voiced criticism of the Urban Programme among respondents in this evaluation — as recorded in Chapter 7 — was that it lacked clear policy guidelines and clarity of aims and goals. Without clear goal statements, without an explicit statement of what the Programme was supposed to be doing, effective use of its funds became largely a matter of chance. Money became dissipated on a very wide variety of projects with widely differing aims and with little hope of cumulative effect, experience, or knowledge. That the Programme initially lacked and subsequently failed to develop clear and explicit aims can be attributed in part to the haste with which it was constructed and, also in part, to the failure to construct the problem of 'urban deprivation' in a cogent and rigorous way. The issues of goal statement and problem construction are clearly inextricably linked and mutually reinforcing.

In Chapter 8 it was argued that the formulation of more effective programmes would depend upon the disaggregation of the social problem of urban deprivation into its constituent parts and its reconstruction in such a way as to distinguish between those elements that can be traced back to causes located within urban areas themselves, and those where the determining factors reside in the wider structure of economic and social markets and processes or in the latent effects or the externalities of existing economic and social policies. A clear implication of this is that programmes potentially effective in meeting urban deprivation must take full account of this disaggregation and reconstruction. A more specific implication is that policies or programmes designed to operate at the area level (and this would of course include area-specific positive discrimination programmes) should have goals that are confined to the alleviation of those social problems or conditions that research would indicate *are* amenable to local intervention. This does not imply that *area-directed* policies should not be employed, because, clearly, encouraging industry to move into areas with poor economic infrastructures could be beneficial. It does imply, however, that the injection of a housing aid and advice centre into an inner-city area of bad housing will do little to solve the housing problems of that area unless backed up by broader and not necessarily area-based initiatives, to (say) influence building society mortgage allocation procedures or red-lining policies or a local authority's housing allocation procedures. It also means that inducements to industry to invest in the area will fail if the only industries that respond are low-paying, and nothing is done at the same time to ensure adequate minimum wages in them. (The question might also be raised as to whether inner-city residents *want* firms to be imported into their areas. Are inner-city residents necessarily any different from suburban residents who might react with considerable disfavour to the importation of industry to their areas? Might it not be possible that inner-city residents would much prefer to be payed wages adequate to enable them with ease to pay the costs of transport to work *outside* their area? The inner-city debate — especially as synthesized in the 1977 White Paper — has taken little account of what social justice requires.)

The formulation of area-specific programmes, therefore, would be more wisely undertaken if it was preceded by or incorporated research into those aspects of 'urban deprivation' that might be amenable to alleviation by local intervention. Such programmes might then be confined to dealing only with those problems so identified and be based on clear statements of aims to that effect.

Central direction and local autonomy

One of the major dilemmas that the Urban Programme faced during its early years was the relative significance of central government direction of funds and local autonomy to decide on spending priorities. That this led to confrontation between central and local government has been shown in Chapter 5. In the case of the UP, the specific manifestation was that of the prioritization of project bids from local authorities and the acceptance of these priorities by central government. But the issue is a more general one and no doubt endemic in programmes of action involving both central and local government activity. The issue was 'solved' (or conceded) in the Urban Programme by an undertaking on the part of central government to accept local authorities' highest priority bids. What local authorities won by way of freedom to determine their own spending priorities, central government lost by surrending its power to impose an overall direction on the Programme.

If urban deprivation policies were to develop in the direction of bipartite initiative — that is, policy on the one hand concerned with the roots of the forms taken by the economic and social structure and processes of urban deprivation, which would, in all probability, not be area specific, and, on the other, area-based programmes directed at those aspects of deprivation that might be amenable to alleviation by local intervention — then the respective roles of central and local government might become clearer. In so far as national policies or prescriptions would be seen to be relevant, then clearly central government direction would not only be expedient — it would also be necessary. In the case of area-specific programmes, however, it could be argued that local authorities would be best placed to decide the nature and magnitude of their own particular problems, and should be able to select their own priorities for action from among the specific programmes of support offered by central government. It would remain to central government — though drawing upon local authority's experience, and research resources — to give direction to the investigation of those aspects of urban deprivation that might be capable of being solved by local intervention, and to devise and adapt programmes to this end.

Voluntary agency involvement

The role of voluntary agencies in the Urban Programme has never been satisfactorily defined and voluntary agency involvement has been a constant source of friction. The nature and causes of the problems of voluntary agency involvement have been detailed in the body of the book and do not require repetition here. As long as voluntary agency participation in urban deprivation policies and programmes is deemed expedient, wise, or necessary, then some way of making this involvement satisfactory for those agencies, acceptable to local and central government, and, at the same time, effective must be worked out.

The major stumbling-block within the Programme proved to be the relationships between local authorities and the voluntary agencies in their area. In some authorities the relationship was satisfactory and mutually beneficial. In many others it was far from happy and led to dissatisfaction and even acrimony between the parties involved. The evidence in Chapter 7 suggests that many local authorities would view with alarm any direct relationship (especially a financial one) between central government and voluntary agencies that did not also involve them. At the very least (it was argued) it would lead to unnecessary duplication of effort between voluntary agencies and local authorities. There were other less explicitly-stated but no less serious misgivings on the part of some authorities about a central government/voluntary agency relationship that excluded them. It is equally clear from Chapter 7 that, as far as many voluntary agencies are concerned, their involvement in programmes like the UP will be partial, limited, and less than effective if the terms of that involvement are allowed to be dictated by the local authorities. Central government respondents — especially Civil Servants — were clear in their unwillingness to deal financially with voluntary agencies other than through local authorities.

The issue remains unresolved (and unresolvable to the satisfaction of all parties) but if central government is to commit itself to the inclusion of voluntary action in urban deprivation programmes or policies then it must recognize that any commitment on terms that remain unacceptable to voluntary agencies themselves must seriously detract from the usefulness and effectiveness of their contribution.

Appendix II: Local Government Grants (Social Need) Act 1969

The Secretary of State may out of monies provided by Parliament pay grants, of such amounts as he may with the consent of the Treasury determine, to local authorities who in his opinion are required in the exercise of any of their functions to incur expenditure by reason of the existence in any urban area of special social need.

Grants under this section may be paid at such times, subject to such conditions and on account of such expenditure (for the year 1968-69 or any later year) as the Secretary of State may determine.

Appendix III: Card index system: data coded

Project types: full and condensed lists
1 Pre-school playgroups (including play leaders and organizers) (PPG)
2 Children's homes (CH)
3 Day nurseries and other forms of day care (DN)
4 Nursery education (nursery schools and classes) (NE)
5 Adventure playgrounds (including adventure play leaders) (APG)
6 Other play facilities (including non-specific holiday projects) (OPF)
7 Youth activities (excluding specifically educational projects) (YA)
8 Provision for the elderly (including homes, help, meals, and lunch clubs) (OP)
9 Family planning (FP)
10 Family Advice Centres (FAC)
11 Neighbourhood Advice Centres (NAC)
12 Citizens Advice Bureaux (CAB)
13 Legal Advice Centres (LAC)
14 Housing Advice Centres (HAC)
15 Other advice centres (OA)
16 Community centres (CC)
17 Community workers (CW)
18 General community projects (CP)
19 Volunteer Bureaux (VB)
20 Accommodation for the homeless and other sheltered accommodation (HSA)
21 Language projects (LP)
22 Compensatory, special, or remedial education (SE)
23 General social work projects (GSW)
24 General health projects (GH)
25 Miscellaneous (M)

The condensed list of types of project used in Chapter 6 consists of groups of the above specific project types. The condensed list and constituent specific project types are as follows:

1 Provision for children	PPG
	CH
	DN
	NE
	APG
	OPF
2 Other age-group projects	YA
	OP
3 Advice and information (general)	FAC
	NAC
	CAB
	LAC
	HAC
	OA
4 Community projects	CC
	CW
	CP
	VB
5 Social work, welfare, and health	FP
	GSW
	GH
	HSA
6 Special education	SE
	LP
7 Miscellaneous	M

Type of budget
  capital
  non-capital
  non-capital, once-only

Phase numbers
  1 to 9

Sponsors
  local authority
  voluntary organization
  joint local authority/voluntary organization

Approving central government department
  Home Office
  Department of Health and Social Security
  Department of Education and Science

Department of the Environment
Any joint combination

Costs of approval

£	0	-	1,999
£	2,000	-	3,999
£	4,000	-	5,999
£	6,000	-	7,999
£	8,000	-	9,999
£	10,000	-	11,999
£	12,000	-	13,999
£	14,000	-	15,999
£	16,000	-	17,999
£	18,000	-	19,999
£	20,000	-	29,999
£	30,000	-	39,999
£	40,000	-	49,999
£	50,000	-	59,999
£	60,000	-	69,999
£	70,000	-	79,999
£	80,000	-	99,999
£100,000		-	119,999
£120,000		+	

For the purposes of analysis and presentation in Chapter 6, the cost categories have been grouped as indicated by the underlining.

Types of local authority
county council
county borough
municipal borough
urban district
rural district
London borough
Greater London Council
Inner London Education Authority

Appendix IV: Additional Tables

Table A   *Applications and approvals by project type for seven local authorities for Phases 3, 7, 9 and total approvals by type of project (all local authorities, all phases)*

Type of project	A Applications (sample)[1]		B Approvals (sample)[2]		C Approvals (total)[3]		D Applications approved (sample)[4]
	Number	%	Number	%	Number	%	%
Pre-school playgroups	63	8.2	32	11.1	278	9.5	51
Children's homes	13	1.7	0	0.0	51	1.7	0
Day nurseries, day care	48	6.2	19	6.6	162	5.5	40
Nursery education	159	20.7	53	18.3	574	19.6	33
Adventure playgrounds	25	3.3	15	5.2	117	4.0	60
Other play facilities	40	5.2	3	1.0	362	12.4	8
Youth activities	38	4.9	16	5.5	82	2.8	42
Care of the elderly	41	5.3	12	4.2	114	3.9	29
Family planning	13	1.7	8	2.8	128	4.4	62
Family Advice Centres	10	1.3	2	0.7	61	2.1	20
Neighbourhood Advice Centres	15	2.0	12	4.2	27	0.9	80
Citizens' Advice Bureau	9	1.2	6	2.1	24	0.8	66

Table A *continued*

Type of project	A Applications (sample)[1]		B Approvals (sample)[2]		C Approvals (total)[3]		D Applications approved (sample)[4]
	Num- ber	%	Num- ber	%	Num- ber	%	%
Legal Advice Centres	6	0.8	3	1.0	8	0.3	50
Housing Advice Centres	15	2.0	10	3.5	92	3.1	66
Other advice centres	10	1.3	6	2.1	28	1.0	60
Community centres	31	4.0	13	4.5	81	2.8	42
Community workers	9	1.2	4	1.4	48	1.6	44
General community projects	32	4.2	11	3.8	95	3.2	34
Volunteer Bureaux	11	1.4	8	2.8	34	1.2	73
Accommodation for homeless	35	4.6	16	5.5	88	3.0	46
Language projects	12	1.6	8	2.8	165	5.6	66
Compensatory education	46	6.0	11	3.8	106	3.6	24
General social work	46	6.0	13	4.5	94	3.2	28
General health	10	1.3	3	1.0	30	1.0	30
Miscellaneous	32	4.2	5	1.7	80	2.7	16
All projects	769	100.0	289	100.0	2,929	100.0	37.6
Local authority projects	498	64.8	145	50.2	1,972	67.3	29
Voluntary agency projects	271	35.2	144	49.8	939	32.7[5]	53
Capital projects	393	51.1	115	39.8	1,211	41.4	29
Non-capital/'once-only' projects	376	48.9	174	60.2	1,718	58.6	46

Notes:

[1] All applications, seven local authorities, three phases: percentage of applications falling within each type or project.

[2] All approvals, seven local authorities, three phases: percentage of approvals falling within each type of project.

[3] Total approvals, *all* local authorities, Phases 1-9: percentage of approvals falling within each type of project (this column is a reproduction of *Table 1*, (Chapter 6).

[4] Percentage of applications which were approved within each type of project, seven local authorities, three phases.

[5] Includes joint local authority/voluntary organization projects (0.6% of total).

Table B Project costs (condensed) by types of local authority

Type of local authority

Cost band £		London boroughs		ILEA		GLC		County boroughs		County councils		Municipal boroughs, urban and rural districts		Total	
		Num-ber	%	Num-ber	%	Num-ber	%	Num-ber	%	Num-ber	%	Num-ber	%	Num-ber	%
0-1,999	Number	308	40.3	15	13.2	0	0.0	563	34.6	99	31.2	43	43.4	1,028	35.1
	%		30.0		1.5		0.0		54.8		9.6		4.2		100.0
2-3,999	Number	129	16.9	17	14.9	2	28.6	329	20.2	51	16.1	15	15.2	543	18.5
	%		23.8		3.1		0.3		60.6		9.4		2.8		100.0
4-5,999	Number	84	11.0	9	7.9	3	42.9	145	8.9	25	7.9	11	11.1	277	9.5
	%		30.3		3.2		1.1		52.3		0.9		4.0		100.0
6-7,999	Number	51	6.7	24	21.1	0	0.0	94	5.8	13	4.1	2	2.0	184	6.3
	%		27.7		13.0		0.0		51.1		7.1		1.1		100.0
8-9,999	Number	22	2.9	4	3.5	0	0.0	80	4.9	17	5.4	2	2.0	125	4.3
	%		17.6		3.2		0.0		64.0		13.6		1.6		100.0
10-11,999	Number	26	3.4	4	3.5	0	0.0	76	4.7	23	7.3	3	3.0	132	4.5
	%		19.7		3.0		0.0		57.6		17.4		2.3		100.0
12-13,999	Number	16	2.1	34	29.8	0	0.0	42	2.6	19	6.0	4	4.0	115	3.9
	%		13.9		29.6		0.0		36.5		16.5		3.5		100.0
14-19,999	Number	23	3.0	3	2.6	0	0.0	84	5.2	19	6.0	6	6.1	135	4.6
	%		17.0		2.2		0.0		62.2		14.1		4.4		100.0
20-29,999	Number	31	4.1	1	0.9	1	14.3	92	5.7	16	5.0	5	5.1	146	5.0
	%		21.2		0.7		0.7		63.0		11.0		3.4		100.0
30-49,999	Number	31	4.1	2	1.8	1	14.3	77	4.7	20	6.3	5	5.1	136	4.6
	%		22.8		1.5		0.7		56.6		14.7		3.7		100.0
50,000+	Number	44	5.8	1	0.9	0	0.0	45	2.8	15	4.7	3	3.0	108	3.7
	%		40.7		0.9		0.0		41.7		13.9		2.8		100.0
Total	Number	765	100.0	114	100.0	7	100.0	1,627	100.0	317	100.0	99	100.0	2,929	100.0
	%		26.1		3.9		0.2		55.6		10.8		3.4		100.0

Appendix V: Selection of local authorities for research

There were a large number of possible criteria by which local authorities could have been selected for inclusion in the research, perhaps the most germane being the following:

— extent of involvement in the Urban Programme (high, medium, low)
— size
— geographical location
— social, industrial, and economic characteristics (Moser and Scott's classification of British towns (1961) proved very useful here)
— type (London or county borough, county council, municipal borough, urban or rural district)
— structure and organization (e.g. extent of use of corporate planning techniques)
— extent of voluntary organization activity.

In practice, because of the limited number of authorities it was possible to cover extensively, it proved impractical to sample by all of these variables. The primary criterion adopted, therefore, was that of degree of involvement in the Programme and, to this end, all recipient authorities were first classified *within* local authority type and population size groups into high, medium, and low applicants and recipients. Three alternative means of doing this presented themselves: by adopting arbitrary numbers of projects as cut-off points for high, medium, and low categories; by allocating equal numbers of authorities to each of the three categories; or by making use of scattergrams showing numbers of projects applied for and received by local authority type and size and searching for 'natural clusters' of authorities. The last of these alternatives was adopted. Four separate scattergrams were produced showing the distribution of authorities by:

a number of project applications and type of local authority
b number of project receipts and type of local authority
c number of project applications and size of local authority (population)
d number of project receipts and size of local authority.

Natural groupings of authorities within each of these scattergrams were used to identify cut-off points for high, medium, and low applicants and recipients. (In order to simplify the process, rural districts were eliminated on the grounds that very few had ever applied and those that had had submitted very few projects, and urban districts and municipal boroughs were combined as one group.)

Each authority then had two pairs of labels:

as a high (H), medium (M), or low (L) applicant
as a H, M, or L recipient
— *within its type*

as a H, M, or L applicant
as a H, M, or L recipient
— *within its size band*

Thus, for example, Leicester C.B. was classified as MM for a county borough (i.e. as compared with all other county boroughs it was a medium applicant and medium recipient) and also as MM within its size band (i.e. as compared with all authorities with populations between 201,000 and 300,999). Burton-on-Trent C.B. on the other hand was classified as LM for a county borough but MM for its size band (31,000-70,999).

First selection was then made to draw up a short-list of authorities that represented all combinations of applicant and recipient category, and all types and all sizes of local authority.

It was then decided that the number of projects involved for authorities classified as low applicants or recipients and for all urban districts and municipal boroughs (whatever their classification as for type of local authority) was so small that extensive involvement in them could not be justified. Having eliminated all such authorities from the list, the remainder were grouped according to secondary criteria such as geographical location and social, industrial, and economic characteristics.

Clearly, with such a small number of authorities to select (twelve) and such a large number of selection criteria, any attempt at complete representation of all possible variables was impossible. Final selection from the short-list was therefore made to give representation to the high and medium applicants and recipients, London and county boroughs and county councils, population size categories, geographical location, and predominant industrial structure as the individual variables. No attempt could be made at achieving full representation of one variable within another (e.g. high and medium applicants and recipients *within* any one type of local authority or industrial structure). The final list of authorities does, however, allow representation of a number of different types, sizes, locations, industrial structures, and UP involvement, and thus broadens the scope for the expression of a potentially wide set of views and opinions.

Appendix VI: Respondents

Discussions were held with officials and members in the departments listed under each local authority.

OFFICERS		MEMBERS
Haringey L.B.		
Community services	1	Leader of the council
Corporate planning	1	
Education	2	
Finance	2	
Planning	1	
Recreation services	2	
Secretariat	1	
Social services	1	
Hartlepool C.B.		
Education (written submission)		Leader of the council
Chief Executive Officer		Leader minority group
Public health	1	
Social services	2	
Treasurers	1	
Kensington and Chelsea L.B.		
Housing	1	Voluntary organization liaison
Social services	1	Committee (chairlady)
Town Clerk's department	1	Social services committee (chairlady)

OFFICERS   MEMBERS

Lancashire C.C.

County Clerk's department	1	None
Education	1	
Finance	1	
Social services	1	

Leeds C.B.

Education	1	None
Finance	1	
Social services	1	
Solicitor's department	1	

Leicester C.B.

Education	3	Committee (chairman)
Social services	3	Committee (chairman)
Treasurer's department	1	

Northumberland C.C.

Architect's department	1	None
County Clerk's department	1	
Education	1	
Social services	2	
Treasurer's department	1	

Sheffield C.B.

Education	1	Committee (chairman)
Housing	1	Policy committee (chairman)
Social services	1	
Town Clerk's department	1	
Treasurer's department	1	

Tower Hamlets L.B.

Community services	1	None
Finance	3	
Social services	1	
Town Clerk's department	1	

Walsall C.B.

Clerk's department	1	Education committee (chairman)
Corporate planning	1	Social services committee (chairman)
Education	1	
Housing	1	
Social services	1	

OFFICERS		MEMBERS

Warley C.B.

Clerk's department	1	None
Education	1	
Parks	1	
Social services	1	
Treasurer's department	1	

Yorkshire West Riding C.C.

Architect's department	1	None
Education	2	
Education (divisional)	1	
Education (divisional)	1	
Education (divisional)	1	
Finance	1	
Social education	1	
Social services	2	

Voluntary organization respondents

Local representatives

Discussions were held with representatives of the voluntary organizations listed under each local authority.

Haringey L.B.

Community Relations Officer
Tottenham Community Project

Hartlepool C.B.

None

Kensington and Chelsea L.B.

North Kensington Amenity Trust
North Kensington Neighbourhood Law Centre
People's Association
West London Family Service Unit

Lancashire C.C.

Lancashire Community Council
Preston Council of Voluntary Service

Leeds C.B.

Community Relations Officer
Leeds Council of Voluntary Service

Leicester C.B.

Community Relations Officer
Leicester Council of Voluntary Service
Leicester Family Service Unit

Northumberland C.C.

None

Sheffield C.B.

Sheffield Council of Voluntary Service
Sheffield Family Service Unit
Churches Council

Tower Hamlets L.B.

Community Relations Officer

Walsall C.B.

Joint meeting attended by:
Council for Community Relations
Council for Voluntary Service
Gingerbread
Indian Organization
Pre-School Playgroup Association
Retired Citizens Action Group
Walsall Human Rights Committee
West Indian Association

Warley C.B.

Community Relations Officer
Assistant Community Relations Officer
Walsall Adventure Playground Association

Yorkshire West Riding C.C.

Doncaster Council of Voluntary Service

Major national representatives

Discussions were held with representatives at 'headquarters level' of the voluntary organizations listed below:

Age Concern	(Director)
Child Poverty Action Group	(Deputy Director)
Community Relations Commission	(Chairman)
Family Planning Association	(Acting Director)
Institute of Race Relations	(Director)
National Citizens Advice Bureaux Council	
National Council of Social Service	

Pre-School Playgroup Association	(General Secretary)
	(Research Director)
Shelter	(Director)
Task Force	(Director)
Young Volunteer Force	(Resource Director)

Central government officials

Discussions were held with officials with a present or past interest in the Urban Programme in the following departments:

Department of Education and Science	6
Department of Health and Social Security	2
Department of the Environment	2
Home Office	5
Treasury	2

Also interviewed

Director, Centre for Studies in Social Policy (previously of the Home Office)
Association of County Councils: Under Secretary
National Association of Local Councils: Deputy Secretary

References

Abel-Smith, B. and Townsend, P. (1965) *The Poor and the Poorest*. London: Bell.

Adeney, M. (1972) Urban Aid Grants Go Astray. The *Guardian*, 23 November.

Atkinson, A.B. (1974) Poverty and Income Inequality in Britain. In, D. Wedderburn (ed.), *Poverty, Inequality and Class Structure*. Cambridge: Cambridge University Press.

Bachrach, P. and Baratz, M. (1970) *Power and Poverty, Theory and Practice*. Oxford: Oxford University Press.

Ball, D. (1971) Urban Programme: Imaginative Investments. *New Society*, 21 January.

Balniel, Lord (1970) The Conservative Case. In, McKie, D. and Cooke, C. *Election '70*. St. Albans: Panther.

Barlow Report (1940) Royal Commission on the Distribution of the Industrial Population. Cmnd. 6153. London: H.M.S.O.

Barnes, J. (1974) A Solution to Whose Problem? In, *Positive Discrimination and Inequality*. Fabian Research Series No. 314. London: Fabian Society.

Batley, R. (1976) *The Neighbourhood Scheme: Cases of Central Government Intervention in Local Deprivation*. London: Centre for Environmental Studies, Research Paper 19.

Batley, R. and Edwards J. (1974) *The Phase Seven Exercise*. Leeds: Urban Programme Working Paper 4, University of Leeds.

Becker, H.S. (1963) *Outsiders: Studies in the Sociology of Deviance*. New York: The Free Press.

———— (1966) *Social Problems: A Modern Approach*. New York: Wiley.

Bennington, J. (1971) Community Development. *Municipal Journal 29*, January.

Berry, F. (1974) *Housing: The Great British Failure*. London: Charles Knight.

Beveridge, Sir William (1942) *Social Insurance and Allied Services*. Cmnd. 6404. London: H.M.S.O.

Bourne, J. (1972) Urban Aid and Catch-22. *Race Today* July: 238-39.

Bowlby, J. (1965) *Child Care and the Growth of Love*. Harmondsworth: Pelican.

Brown, R.G.S. (1970) *The Administrative Process in Britain*. London: Methuen.

Bull, D. (ed.) (1972) *Family Poverty*. London: Duckworth.

Burney, E. (1967) *Housing on Trial*. Oxford: Institute of Race Relations, Oxford University Press.

Carrier, J. and Kendall, I. (1972) Social Policy and Social Change. *Journal of Social Policy 2* (3), July.

Central Advisory Committee for Education (1959) *Fifteen to Eighteen* (Crowther Report). London: H.M.S.O.

—— (1963) *Half Our Future* (Newsom Report). London: H.M.S.O.

—— (1967) *Children and their Primary Schools* (Plowden Report). London: H.M.S.O.

Central Housing Advisory Committee (1969) *Council Housing: Purposes, Procedures and Priorities* (Cullingworth Report). London: H.M.S.O.

Central Policy Review Staff (1975) *A Joint Framework for Social Policies*. London: H.M.S.O.

Chapin, F.S. (1961) *The Relationship of Housing to Mental Health*. Geneva: World Health Organisation.

Chapman, R.A. (1973) The Vehicle and General Affair: Some Reflections for Public Administration in Britain. *Public Administration 51*, Autumn: 273-90.

Committee of Inquiry on Local Government Finance (1976) Report (Layfield Report). Cmnd. 6453. London: H.M.S.O.

Committee on the Civil Service (1968) Report (Fulton Report). Cmnd. 3638. London: H.M.S.O.

Committee on Compensation and Betterment (1942) Report (Uthwatt Report). Cmnd. 6386. London: H.M.S.O.

Committee On Higher Education (1963) *Higher Education* (Robbins Report). Cmnd. 2154. London: H.M.S.O.

Committee on Housing in Greater London (1965) Report (Milner Holland Report). Cmnd. 2605. London: H.M.S.O.

Committee on Land Utilization in Rural Areas (1942) Report (Scott Report). Cmnd. 6378. London: H.M.S.O.

Committee on Local Authority and Allied Personal Social Services (1969) Report (Seebohm Report). Cmnd. 3703. London: H.M.S.O.

Community Action (1972) Action Report: The Urban Aid Programme. *Community Action 3*, July/August.

—— (1973) Urban Aid: The Tinkering Continues. *Community Action 6*, January/February.

Community Development Project (1974) *Inter-Project Report*. London: Community Development Project Information and Intelligence Unit.

Community Relations Commission (1974) *Unemployment and Homelessness*. London: Reference Division, Community Relations Commission, H.M.S.O.

Critchley, T.A. (1951) *The Civil Service Today*. London: Gollancz.

Crossman, R. (1975) *The Diaries of a Cabinet Minister* (Vols I and II). London: Jonathan Cape.

Crowther Report (1959) Central Advisory Committee for Education. *Fifteen to Eighteen*. London: H.M.S.O.

Cullingworth, J.B. (1973) *Problems of an Urban Society* (Vol 2). London: Allen and Unwin.

Dahrendorf, R. (1959) *Class and Class Conflict in an Industrial Society*. London: Routledge and Kegan Paul.

Daniel, W.W. (1968) *Racial Discrimination in England*. Harmondsworth: Penguin.

Davies, B. (1968) *Social Needs and Resources in Local Services*. London: Joseph.

Davison, R.B. (1966) *Black British*. Oxford: Oxford University Press.

Department of Education and Science (1972) *Education: A Framework for Expansion*. Cmnd. 5174. London: H.M.S.O.

Department of the Environment (1973a) *Making Towns Better: The Oldham Study: Environmental Planning and Management*. London: H.M.S.O.

_____ (1973b) *Making Towns Better: The Rotherham Study: A General Approach to Improving the Physical Environment*. London: H.M.S.O.

_____ (1973c) *Making Towns Better: The Sunderland Study: Tackling Urban Problems*. London: H.M.S.O.

_____ (1974) *Inner Area Study: Liverpool: Third Study Review* IAS/LI/6. London: H.M.S.O.

_____ (1975a) *Inner Area Study: Birmingham: Interim Review* IAS/B/4. London: H.M.S.O.

_____ (1975b) *Inner Area Study: Lambeth: Poverty and Multiple Deprivation* IAS/LA/IO. London: H.M.S.O.

_____ (1975c) *Census Indicators of Urban Deprivation: Working Note No. 6*. London: H.M.S.O.

_____ (1977a) *Inner Area Studies: Summaries of Consultants' Final Reports*. London: H.M.S.O.

_____ (1977b) *Policy for the Inner Cities*. Cmnd. 6845. London: H.M.S.O.

_____ (1977c) *Housing Policy: A Consultative Document*. Cmnd. 6851. London: H.M.S.O.

Dillon, G.M. (1976) Policy and Dramaturgy. In, *Policy and Politics 5* (1), September: 47-62.

Donnison, D. and Chapman, V. (1967) *Social Policy and Administration*. London: Allen and Unwin.

Donnison, D. (1974) Policies for Priority Areas. *Journal of Social Policy 3* (2): 127-35.

Edwards, J. (1973) *The Other Housing Problem: Access and Accountability*. Birmingham: Centre for Urban and Regional Studies, University of Birmingham.

Edwards, J. and Batley, R. (1974) The Urban Programme: A Report on Some Programme Funded Projects. *British Journal of Social Work 4* (3): 305-31.

Edwards, J. (1974) *The Distribution of Urban Programme Funds Amongst*

London and County Boroughs in England. Leeds: Urban Programme Working Paper, Department of Social Policy and Administration, Leeds University.

—— (1975) Social Indicators, Urban Deprivation and Positive Discrimination. *Journal of Social Policy 4* (3): 275-87.

Field, F. and Piachaud, D. (1971) The Poverty Trap. *New Statesman*, 3 December.

Field, F. (ed.) (1973) *Low Pay.* London: Arrow Books.

Floud, J. (1961) Social Class Factors in Educational Achievement. In, Halsey, A.H. (ed.) *Ability and Educational Opportunity.* Paris: OECD.

Foot, P. (1969) *The Rise of Enoch Powell.* London: Cornmarket Press.

Forder, A. (ed.) (1971) *Penelope Hall's Social Services of England and Wales.* London: Routledge and Kegan Paul.

Fuller, R. and Myers, R. (1941) The Natural History of a Social Problem. *American Sociological Review*, June.

Gaine, M.B. (1971) In, Forder, A. (ed.) *Penelope Hall's Social Services of England and Wales.* London: Routledge and Kegan Paul.

Garrett, J. (1969) Planning Government Action. *Management Decision*, Autumn.

—— (1972) *The Management of Government.* Harmondsworth: Penguin.

George, V. and Wilding, P. (1976) *Ideology and Social Welfare.* London: Routledge and Kegan Paul.

Glennerster, H. and Hatch, S. (1974) *Positive Discrimination and Inequality.* Fabian Research Series No. 314. London: Fabian Society.

Goldthorpe, J. (1974) Political Consensus, Social Inequality and Pay Policy. *New Society 27* (588): 55-8.

Gordon, M.R. (1971) Civil Servants, Politicians and Parties. *Comparative Politics iv*, October: 29-58.

Gray, J. (1975) Positive Discrimination in Education, A review of the British Experience. *Policy and Politics 4* (2), December.

Greve, J. (1973) Community Development in the Context of Urban Deprivation. Paper prepared for the European Study Group in Community Development and Urban Deprivation, Oxford. United Nations Division of Social Affairs.

Greve, J., Page, D., and Greve, S. (1971) *Homelessness in London.* Edinburgh: Scottish Academic Press.

Griffiths, P. (1966) *A Question of Colour?* London: Leslie Frewin.

Guardian, The (1973) Four Million Pounds Aid for Communities in Distress. The *Guardian*, 28 September.

Hall, A.S. (1974) *The Point of Entry: A Study of Client Reception in the Social Services.* London: Allen and Unwin.

Hall, P., Land, H., Parker, R., and Webb, A. (1975) *Change, Choice and Conflict in Social Policy.* London: Heinemann.

Halsey, A.H. (ed.) (1961) *Ability and Educational Opportunity.* Paris: OECD.

—— (ed.) (1972) *Educational Priority.* London: H.M.S.O.

—— (1973) In, *The Times Educational Supplement*, 9 February.

Hansard (1961) 5 December: cols. 1172-73.
___ (1968) 22 July: col. 40.
___ (1968) 2 December: cols. 1107-66.
___ (1972) 27 July: col. 253.
___ (1972) 11 December: col. 267.
___ (1973) 14 June: col. 342.
___ (1973) 1 November: col. 337.
___ (1973) 6 December: col. 1484.
___ (1974) 24 January: col. 1877.
___ (1974) 4 July: cols. 243-47.
___ (1974) 29 July: cols. 237-53.
Harloe, M., Issacharoff, R., and Minns, R. (1974) *The Organisation of Housing: Public and Private Enterprise in London.* London: Heinemann.
Harrington, M. (1968) *The Other America: Poverty in the United States.* Harmondsworth: Penguin.
Harrison, P. (1975) Urban Aid. *New Society*, 30 January.
Hatch, S. and Sherrott, R. (1973) Positive Discrimination and the Distribution of Deprivations. *Policy and Politics 1* (3), March.
Heclo, H. and Wildavsky, A. (1974) *The Private Government of Public Money: Community and Policy in British Government.* London: Macmillan.
Hepworth, M.P. (1971) *The Finance of Local Government* (2nd edn.). London: Allen and Unwin.
Hill, M.J. (1969) The Exercise of Discretion in the National Assistance Board. *Public Administration*, Spring.
___ (1972) *The Sociology of Public Administration.* London: Weidenfeld and Nicolson.
Holman, R. (1969) The Wrong Poverty Programme. *New Society*, 20 March.
___ (1971) The Urban Programme. *Venture*, January: 11-14.
___ (1973) Poverty: Consensus and Alternatives. *British Journal of Social Work 3* (4): 431-46.
Home Office (1965) *Immigration from the Commonwealth.* Cmnd. 2739. London: H.M.S.O.
___ (1968) *Urban Programme Circular No. 1.* 4 October. London: Home Office.
___ (1969) *Urban Programme Circular No. 2.* 7 February. London: Home Office.
___ (1970) *Urban Programme Circular No. 3.* 20 April. London: Home Office.
___ (1972) *Urban Programme Circular No. 7.* 10 May. London: Home Office.
___ (1973) *Urban Programme Circular No. 9.* 20 February. London: Home Office.
___ (1974) *Urban Programme Circular No. 11.* 22 April. London: Home Office.
Hornsby-Smith, P. (1968) (on the immigration issue) *Daily Herald*, 3 May.

Horowitz, I.L. (ed.) (1963) *Power, Politics and People: The Collected Essays of C. Wright Mills*. Oxford: Oxford University Press.

Housing and Urban Development, Department of (1965) *Improving the Quality of Urban Life*. Washington D.C.: HUD.

Hudson, R. (1974) A Finger in the Dyke. *Municipal and Public Services Journal 82*, (41), 11 October: 1255-57.

Hughes, J. (1972) Low Pay: A Case for a National Minimum Wage? In, Bull, D. (ed.) *Family Poverty*. London: Duckworth.

Jenkins, R. (1972) *What Matters Now*. London: Fontana.

Johnson, L.B. (1964) Address to Joint Session of Congress. January.

Johnson, N. (1965) Who Are the Policy-Makers? *Public Administration XLIII*, Autumn.

Jordan, W. (1974) *Poor Parents: Social Policy and the Cycle of Deprivation*. London: Routledge and Kegan Paul.

Joseph, Sir K. (1972) Speech. Pre-School Playgroups Association Conference. 29 June.

―― (1973) The Cycle of Deprivation. Speech. Association of Directors of Social Services Conference, Brighton. 27 March.

Kelsall, R.K. (1955) *Higher Civil Servants in Britain*. London: Routledge and Kegan Paul.

Kincaid, J.C. (1973) *Poverty and Equality in Britain*. Harmondsworth: Pelican.

Kramer, R.M. (1969) *Participation and the Poor*, Englewood Cliffs: Prentice Hall.

Kravitz, S. (1969) In, Sundquist, J.L. (ed.) *On Fighting Poverty*. New York: Basic Books, Inc.

Labour Party (1964) Manifesto: *Let's Go With Labour*. London: Labour Party.

Lambert, R. (1964) *Nutrition in Britain, 1950-60*, Occasional papers in Social Administration No. 5. Welwyn: Codicote Press.

Lansley, S. and Fiegehen, G. (1973) *Housing Allowances and Inequality*, Young Fabian Pamphlet No. 36. London: Fabian Society.

Lees, R. and Smith, G. (1975) *Action Research in Community Development*. London: Routledge and Kegan Paul.

Lister, R. (1974) *Take-up of Means-Tested Benefits*. Poverty Pamphlet No. 18. London: Child Poverty Action Group.

Local Government Grants (Social Need) Act 1969.

Lockhead, A.V.S. (ed.) (1968) *A Reader in Social Administration*. London: Constable.

Lynes, A. (1963) *National Assistance and National Prosperity*. Occasional Papers in Social Administration No. 5. Welwyn: Codicote Press.

Marris, P. and Rein, M. (1971) *Dilemmas of Social Reform*. London: Routledge and Kegan Paul.

McKie, D. and Cook, C. (1970) *Election '70*. St. Albans: Panther.

Meacher, M. (1974) The Politics of Positive Discrimination. In, *Positive Discrimination and Inequality*. Fabian Research Series No. 314.

Merton, R.K. (1957) *Social Theory and Social Structure*. New York: Free Press.

Miller, S.M. and Rein, M. (1966) Poverty, Inequality and Policy. In, Becker, H. (ed.) *Social Problems: A Modern Approach*. New York: Wiley.

Milner Holland Report (1965) Committee on Housing in Greater London. Cmnd. 2605. London: H.M.S.O.

Ministry of Pensions and National Insurance (1966) *Financial and Other Circumstances of Retirement Pensioners*. London: H.M.S.O.

Moser, C.A. and Scott, W. (1961) *British Towns*. Edinburgh: Oliver and Boyd.

Moynihan, D. (1969) *Maximum Feasible Misunderstanding*. New York: Free Press.

_____ (1969) In, Sundquist, J.L. (ed.) *On Fighting Poverty*. New York: Basic Books, Inc.

Municipal Review (1973) Minutes of meeting of the Association of Municipal Corporations. November.

Murie, A., Niner, P., and Watson, C. (1976) *Housing Policy and the Housing System*. London: Allen and Unwin.

New Society (1975) Urban Aid. 30 January.

Newsom Report (1963) Central Advisory Committee for Education. *Half Our Future*. London: H.M.S.O.

Nicholson, J.L. (1974) The Distribution and Redistribution of Income in the United Kingdom. In Wedderburn, D. (ed.) *Poverty, Inequality, and Class Structure*. Cambridge: Cambridge University Press.

North West Interprofessional Group (1975) *Local Authority Needs and Resources — the Effect of the Rate Support Grant in the North West*. London: Centre for Environmental Studies, Research Paper 12.

Olsen, M. (ed.) (1970) *Power in Societies*. London: Macmillan.

Pahl, R. (1970) *Whose City?* London: Longmans.

Pinker, R. (1968) The Contribution of the Social Scientist in Positive Discrimination Programmes. *Social and Economic Administration 2* (4): 227-41.

_____ (1971) *Social Theory and Social Policy*. London: Heinemann.

Plowden Report (1967) Central Advisory Committee for Education. *Children and their Primary Schools*. London: H.M.S.O.

Powell, E. (1968) Speech. Birmingham. 20 April.

Price, J.R. (1974) Deprived Areas: Britain's Non-Policy. *Community Care,* 29 May.

Quest News Service (1973) The Urban Programme. *Quest*, 16 March: 4080-83.

Rex, J. and Moore, R. (1971) *Race, Community and Conflict*. Oxford: Oxford University Press.

Rex, J. (1973) *Race, Colonialism and the City*. London: Routledge and Kegan Paul.

Roach, J.L. and Roach, J.K. (eds.) (1972) *Poverty*. Harmondsworth: Penguin.

Robbins Report (1963) Committee on Higher Education. *Higher Education*. Cmnd. 2154. London: H.M.S.O.

Rodgers, B. (1969) *The Battle Against Poverty*. London: Routledge and Kegan Paul.

Rose, E.J.B., Deakin, N., Abrams, M., Preston, M., Vanags, A.H., Cohen, B., Gaitskell, J., and Ward, P. (1969) *Colour and Citizenship: A Report on British Race Relations.* Oxford: Oxford University Press.

Rose, S.M. (1972) *The Betrayal of the Poor.* Cambridge, Massachusetts: Schenkman Publishing Company.

Royal Commission on the Distribution of the Industrial Population (1940) Report (Barlow Report). Cmnd. 6153. London: H.M.S.O.

Royal Commission on the Distribution of Income and Wealth (1975a) Report I. *Initial Report on the Standing Reference.* Cmnd. 6171. London: H.M.S.O.

———— (1975b) Report II. *Income from Companies and its Distribution.* Cmnd. 6172. London: H.M.S.O.

Runciman, W.G. (1966) *Relative Deprivation and Social Justice.* London: Routledge and Kegan Paul.

Rutter, M. and Madge, N. (1976) *Cycles of Disadvantage.* London: Heinemann.

Schaffer, B. and Huang Wen-Hsien (1975) Distribution and the Theory of Access. *Development and Change vi* (2), April.

Schorr, A. (1964) *Slums and Social Insecurity.* Sunbury on Thames: Nelson.

Scott Report (1942) Committee on Land Utilization in Rural Areas. Cmnd. 6378. London: H.M.S.O.

Seebohm Report (1969) Committee on Local Authority and Allied Personal Social Services. Cmnd. 3703. London: H.M.S.O.

Seldon, A. (1968) Welfare by Choice. In, Lockhead, A.V.S. (ed.) *A Reader in Social Administration.* London: Constable.

Self, P. (1972) *Administrative Theories and Politics.* London: Allen and Unwin.

Sellover, W.C. (1969) In, Sundquist, J.L. (ed.) *On Fighting Poverty.* New York: Basic Books, Inc.

Shelter Neighbourhood Action Project (1972) *Another Chance for Cities.* Liverpool: SNAP.

Simon, H.A., Smithburg, D.W., and Thompson, V.A. (1950) *Public Administration.* New York: A.A. Knopf, Inc.

Sinfield, A. (1973) Poverty Rediscovered. In, Cullingworth, J.B. *Problems of an Urban Society* (Vol III). London: Allen and Unwin.

Smith, B. (1976) *Policy Making in British Government.* London: Martin Robertson.

Smith, J. (1972) Understanding Special Areas. *Spectator,* 21 October.

Smith, G. and Smith, T. (1971) Urban First Aid. *New Society,* 30 December: 1277-80.

Social Science Research Council and Department of Health and Social Security (1974) *First Report of the SSRC/DHSS Joint Working Party on Transmitted Deprivation.* London: Social Science Research Council.

Spectator, The (1972) 21 October.

Stewart, J., Spencer, K., and Webster, B. (1974) *Local Government and Urban Deprivation.* London: Home Office Urban Deprivation Unit.

Sundquist, J.L. (ed.) (1969) *On Fighting Poverty*. New York: Basic Books, Inc.

Syson, L. and Young, M. (1974) Poverty in Bethnal Green. In, Young, M. (ed.) *Poverty Report 1974*. London: Institute of Community Studies.

Tawney, R.H. (1974) *Equality*. London: Allen and Unwin.

Taylor, R.H. (1967) US Department of Housing and Urban Development. Speech. Regional Conference on Model Cities.

Times, The (1968) Editorial. 2 March.

_____ (1971) Help for Decaying City Centres (editorial). 14 April.

_____ (1972) Complex Needs of Cities (editorial). 6 April.

_____ (1975) Group Fear Urban Aid Projects may be cut by Councils in Need (article). 25 January.

Times Educational Supplement, The (1969) Money for Cities (editorial). 4 July.

_____ (1975) Gleam of Hope for the Touchstone Kids (article). 24 January.

Titmuss, R. (1964) Introduction. In, Tawney, R.H. *Equality*. London: Allen and Unwin.

_____ (1965) Poverty Versus Inequality: Diagnosis. *Nation 200*.

_____ (1968) *Commitment to Welfare*. London: Allen and Unwin.

Townsend, P. (1974) Poverty as Relative Deprivation: Resources and Style Of Living. In, Wedderburn, D. (ed.) *Poverty, Inequality and Class Structure*. Cambridge: Cambridge University Press.

_____ (1974) Speech. National Conference of the British Association of Social Workers. April.

_____ (1975) *Sociology and Social Policy*. London: Allen Lane.

Uthwatt Report (1942) Committee on Compensation and Betterment. Cmnd. 6386. London: H.M.S.O.

Wafford, J.G. (1969) In, Sundquist, J.L. (ed.) *On Fighting Poverty*. New York: Basic Books, Inc.

Warren, R.L. (1971) *The Model Cities Programs: Assumptions, Experience, Implications*. Paper. Annual Forum Program, National Conference on Social Welfare, Dallas, Texas. 17 May.

_____ (1973) *Community Change: Some Lessons from the Recent Past*. Paper. Louis and Gillian Goldstein Memorial Lecture, School of Social Work, University of Connecticut. 10 April.

Wedderburn, D. (1974) *Poverty, Inequality and Class Structure*. Cambridge: Cambridge University Press.

Weir, S. (1976) Red Line Districts. *Roof*, July: 109-14.

Wilson, H. (1968) Speech. Birmingham. 5 May.

_____ (1971) *The Labour Government 1964-1970: A Personal Record*. London: Weidenfeld and Nicolson.

Wright, M. (1973) The Professional Conduct of Civil Servants. *Public Administration 51*: 1-15.

Young, M. (1974) *Poverty Report 1974*. London: Institute of Community Studies.

Name index

Subject index